A Choice of Futures

A Choice of Futures

Politics in the Canadian North

Gurston Dacks

Methuen

Toronto   New York   London   Sydney   Auckland

Copyright © 1981 by Methuen Publications
(A division of The Carswell Company Limited)

Canadian Cataloguing in Publication Data
Dacks, Gurston, 1945-
    A choice of futures

Bibliography: p.
Includes index.
ISBN 0-458-95190-0 bd.
ISBN 0-458-94960-4 pa.

1. Canada, Northern—Politics and government.*
2. Canada, Northern—Economic policy.* I. Title.

FC3963.D32   971.9'03   C81-094646-7
F1060.92.D32

Cover design by Michael van Elsen Design Inc.
Cover photo courtesy the Department of Information,
    Government of the Northwest Territories

Printed and bound in Canada
1 2 3 4 5 81 86 85 84 83 82

Contents

Preface

This book has grown out of teaching a seminar on public policy in the Canadian North. In selecting readings, I found many that were illuminating and some that were inspiring. However, much of the literature was narrowly focused on particular topics and written primarily for an expert audience, quite partisan, or outdated. Many useful items were unpublished, hence unavailable to the general public. In reviewing this literature I concluded that a volume was needed to present a variety of basic northern issues in the context of an integrated analysis. The volume needed would not only promote an understanding of the past and present, but also provide the means to assess future developments in the evolution of the North. This latter criterion seemed extremely important because the essential element of northern public policy in the 1980s is change, change both in the specifics of policies and in the responsibilities and relationships among the governmental agencies active in the North. The fact of this rapid change demanded a methodology that would focus on underlying and more permanent relationships instead of on the ephemeral details of day-to-day events. For myself, political sociology and public-policy analysis are the methodologies to meet this challenge.

In undertaking this book, I have been humbled by the realization that hundreds of men and women have devoted lifetimes to the study and development of the policies on which my account touches. In the face of their contributions, this work can only represent the merest beginnings of an attempt at understanding. Indeed, at stages during its preparation I have despaired at what has had to be omitted for reasons of space and wondered whether what remained was sufficient to justify publication. As should be obvious, I concluded that it was, particularly because the increasing importance of northern issues made the unavailability of a comprehensive and timely political analysis an increasingly serious gap in the literature on Canadian issues. While a book such as this cannot be definitive, it will serve an important purpose if the themes it presents provide a context and suggest directions for the evolution of the North that will prepare the reader to delve more deeply into northern issues. To assist the reader to inquire further, I have tried as much as possible—and, where arguments require substantiation by reference to specialized documentation, it was not possible—to emphasize

in the notes those sources that ought to be readily available in public c
university libraries.

Northern issues are intense issues. They touch the most element;
aspects of the lives of people who often face one another across the enormou
gulf of their cultural differences. Such issues invite the caricaturing or th
attribution of malice of those with whom one disagrees. Equally, they ca
encourage readers to find such attributions where they were not intended.
hope in this book to present my conclusions on the possible directions o
northern development. In this sense, my approach is not neutral, although
hope that it is balanced. I offer my own view of right and wrong, but I prefe
to leave judgments about malice and sincerity to others, or at least to othe
discussions. In my view, as I indicate in the Appendix, effective politic;
analysis requires empathy. The views of participants in policy processe
must be seen as resulting from the socialization they have undergone in th
roles that involve them in the processes and in their life histories in genera
Their socialization and their reasons for their positions lead them to vie
their actions as right and proper. In understanding them, it is mo
important to appreciate how they come to their conclusions than it is t
attack them, which is a partisan exercise that is not my purpose here.

I have incurred a great many debts in preparing this book, particularl
since its purpose is to provide a relatively comprehensive tour of th
northern-policy horizon. The breadth of this task took me into policy area
concerning which I was previously little more than a layman. In these areas
relied greatly on the assistance of those whom I interviewed, people who liv
and work with the situations and policies I was examining. I was no
disappointed: many public servants, both territorial and federal, proved to b
unfailingly generous with their time and insights. In not naming any, an
thus avoiding overlooking the kindness of any particular individual, I do no
want it to be thought that I do not appreciate the efforts that many officia
made to enlighten me. To the contrary, whatever insights of value this boo
contains are largely due to the candor, patience, and sympathy of the publi
servants I interviewed; I am very grateful for their assistance. Similarl
individuals, often associated with interest groups, proved most generou
with their time and opinions. Without all these people, this book could no
have been written.

At the University of Alberta I was fortunate to receive the kind support c
Robbie Jamieson, the Director of the Boreal Institute of Northern Studie
and the sympathetic administrative help of Anita Moore. The staff of th
Boreal Institute Library, headed by Mrs. G. A. Cooke, were most gracious i
making available to me the resources of what is undoubtedly one of the mos
comprehensive collections of materials on the Canadian—indeed, th
circumpolar—North anywhere. I am indebted to the University of Alberta fo
providing me with study leave to accommodate much of the preparation c
this volume. Roberta McKown, the chairman of the Department of Politica

Science, encouraged my work at every stage and at a crucial point generously arranged for course relief to permit the completion of the final stages of the manuscript. Darlene Nosko achieved heights of clairvoyance in deciphering my very rough rough drafts and some subsequent drafts without once losing her patience or her characteristic cheerfulness. Janet Southoff typed a later draft with equal accuracy and good humour.

Larry Pratt shared with me a variety of documents on energy topics and proved a willing and helpful testing ground for some of my ideas on the political economy of northern energy projects. Michael Asch, Don Stewart, Mikell Montague, and Robert Page read the manuscript in whole or in part and I benefited greatly from their careful comments, although I did not incorporate all of them in what follows, for which I alone am responsible. Peter Milroy of Methuen has been a part of this project from the start. I am grateful for his exemplary job of guiding it and me conscientiously and supportively through the shoals of the Canadian publishing industry and for the added assistance of Judy deBacker of Methuen.

Finally, my deepest thanks go to my wife, Barb, who not only took up the slack in my familial responsibilities during my research travels, but, more importantly, focused her intuition and flair on aspects of this project as diverse as research strategy and text editing. She knew when to be patient with my preoccupation and when to prod my procrastination. Her strength always inspires me and this book is no exception; it owes far more to her than she can imagine, and it is dedicated to her.

GURSTON DACKS

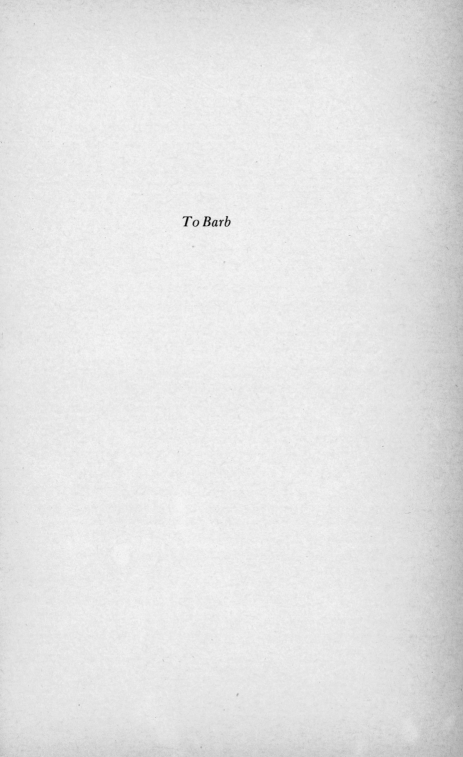

To Barb

1/Approaching the North

The 1970s thrust the North into the Canadian consciousness. The North has been part of the Canadian mythology and Canadians have referred to it when pressed to define their nationality and its distinctiveness. Still, for most Canadians, urban dwellers living within 350 km of the American border, the North used to seem as distant as the new states of the third world—and about as important. With so few people and apparently so little to contribute to the national economy, it is not surprising that the North captured the interest of Canadians only intermittently. The Klondike Gold Rush, the building of the Alaska Highway, the northern vision of John Diefenbaker—all stirred the imagination of Canadians, but before long were pushed into the background by events closer to home.

In the 1980s, Canadians no longer feel indifferent about the North. They have stopped thinking of it as a last refuge for romantic images, a forbidding land in which noble primitives struggle against the unrelenting wilderness. They are beginning to comprehend that the North can make an economic contribution to the rest of Canada that is not only significant, but also more enduring than the dramatic interludes in northern history. Canadians are also beginning to recognize the complexity of northern society, and the implications and difficulty of some of the political issues evolving in the North. They are coming to acknowledge the ethical responsibility of all Canadians because the North is a colony of southern Canada. Southern Canadians will continue to be preoccupied with national unity, Canada's persistent economic anemia, and other southern issues. However, southern Canadians will be paying more attention to the northern issues they used to deal with "in fits of absentmindedness,"[1] if at all.

What they will find is that each northern issue involves an unresolved debate about the future of the North. The North is a frontier in the process of becoming integrated into Canada, much as the West was during the late nineteenth century. Decisions taken then still define the West today. Decisions taken in the North today will define it long into the future. This fact adds greatly to the significance of contemporary northern issues and to the heat that northern politics can generate. However, the very importance of the issues requires that they be approached as carefully and systematically as possible, so that they can be fully rather than romantically understood. To

1

achieve a systematic understanding of the North in general and of individual issues in particular, three perspectives need to be applied. These perspectives—political sociology, the colonial model, and public-policy analysis—are discussed in the appendix on methodology at the end of this book. Readers who feel comfortable with political analysis may find this discussion of the basics unnecessary and may prefer to plunge directly into the narrative of the North and to consider the material in the appendix in the light of the evidence provided in the book. Others may feel that the framework for a political analysis contained in the appendix will be sufficiently helpful in dealing with the main argument of the book that they should turn to it before proceeding further.

Public Policy in the Canadian North

The role of the state is as fully developed north of the sixtieth parallel as it is in the rest of Canada. Northern residents receive the full range of services and bear the same regulatory burdens as do all Canadians. While factors of distance, sparse population, climate, and the ethnic makeup of the North cause these government activities to vary somewhat from their southern counterparts, by and large they are cut from the same policy cloth as southern programs. These policy areas raise interesting questions and display a northern flavour to varying degrees. However, to the extent that the issues concerning them are not fundamentally northern issues, they are not particularly interesting for a study of specifically northern policy issues. For this reason, this book examines such issues only in the context of their relationship to the particular politics of the North.

This book addresses the three interrelated issues that form the heart of northern politics—native claims, political development, and the future of the northern economies. These issues will be discussed in detail in the following chapters. However, as these chapters will demonstrate, the issues cannot be understood fully if they are viewed independently. What must be appreciated is that issues in the North tend to take on a significance and produce more hostility and much tougher bargaining than the terms of the issue would seem to justify simply because they are in the North. While an issue in the South will tend more to be decided on its merits, in the North the issue will be argued in terms of its implications for the basic northern issues to which it is seen to be related. This interdependence of key issues defines northern politics. It tends to bring northern political debate regularly back to first principles and invariably those first principles have to do with the basic question of what is the most desirable future for the North.

Before the next chapters set out the variety of opinion on that question, it is important to appreciate just how the three policy issues will combine to produce its ultimate answer. Without question, the future economic structure of the North will affect all aspects of its life. Any type of economic emphasis will differ from others in:

1. Whom it benefits most: some people will be particularly prepared to take advantage of a certain type of system, while others will not be so well suited to it, whether in terms of academic preparation, other training, financial resources, temperament, or tradition;

2. The options it offers to northerners and the options it forecloses; and

3. The cultural implications of the first two consequences, particularly if people find that they must adjust to a new economic situation so radically different from the former system that their abilities to cope are very severely tested.

Understandably, northerners want to maximize their control over these impacts and to be able to provide the kinds of cushioning services that respects the outlook of the people experiencing them. This desire has led northerners to seek a loosening of the constitutional bonds with Ottawa. They have of course been moved by the principled wish for self-government that comes from the democratic tradition, but they have also been aware that their wellbeing depends on their abilities to use the tools of economic promotion and regulation and of social policy to fashion a North in their own image. Non-native northerners who are active in this effort fasten their hopes on the territorial governments so that the cry for provincehood in the Yukon and more responsible government in the N.W.T. is really a cry for the power to create a society that, it is felt, can only be achieved if more power is vested in northern governments. However, the bulk of politically active native people wish a substantial degree of political power—but not for the territorial government, which can too easily be controlled by non-natives. Rather, they wish the power over their social and economic future to be held by the structures to be provided for in the settlements of their native claims. Thus, their claims imply a future social and economic direction for their people—a future that will profoundly affect the larger territories in which they live, given their numbers. At the same time, they potentially challenge the thrust towards attainment of greater power by the territorial governments. As Chapter 2 argues, the native people see their claims as a last chance, an opportunity to regain their feet. They place the highest priority on their claims and resist constitutional changes that precede them. For example, they urged the dissolution of the Drury Inquiry precisely because it assumed a separation of political and constitutional development from the question of native claims. They also oppose approval of economic activities, particularly large-scale resource developments, which they feel will reduce their choices in the future once their claims are settled. In this way, the native concern for their claims involves both economic goals and a vision of political means that stand in opposition to those of the proponents of constitutional development. For their part, these proponents, in order to succeed, must press for a settlement of the native claims that will not limit the ability of northern governments to create a northern future most congenial to them.

Obviously, this thumbnail sketch contains many simplifications, the most obvious of which is the suggestion that only two positions exist on the many complex issues surrounding the future of the North and that these positions are poles apart. The reality is more complicated and subtle by far. However, what counts here is the intimate relationship among the themes of economic development, the evolution of political institutions and native claims, the absolutely fundamental nature of the issues being debated, and the fact that the North is currently passing through a particularly formative period. Northern politics today are truly a struggle over the shape of the future. Once the choice of future is made, it will prove to be a very enduring choice. This recognition of these realities among northerners has given their politics a unity and an intensity that have rarely been equalled elsewhere in Canada. For this reason, any attempt to understand a particular policy in the North requires not only the application of the three perspectives set out in this Appendix, but also the linking of the issue in question to the broader political debate of which it forms a part.

The Land and Its Peoples

Three qualities define the Canadian North in the 1980s—change, variety, and complexity. Together they make northern politics as dynamic as any in Canada. The speed of change in the North has had a wrenching effect on groups of peoples whose assumptions often diverge much more widely and in much more fundamental ways than is the case in southern-Canadian politics. As a result, the task of sorting out the consequences of change on the relations among these diverse groups raises especially fundamental issues. This chapter will describe first the physical environment that gives the issues their particularly northern tone and then the social and economic structure of northern society that shapes the issues.

How Far North Is North?

Many different boundaries have been suggested to delimit the southern edge of the Canadian North. The treeline is often thought to define the boundary that separates what is truly the North from adjacent regions that, while sharing many climatic traits with more northerly areas, differ in terms of vegetation and the ways in which their native peoples have evolved economic and social structures in response to the demands of these different environments. Other definitions depend on various factors of climate, accessibility to southern Canada, and the nature of the economic activity. Because each of these indicators by itself only tells part of the story, Louis-Edmond Hamelin, a noted geographer and former member of the Northwest Territories Council, has developed a complex calculation of "polar units" that provides a single index of the degree of northernness of any particular site. He argues that much of the area of the provinces should be considered to be northern in terms of the factors that comprise his index.[2]

Hamelin's approach is valuable, for it permits an intelligent comparison of the northernness of various locations, which is useful in deciding such questions as isolation-pay supplements for workers. However, his approach of stipulating a particular cutoff point in terms of a reading on his index as the boundary of the North is arbitrary because a given location may be quite northern in some respects, such as vegetation, but less northern in others, such as social structure. Because any single index will suffer from this arbitrariness, it is much better to select a boundary for the North that reflects the particular reason for raising the question of northernness in the first place. Thus, the forestry expert, the meteorologist, and the economist each ought to select the northern boundary most useful for his or her particular area of study. In this way, the selection of the boundary will promote rather than obstruct understanding.

This criterion makes the sixtieth parallel (60°N) the obvious political boundary of the North. (See Figure 1-1). The dominant political fact in the North is its territorial status. This status sets the North apart from the rest of Canada in all three of the issues this book focuses on. Rightly or wrongly, debate on political development in the North focuses on the evolving terms of the colonial relationship between the territorial governments and Ottawa. This is not the same as the debate surrounding federal-provincial relations because of the hard fact of the federal government's legal supremacy over the territories. In addition, the question of the political development of the provinces is assessed, if at all, only by the occasional academic, because it seems inappropriate for civil servants or politicians to judge the maturity of an autonomous government. In contrast, the colonial status of the territories invites judgments about their political maturity and readiness for further self-government.

The native-claims issue in the North differs profoundly from that of the South, in that the federal government both recognizes an obligation—although undefined—to the native people and controls the land they claim. In the North, a settlement of a native claim legally requires only the agreement of the federal government and the native claimants. In the South, the federal government must negotiate with the native people, but the land about which it negotiates falls under the jurisdiction of the provinces. For this reason, some aspects of the settlement will have to be approved by a party, the provincial government, that may not be legally or feel morally bound to concede anything to the claimants. Clearly, negotiating claims in the North is simpler, though not necessarily easier, than in the South.

The third major focus of this book is the economic future of the North. Part of this economic future depends on huge resource-development projects. The federal government in Ottawa has it solely within its power to determine how many such projects will proceed and when. This contrasts profoundly with the situation in the provinces in which Ottawa's role, while important is more limited. Thus, whether the issue involves political, economic, or native questions, Ottawa plays a paramount role, and the southern boundary of that role is the sixtieth parallel.

It must be emphasized that the political relevance of this boundary says very little about its relevance for other questions. The sixtieth parallel in no way respects geographical features because it cuts across mountain ranges and river basins. It does not match any clear break in weather, vegetation, or animal habitat. The social problems found north of the sixtieth parallel also plague communities in the northern parts of the provinces. Still, governmental responses to the similar conditions on both sides of the line differ substantially because of the political fact of the line. For this reason, while recognizing that issues in the northern parts of the provinces raise important questions,[3] this book will concentrate on policies and politics north of 60°.

The Northern Climate[4]

The most obvious features of the northern climate are the intensity and duration of the winter. For example, the mean daily temperature for December through March at Frobisher Bay lies between -30°C and -35°C. Even the relatively southern Yellowknife averages temperatures of below -20°C for those months.

The intense cold creates a variety of problems for engineers. Foremost among them is the phenomenon of permafrost, permanently frozen ground lying beneath a thin "active layer" of soil that thaws and freezes in a yearly cycle.[5] Permafrost poses severe problems for engineers, in that it can begin to melt if it is disturbed—whether by piles being driven into it to support a building, a pipeline whose contents are warm (crude oil will not flow well when cold), or the scraping away of the active layer or the cover of vegetation that protects the permafrost. Particularly if the soil has a high water content, it may flow away once melted, causing the land to subside. This could cause a building to collapse or undermine a pipeline enough to rupture it.

To avoid such mishaps, engineers must design special northern adaptations for their projects. For example, they may construct buildings or hot oil pipelines on stilts or gravel pads to keep the heat generated by the buildings away from the permafrost, sink refrigerated columns into the ground, and refrigerate natural gas carried by pipelines. All of these designs add to the cost of northern construction and some have their own problems. The most notorious problem is the "frost heave" caused when refrigerated gas in a pipeline flows through an area of unfrozen ground, causing it to freeze and heave upward, possibly breaking the pipeline. The failure of the Canadian Arctic Gas Pipeline consortium to prove that it had developed techniques for dealing with this problem was one of the factors that undermined its proposal.[6]

A final set of engineering problems posed by the cold is the difficulty of

Figure 1-1

Canada North of the Sixtieth Parallel

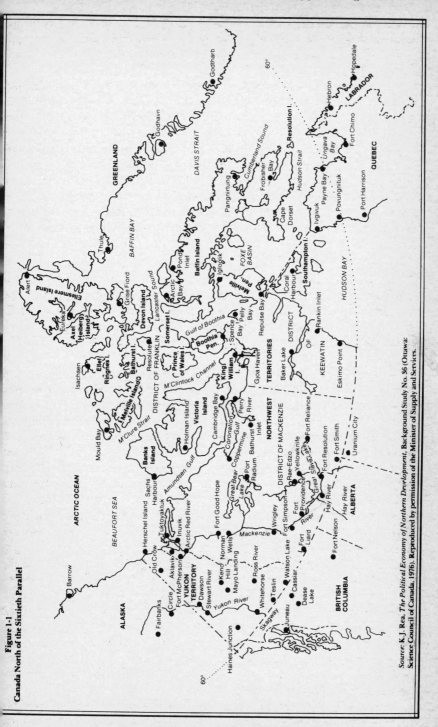

Source: K.J. Rea, *The Political Economy of Northern Development*, Background Study No. 36 (Ottawa: Science Council of Canada, 1976). **Reproduced by permission of the Minister of Supply and Services.**

operating in the ice-infested waters of the Arctic.[7] Artificial islands built in
the shallow water of the Beaufort Sea must withstand the enormous pressure
of tons of wind-driven ice. Shipping must be specially adapted to operate in
thick ice. The dawning of a new era of nonrenewable-resource development
in the high Arctic will depend on the extent to which a new generation of
icebreakers and reinforced freighters now in the planning stages actually
leaves the drawingboards and becomes reality.[8]

Gouges on the ocean bottom called "scour marks" indicate that ice
formations can extend as far as thirty metres below the surface and, as they
move, can dig out troughs up to eight metres deep in the sea bottom.[9] Any
underwater pipeline or wellhead facilities built in the North will have to be
buried wherever scour marks indicate that they might be damaged by passing
ice formations. The proposals for both the Arctic Pilot Project and the Polar
Gas pipeline project envision special—and expensive—engineering responses to the problem of ice scours.

Despite the fact that the cold is the definitive feature of the northern
climate, the North does enjoy a summer, albeit a brief one. For the parts of the
North that experience a truly arctic climate because they are close enough to
the Arctic Ocean to have their weather influenced by it, summer tends to be
cool and bleak with frequent fog. The subarctic weather pattern of the more
inland areas gives them relatively warm temperatures in which to enjoy the
long hours of sunshine.

However, this warm interlude is really only a brief respite from winter
and a return to its intense cold and to its darkness. In December, the residents
of Inuvik carry on their daily lives in about fourteen hours of darkness and ten
hours of twilight. The depth of winter in Yellowknife offers about six hours
of thin daylight, with the sun only about eight degrees about the horizon at
noon.[10] The major consequence of the darkness is psychological depression,
particularly among newcomers to the North who are unaccustomed to it.[11] A
second consequence is that it can complicate construction and drilling
operations by requiring people to work longer hours under artificial light
than is usual in the South.[12]

Because the North is so cold for much of the year, the winter days so
short, the sun so oblique, and the winter snow and ice cover reflect so much of
what solar energy does reach the ground, relatively little evaporation occurs
for much of the year. With little evaporation, there tends to be little
precipitation. The annual precipitation at Eureka on Ellesmere Island, for
example, is only 61 mm, the lowest reading in Canada.[13] While this is an
extreme example, much of the North can be considered desert in terms of the
precipitation it receives.

Northern Ecology

Despite the millions of dollars spent on studying the North, northern
ecosystems are still not well understood. However, it is clear that what Justice

Berger referred to as the northern "biome" differs significantly from that of the South and that the major difference is its greater sensitivity. This sensitivity results from the following factors:

1. Northern ecosystems are simpler than those found farther South, in that the North contains many fewer species. As a result, the extinction of one species may lead to the eradication of species higher up the food chain that depend on the extinct species, because those higher species may be unable to find another species to replace the one that has become extinct.

2. Because of low temperatures and the general scarcity of food, it takes much longer for fish and wildlife to grow and reproduce than in the South. As a result, if a disaster such as a winter when particularly little food is available or where a river is polluted and spawning grounds in it are thereby disturbed, it will take much longer for the stock of wildlife or fish affected to recover (if recovery occurs at all) than would be the case in the South. This factor adds to the delicacy of an ecological balance already precarious because of the biological simplicity.

3. Pollution tends to linger in the North because the cold retards the organisms that decompose certain kinds of pollutants and can freeze pollutants in the ice for much of the year. This latter possibility particularly complicates the task of cleaning up oil spills in ice-covered Arctic waters.[14] After its 1976 decision to permit drilling in the Beaufort Sea and to prepare for the oil spills whose likelihood is increasing as the pressure to develop the oil reserves of the North intensifies, the federal government created the Arctic Marine Oilspill Program (AMOP) in 1977. In 1980, the Manager of the Program acknowledged, "It is universally recognized that the general state-of-the-art for dealing with major oil spills is inadequate and unsatisfactory." However, he did hold out the promise that after the completion of AMOP's research ". . . we will be in a better position than we are today to deal with a large oil spill in an ice-infested Arctic environment."[15]

Because science has not produced all of the answers concerning the nature and depression of northern ecosystems and their responses to external disturbances, it cannot be dogmatically asserted that any and all northern development possess unacceptable environmental risks. For the same reason, it would be unwise to proceed simply because it cannot be proven that environmental damage will in fact occur. What is necessary because of the sensitivity of the northern environment is to attempt to improve our understanding of northern life processes and to approach northern development with the greatest of caution until much more is known.

These subjects will be discussed in Chapter 5, as will the extent of the fish and wildlife resources of the North. Because vegetation will not be discussed there, it may be helpful to offer a few notes here. The first is that the North can be divided into two zones, separated by the treeline. This is not in reality a line but a transitional zone. To the south lies the boreal forest, sometimes referred to as the taiga. Coniferous trees are the most common species in it, although birch and poplar become more plentiful the farther south one goes. North of the treeline is the treeless tundra, sometimes called the barrens. The vegetation in the tundra is limited to lichens, mosses, grasses, and low shrubs. The eastern Arctic and the Arctic Islands that lie north of the treeline are much less biologically productive than are the western parts of the North because the factors contributing to low environmental productivity operate more strongly in the east. Accordingly, these areas are particularly sensitive environmentally and they cannot support nearly the same intensity of hunting, fishing, and trapping activities that the western Arctic can support.

Northern Geography

While the geography of the North is extremely varied, it can be summarized in terms of four major regions—the Precambrian Shield, the Arctic Islands, the interior plains, and the Cordillera. (See Figure 1-2.) The Precambrian Shield covers 1 813 000 km² of the Northwest Territories, more than half its total area of 3 379 950 km².[16] It extends from Great Bear Lake and Great Slave Lake in the west to Baffin Island in the east and its northern edge cuts across the southern Arctic Islands. The shield is generally low, rugged land that does not support much wildlife harvesting, but is becoming increasingly important economically because of its mineral wealth—particularly its gold, silver, lead, zinc, and uranium.

The Arctic Islands encompass a great variety of landforms. The eastern islands, from Ellesmere to Baffin, feature high mountains of Precambrian rock. To the west, the islands are lower. In the Innuitian region, north of the Shield, high sedimentary mountains mark the islands.

The interior plains are a continuation of the midcontinental plain around both sides of the Shield. In the east, the plains lie under Hudson Bay and Fox Basin and take in the islands of these areas. In the West, the plains form the Mackenzie Valley. Because the plain slopes gradually, the Mackenzie River, which flows down it, is navigable for its entire length of 2253 km. It serves as a major transportation link in the western Northwest Territories, particularly for the transportation of heavy bulk cargoes. Historically, it has facilitated communication among the native people of the Valley, thus providing a basis for their view of themselves as a single people, the Dene.

The Cordilleran backbone of the continent runs through the Yukon as a series of mountain ranges, the highest of which are the Saint Elias Mountains in the southwest Yukon. Because the western portion of the Yukon escaped the ice age, its upland plateaus have not lost their cover of soil. While they support very little agriculture, their fertility has produced abundant timber and animal life.

The Yukon River flows from British Columbia in a northwesterly direction through the Yukon and into Alaska. Unlike the other rivers in the

Figure 1-2
The Physiographic Regions of Northern Canada

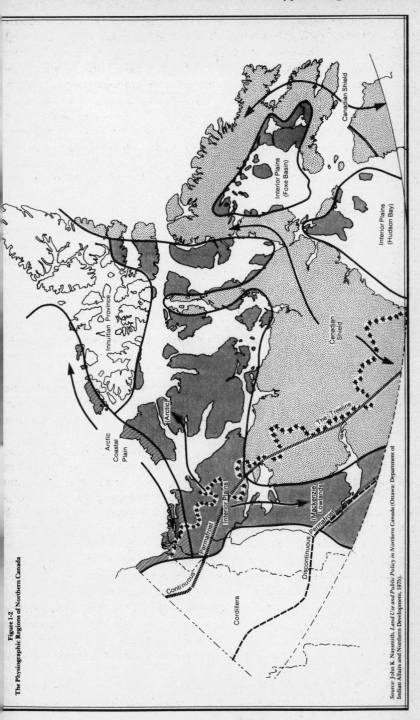

Source: John K. Naysmith, *Land Use and Public Policy in Northern Canada* (Ottawa: Department of Indian Affairs and Northern Development, 1975).

Territory, the Yukon is navigable for most of its length, although it lost its significance as a commercial waterway with the drop in freight traffic after the gold rush. In general, northern rivers are exceedingly important geographic forms, whose significance has been summarized as follows:

1. They contain kinetic energy that, depending on the river profile, may be harnessed.
2. They are a medium of transportation for a variety of living organisms including people.
3. They are a medium of nutrient supply and deposition and are therefore areas of relatively rich soils, especially compared to the rest of the North.
4. They allow the extension northward of the range of some plant and animal communities.
5. They are an essential habitat for fish, waterbirds, and semiaquatic mammals and for the migration and dispersal of these animals.
6. For all the foregoing reasons, they are traditionally associated with settlements.
7. They are a source of water supply for settlements and a medium for waste disposal of various kinds.
8. They have a strong esthetic, emotional, and intellectual appeal to many people.[17]

The Economies of the North

Northern economics are colonial economics, as reflected in the North's dual economy. The two northern economies overlap and many individuals participate in both, but they represent distinct foci of economic activity and proceed on the basis of contrasting assumptions. For this reason, they are analytically separate.

The "traditional" economy is the economic life centred on hunting, fishing, and trapping.[18] This economy is almost exclusively native, is highly labour intensive, and involves relatively low capital investment. It is not completely satisfying to call this economy traditional, in that it is not identical to the kind of activity in which native people participated in antiquity: that activity was primarily devoted to subsistence, whereas the hunting, fishing, trapping economy of today's natives has an important commercial component. Indeed, one of the major issues in native claims is to have natives' largely unlimited freedom to hunt, fish, and trap for subsistence purposes extended to their commercial wildlife-harvesting activities. Historically, the land economy was the only way for native people to gain the necessities of life. Now they also rely, to degrees that vary from region to region and from individual to individual, on cash income from a variety of sources. Moreover, the technology of high-powered rifles and snowmobiles has substantially altered customary hunting practices and the forms of social life that grew up around them. Still, hunting, fishing, and trapping are traditional, in that they bring native people into intimate contact with the land, providing an experience that reaffirms the traditional link they feel with the land.

Hunting, fishing, and trapping cannot be understood solely as economic activities. Often northern natives undertake them with little expectation of cash profit. This behaviour appears irrational to the non-native observer, but in reality it is perfectly reasonable: the hunter derives a spiritual as well as a material benefit from being on the land. By the same token, many native people who are employed—and therefore do not have an economic need to do so—continue to hunt, fish, or trap in their spare time or in interludes between periods of wage employment. To some extent, this can be explained in terms of the same factors that lead many non-natives to hunt and fish—that is, to obtain free meat and to enjoy a recreational pastime. However, for the native people, the traditional tie to the land is also prominent. For them, being on the land feels right; it is a spiritually meaningful activity.[19]

The innocent newcomer to northern politics who asks the apparently straightforward question, "How large is the traditional sector of the northern economy?" will be startled by the heat of the controversy this question provokes. This debate will be examined in Chapter 5. However, for the purposes of the overview presented in this chapter, it is enough to note that, while only a minority of native people support themselves by hunting, fishing, and trapping, these activities remain very important to native people. Besides income, these activities provide food, which reduces the amount of expensive food that must be purchased, is itself nutritious,[20] and is greatly preferred by native people.[21] For example, the land-use studies by the Inuit Tapirisat of Canada and the Committee for Original Peoples' Entitlement indicate that more than 60 per cent of the goods consumed by Inuit comes from wildlife harvesting.[22]

While the traditional economy remains important for many native people, it is overshadowed in several senses by the wage economy. The focus of the wage economy is the large-scale, capital-intensive, high-technology "megaprojects," which will be discussed in Chapter 4.[23] The following are the fundamental elements of this economy.

1. Staple Base

The economy of the North is based on the export of staples to the metropolis, be it southern Canada, Europe (in the case of the Nanisivik mine), or (as has been proposed for Beaufort Sea oil) Japan. Staple goods are materials that are exported in relatively unprocessed form and that tend to be far and away the major source of economic activity in the area that produces them.[24] They are so important that their impact extends far beyond the realm of economics; social and political patterns tend to be profoundly influenced by the nature of the staple and by the relationships among all those—independent producers, employees, employers, government regulators, and consumers—who are involved in any way with the staple. For example, a staple such as furs can be developed without substantially altering the lifestyle of native people; a staple such as mining cannot. To carry the example further, fur traders imposed their will much less on the natives with whom they dealt than do mine foremen on native miners today. The point is that the technology of producing the staple shapes the lives of those involved in its production.

2. The Colonial Link

The most important relationship created by a staple economy is the colonial link between the frontier hinterland and the staple-consuming metropolis. The essence of this relationship is that factors outside the colonial economy determine the economic viability of the staple. A northern resource only becomes a staple commodity when the factors of technology and the needs of the metropolis come together so that it is possible to extract the staple from the North at a price the South is willing to pay. For example, the disruption of oil supplies because of Middle East politics in the mid-1970s has made Canadians willing at least to consider paying sufficiently higher prices for oil and gas to justify active exploration for them in the North. Similarly, the discovery of reserves in southern Canada or elsewhere may quickly take the heat out of the northern "energy play." More specifically, the discovery of promising finds off the east coast of Canada may well upset the timetable of northern exploration and development. Whatever the outcome of this particular case, the important factor is that the decision will be made outside the North in response to needs as they exist outside the North. This is the essence of economic colonialism.

3. The Role of Multinational Corporations

The economic symbols of this colonialism are the multinational corporations[25] whose involvement in northern megaprojects is an inevitable result of the scale of these projects. Firms such as Urangesellschaft and Cominco, a Canadian-based multinational, are leaders in the mining and mineral-exploration industry of the North. While Canadian firms such as Panarctic and Petro-Canada are active in the search for northern oil and gas, some large multinational firms have also been exploring actively. For example, in 1980 Esso Resources announced plans to add $30 million to the $70 million already invested in constructing and drilling from the Issungnak artificial island in the Beaufort Sea, and to carry out a $460 million expansion program of its Norman Wells oilfield.[26]

The significance of these sums of money and of the presence of multinationals is that they emphasize how powerful are the external forces that the North must confront if it is to control its own destiny. The multinationals possess tremendous resources of money, technology, marketing ability, and management skills. These economic resources become political to the extent that Ottawa comes to rely on them as the vehicle for the northern development that it is eager to see take place. The dependence is all the greater because the multinationals can credibly threaten to transfer their activities to other parts of the globe if Ottawa denies them the concessions they seek. However, the multinationals have not usually had to resort to such crude tactics because their other political resources are substantial. They have access to large amounts of information even Ottawa does not possess. Accordingly, they are in a position to put their proposed projects in the best possible light. In effect, their expertise enables them to act as initiators of the policy process and to force government into the role of reacting rather than leading. The multinationals also enjoy the access resulting from the social status of their senior members. Their lobbyists and their supporters in the business and financial community cultivate the more political levels of government and their experts work closely with the technical levels. The Canadianization provisions of the 1980 National Energy Program seem intended to reduce Canada's dependence on the foreign-owned multinationals; however, the resources of the multinationals seem likely to assure them of continued influence in Ottawa.

4. High Costs

The costs of living and doing business in the North are high. It costs on the average 50 per cent—and in some places 90 per cent—more to live in the N.W.T. than in Edmonton.[27] Because the Yukon enjoys better transportation links with the South, its price differential, while still severe, is not quite so breathtaking: Whitehorse prices average 30 per cent above those of Edmonton; Dawson prices, 50 per cent.[28] A contributor to these high costs is the high rates charged by the Northern Canada Power Commission. Because the charter of this crown corporation requires that it not operate at a loss, it is forced to pass on to its customers the high costs associated with serving a small and scattered population. The resulting high electricity rates have from time to time become a political issue because they not only raise the cost of living, but also limit the development of any industry that would require substantial amounts of electricity, yet is not large enough to justify creating a huge power project.[29]

Business costs are raised by the high cost of living, by the need to pay salaries to compensate workers for the isolation and physical discomfort of working in northern locations, and by the cost of the rotation of crews working on certain megaprojects. Transportation of supplies is expensive because the distances are great and the ability of the transportation industry to service many points is limited. From freezeup to breakup, many communities must be served by air, an expensive mode of transportation. Firms must either pay the price or wait for the short shipping season to permit resupply by ocean freighter or by barge on the Mackenzie. The problem with relying on the shipping season is the financial charges that the firm must pay for goods in storage that may not be used for half a year or longer. Similarly, the firm is paid only when its produce—for example, ore from a mine—is actually delivered to market. In this way, the interval between spending the money and receiving the income can be much greater in the North than in the South. Icebreaking freighters and tankers will reduce this problem in some instances, but they still involve higher costs than are associated with the usual forms of shipping in southern waters.

While these problems are less acute in the Yukon and the southwestern corner of the N.W.T., which are served by all-weather roads, and while they may diminish for the Mackenzie Delta with the completion of the Dempster Highway, the costs anywhere in the North remain high. Northern businesses suffer particularly because to the problem of high cost must be added the fact that the markets they service are too small to permit them to achieve economies of scale. They often find that larger southern firms, for which the North is just a sideline, can underbid them in contract competitions for northern business.

These problems make the northern economy particularly precarious: opportunities must be extremely lucrative to overcome the cost factor. But not many such opportunities exist; those that do may only be lucrative enough to permit them to last for a short while. All of these factors dampen economic activity in the North.

5. Boom and Bust

Because the North can itself sustain little economic activity—that it is a high-cost and low-demand economy—explains why the waxing and waning of the South's economic needs have created a boom-and-bust cycle in the North. At the peak of the Klondike Gold Rush, Dawson boasted a population of 25 000;[30] today it is little more than a tourist attraction with a population of less than a thousand. Another example is Rankin Inlet, which became a boom town with the opening of a mine in 1957. Native people were encouraged to move to Rankin Inlet from their dispersed camps and to work in the mine. Their reward was mass unemployment when the mine shut down in 1962.[31] Looking into the future, the likeliest boom-and-bust situations will probably be associated with the construction of pipelines. While these projects require large construction crews and pay very well, they need relatively few people to operate them after completion. The majority of their builders will leave the North and most of the northerners who worked on them will be forced to make a difficult adjustment. Some will have to leave the North to find work to pay them the substantial salary to which they will have grown accustomed. Others will have to leave the North to find any wage employment at all. Many will have to accept jobs at rates of pay they consider unsatisfying. Northern society as a whole will have suffered the social dislocation of the boom and will have had to spend large sums of money on facilities to service the boom. However, subsequently, it may find that the project does not provide it with the resources either to sustain the facilities or to properly redress the social ills created by the project. In this way, the boom-and-bust cycle affects both individuals and societies.

The importance of this type of problem has now been recognized. For example, Ottawa requires that proposals for large-scale projects include assessments of their socioeconomic impacts. The National Energy Board for the first time considered these impacts in ruling on the northern pipeline question in 1977.[32] The Northern Pipeline Agency has issued a set of socioeconomic terms and conditions to govern the construction and operation of the Alaska Highway Pipeline, and the federal EARP (Environmental Assessment Review Process) is increasingly considering social and economic impacts. However, while Ottawa has begun to address the problems of boom and bust, its success in dealing with them remains to be seen. One obstacle is that impact assessment of very large-scale, one-of-a-kind projects is still in its infancy. Probably more important, it is not yet clear what priority Ottawa will attach to anticipated social costs, such as the boom-and-bust phenomenon, if it felt that a project was important to meeting some southern need. Ottawa's priorities are indicated by the selection of the Alaska Highway pipeline route, in that it is likely to affect most of the native communities of the Yukon more than a pipeline in the Mackenzie would have affected Dene communities. If social costs were Ottawa's first concern, neither route would have been selected.

6. The Lack of Internal Economic Linkages

If the northern economy were a fully developed economy, the creation of megaprojects would lead to substantial growth. Wages and corporate purchasing would buoy up the northern economy by providing jobs and profits in its manufacturing and service sector. Profits earned by megaprojects would be available to invest in further economic activities in the North. Depending on Ottawa's willingness to share resource revenues, royalties would add to the territorial governments' income and increase their ability to undertake economic-development programs. Canadians have come to expect these spinoff benefits when an industry based on natural resources is created in southern Canada.[33] However, the colonial economy of the North gains fewer of such benefits because mineral-exploration and oil-and-gas-drilling firms receive much of their supplies directly from southern Canada and employ crews who are mostly recruited in the South and flown directly to the North. Northern businesses therefore lose opportunities to supply these projects and to earn the profits that might permit them to flourish; instead, they have to restrict themselves to scrambling after crumbs while the cream of business opportunities is skimmed off in the South. The northern economy also loses potential wages: this purchasing power ends up in Edmonton, Calgary, or wherever workers go when they are off their shift or finished their job. This is particularly true of operations supplied directly from the South, such as Arctic Island sites. However, it also applies to less self-contained projects such as mines. The Northwest Territories government has estimated that in the mining sector "one job creates between 0.3 and 0.6 jobs in the rest of the economy, when all effects have been taken into account,"[34] a very small multiplier effect compared to those attributed to manufacturing or even primary-resource industries in southern Canada.

Undoubtedly, profits earned in the North are in many instances reinvested in the North in the form of expanded or improved facilities. However, the profits and dividends that do flow out of the North into the hands of southern investors are not necessarily made available for investment in other northern ventures. This pattern breaks the link between profit and investment, which is so important to the growth and development of economic systems; therefore, financial institutions based in the North are weak—indeed, virtually nonexistent. Here again, the structure of the northern economy prevents the success of one sector spilling over into others. In this type of situation, it is almost unavoidable that the economies of the North perform sluggishly.

7. Economic Structures

Relatively developed economic systems display some balance, in that they possess substantial primary, secondary, and service sectors. The North does not match this pattern: it has large primary and service sectors, but only a very small manufacturing sector. Because manufacturing tends to be labour intensive, the lack of a manufacturing sector makes it all the more difficult for the territories to find employment for their increasing numbers of workers. The manufacturing sector is unlikely to grow because its size and vigour are intimately related to the efficiency of transportation. If transportation is slow, expensive, or unreliable, then it may be possible to establish a small manufacturing industry, even if it does not enjoy the economies of scale that give southern industry an advantage. However, as transportation improves, it poses less of a cost or reliability barrier to the import of southern goods, which can then compete more successfully with northern manufactured products. It is thus paradoxical but true that an improvement in one economic sector, transportation, has dampened another, manufacturing. Since northern transportation is likely to continue to improve in the future, the prospects for growth in the manufacturing sector will continue to be poor.

The service sector in the North is unusually large. Much of this can be attributed to the large numbers of workers employed by government: in 1978-79, the Yukon government provided 1461 man-years of employment; the N.W.T. government, 3226 man-years; and Ottawa, about 3700 man-years.[35] The number of public servants—both federal and territorial—per capita serving in the North is more than three times the national average.[36] Some northerners cite this comparison to prove that they are grossly overgoverned.

They may well be, but the argument cannot be demonstrated by these statistics. The reason is that the figures are not comparable. Many public servants in the North perform functions that are not really governmental. For example, nurses in the North are classed as public servants, but their activities can hardly be considered governmental. Others, such as teachers, who are classed as public servants in the North, would be employed at the local level in the South and would not figure in the statistics of federal and provincial employees. These examples, which involve large numbers of public servants, suggest that the argument that the North is overgoverned will require a more sophisticated form of proof than simple numerical comparisons.

8. The Role of Government

Not only is government a major employer in the North, but it also feeds the northern economies through its spending, budgeted at $714 million for 1978-79.[37] This figure has grown rapidly in recent years; for example, the comparable figure for 1973-74 was $347 million. This growth has undoubtedly been a major source of whatever economic growth has occurred in the North. Beyond its spending, government is also economically important because it can breathe life into proposed northern developments, either by creating favourable regulations or by providing a variety of forms of support. As Chapter 4 will detail, proposed northern projects must receive approval on a variety of their aspects before they may proceed. The stringency of the standards that developers must meet often makes the difference between ventures' proceeding or being shelved. The result is the now-familiar public-bargaining process in the form of environmental and social-impact hearings at which the proponents of projects seek the most favourable regulatory climate and public-interest groups argue for full and careful regulation.

Government can provide other forms of support in addition to regulation sympathetic to developers. The most important of these are incentives to prospective northern developers. The high costs of doing business in the North and the often-enormous exploration, application, and startup costs of large-scale projects mean that many economic activities that would be viable elsewhere simply cannot turn a profit on their own in the North, or involve too great a risk to be attractive to developers. Here government enters the picture. It provides generous tax allowances to encourage northern development. For example, Ottawa has encouraged oil and gas development by offering exploration leases at terms very favourable to the industry. In addition, the "super-depletion" allowance applied to northern oil and gas exploration from 1976 to 1980 meant virtually that the taxpayers of Canada were paying for northern drilling, not the oil industry itself.[38]

When a project is actually launched, government frequently greases the way by contributing to the expensive infrastructure the project must have in order to operate. For example, Ottawa devoted $25 million for access roads, electrical-generating capacity, communications, a townsite, and a worker-training program for the Cyprus Anvil mine that opened in the Yukon in 1969.[39] Ottawa paid for $8.8 million of capital investment associated with the opening of the Nanisivik Mine on Baffin Island and loaned a further $7.9 million.[40] These are very large sums of money. They put the federal government into the league of the multinational corporations for determining the pace of northern economic development. However, as Chapters 4 and 5 will argue, the fact that Ottawa plays a very important economic role in the North does not necessarily mean that it acts on the basis of a coherent economic plan.

Summary

To summarize, the wage economy of the North is a colonial economy, directed by multinational corporations and the federal government. Its staples basis necessarily makes it a boom-and-bust economy and its lack of internal economic links acts as a brake on its development. These factors make the North economically weak and dependent; thus, its vulnerability to outside forces is perpetuated.

There are, then, two economies in the North, the traditional economy and the wage economy. The differences between them are obvious: it might be thought that they operate in separate spheres and with relatively little influence on each other. Nothing could be farther from the truth: in practice the two economies clash in a variety of ways. The first and most obvious is that they may involve conflicting land uses. Pipeline and highway construction can divert herds of migrating animals away from the villages, whose people have traditionally hunted them, or may actually reduce the herd by interfering with the animals at a particularly vulnerable point in their life cycle, such as the calving season. Oil spills in arctic waters could cause massive kills of the tiny plants and animals on which northern marine food chains are based. Some of the icebreaking tanker and freighter routes being contemplated for northern waters may produce channels in what would otherwise be frozen expanses. These channels could cut native hunters off from their traditional hunting grounds.

The wage economy can also undermine the traditional economy by enticing natives to work on megaprojects that turn out, as in the case of the Rankin Inlet mine, to last only a few years. These native people may find it difficult to return to traditional employment and may be relegated to a life of welfare in the towns to which they have been attracted, but which offer them few employment opportunities.

Even when it is steady, wage employment can upset the social relations among native people in at least four ways.[41] The first is that it may cause workers or families to leave their homes to take up residence in a place where the social support system of friends and extended family is not available. In such a situation, the native worker and family may find that they lack the psychological backup they need to deal with the stress of the new situation. This problem should not be overstated, for many of the locations in which northern natives now live are the result of their having been uprooted and do not supply the kind of support system of traditional camps.

The second problem with wage labour is that it gives the native worker a social status that conflicts with the status traditionally assigned on the basis of factors other than cash income. For example, tension can arise between generations when the elders feel that they are denied their rightful status based on age and when the young feel that they are not receiving credit for their successes.

Third, wage labour individualizes economic activity. Whereas hunting, fishing, and trapping involve varying degrees of cooperation among the members of a family, who share the fruits of their common labours, wage employment means a paycheck for a single individual for whom sharing means giving without receiving in return anything equally tangible. As a result, wage employment can lead the individual to see his interests in competition with the interests of others with whom he would normally wish to share. This feeling can erode the sense of community so basic to native social organization.

Finally, the wage economy undermines the traditional economy by its very presence in the North. The coming of non-natives has largely invalidated native lifestyles by imposing southern institutions and even place names on them, by denying the native claim to the land, and by repudiating native religion and language. The marginality of native people in the new society of the North cannot help but have undermined all aspects of native life and weakened the confidence and sense of personal efficacy of individual native people.[42]

The wage and traditional economies interact, then, in such a way that the former undermines the latter. Indeed, the common prescription that industrial development is needed in the North to provide jobs for native people may in some situations in the long run be a formula for less rather than more employment.[43] Wage employment is far from the only cause of the present economic plight of northern natives, but it is sufficiently important that, as Chapter 2 will point out, one of the most important parts of the northern native claims is the political power to control the impact of the wage economy on the traditional economy.

The colonial nature of the northern economies has affected the northern labour force in several distinct ways. The first is that there are in effect two labour forces in the North. The first labour force is made up largely of non-natives, most of whom either have steady employment in government or private wage employment or operate their own business or professional practices. Unemployment in this labour force tends to be low, in part because its skills are in demand and in part because of its high mobility. Individuals usually come north to take jobs for which they have been hired in the South and return south when their employment ceases. Those who come north i search of work usually leave quickly if they cannot find it.

In contrast, the native labour force suffers from high unemployment i the wage sector of the economy, where natives tend to work at relativel unskilled jobs for limited periods of time, usually for low pay. Assessin native unemployment in the North is a complicated task, for several reason The first is that many native people who are only seasonally employed in th wage economy or not employed in it at all may not think of themselves a unemployed when they are hunting, fishing, and trapping as a matter o preference. Indeed, one characteristic of the native labour force is that it members often prefer short-term employment so that they can hunt or tra during the appropriate periods of the year. In this way they gain thei livelihood from a combination of sources—wages, wildlife harvesting, an (often) transfer payments from governments, such as welfare, family, or old age allowances.

Similarly, native people who hunt, fish, or trap with the intention o selling some or all of their harvest tend not to interpret a low financial retur from these sources as evidence of underemployment, as non-natives migh Not only do they consume some of the harvest, they also tend to see th harvesting activities themselves as worthwhile and not to be judged solely b the revenue they produce. The native pattern of participation in th economy—and it must be stressed that there are many exceptions: native who are employed full time for years or who hunt or fish only ver occasionally, and others who receive good incomes from trapping[44]—doe enable natives to undertake certain activities that are culturally important t them. However, there can be no denying that northern native people tend t be very poor and that the wage economy does not come close to providin them with the employment opportunities they seek.

In reality, unemployment among northern natives is even greater than i appears to be. This is a second reason for being wary of official unemploy ment statistics. Official versions of the unemployment rate anywhere i Canada only count as unemployed those workers who are actually seekin work and who have not yet found it—in other words, only the members of th "active labour force." The statistics do not report individuals who have com to view their prospects as so poor that they have given up seekin employment. Many native northerners fall into this category simply becaus jobs are so scarce. For example, Baker Lake can supply only one job for ever four or five employable natives.[45] The Council for Yukon Indians views th unemployment situation in the Yukon native communities outside o Whitehorse as almost as serious.[46]

The overall situation can be appreciated by means of labour-forc participation statistics. Using the narrow Indian Act definition of a nativ person, the 1980 population of the N.W.T. was composed almost equally o natives and non-natives.[47] However, there were two and a half times as man non-natives in the active labour force as there were natives.[48] The native participation rate—the percentage of natives of working age actually in the active labour force—was 38 per cent, while the rate for the total N.W.T. including native labour was 56 per cent.[49] In this way, the unemployment figure understates the true extent of native unemployment.

The basic problem is that the towns to which the native people moved or were moved from their hunting camps hold very few jobs. Manufacturing is not likely to establish in them, government offers little employment for natives, and megaprojects are few in number and may not encourage native employment.[50] However, the traditional economy has been undermined by the movement to the towns, in that the land immediately adjacent to them cannot possibly support wildlife harvesting by all the people of the settlement. The low regenerative capacity of the land historically led the native people to live in a highly dispersed pattern. Now that they are clustered, the land cannot support them as it once did, although it does permit some hunting, fishing, and trapping.[51]

To make matters worse, unemployment seems likely to rise, particularly in the N.W.T., because of changes in the native population. Since the population is so young, primarily a result of the very high rate of natural increase within the native population in the last two decades, large numbers of young people are entering the labour force. The N.W.T. labour force is expected to grow by 20 per cent from 1980 to 1985, while employment is expected to increase by only 2 per cent, barring some unforeseen development.[52] Over those five years, the unemployment rate for the whole N.W.T. labour force is expected to rise from 15.6 per cent to 27 per cent,[53] with the figures for the native labour force certain to be much higher. This increased unemployment will continue the cycle of personal and family breakdown that has plagued northern natives and seems likely to be passed on to yet another generation.

This brief summary identifies three basic economic features of the North. First, its colonial status weakens its economy. Second, the tension between its two different economic emphases complicates it. Third, the northern economies are volatile: change is basic to them. At the start of the 1980s both the Yukon and the Northwest Territories were still colonial economies and were in the economic doldrums; however, the changes of the recent past ought not to be discounted. For example, total personal income in the N.W.T. increased by 547 per cent between 1967 and 1977, as contrasted with 341 per cent for all Canada.[54] The role of government in the North mushroomed during the 1970s. The government of the N.W.T.'s spending totalled $4.6 million in the fiscal year 1967-68 and $269.8 million in 1978-79.[55] The Yukon government's spending grew from $13.9 million to $108 million during the same span.[56]

Looking to the future, native unemployment seems likely to increase substantially. An increased emphasis on traditional activities might cushion

the shock of this unemployment to some extent, but the place of renewabl
resources in the northern economy has yet to be finally determined
Megaprojects may come into being, which could increase employment an
add greatly to governmental revenues. However, megaprojects might under
mine the hunting, fishing, and trapping economies and further strain th
social fabric of the North, particularly if the native people feel that they ar
not receiving a fair share of the jobs created by the projects. Accommodation
may be found between the two contrasting approaches to the economic futur
of the North. Nonetheless, differences on economic questions will pos
particularly formidable challenges to northern policy makers, because th
contrasts are so fundamental and because the colonial economy of the Nort
probably does not have the wealth to underwrite satisfactory compromises.

Northern Social Structure

Because the political and economic forces that dominate the North ar
directed from outside the North, a description of the structure of the North
colonial society should begin in the South, with the multinational corpora
tions and the government of Canada.

1. Multinational Corporations

As has been noted, the cost of northern megaprojects virtually necessitates th
participation of powerful multinational corporations. Their political goa
in the North is to seek an environment in which to maximize profit an
growth and to minimize risk. They support a quick resolution of nativ
claims because the uncertainty until their settlement increases risk—of eithe
violence[57] or delays through litigation. This uncertainty makes it difficult fo
the multinationals to weigh probable costs against probable incomes whe
they make corporate decisions. Uncertainty over native claims also makes i
difficult for the multinationals to persuade investors to advance the hug
sums of money needed to finance megaprojects. However, while they suppor
claims settlements, the multinationals do not wish these settlements to giv
powers to native people that might stand in the way of their projects. Thei
interests require that native land ownership be as restricted as possible an
apply only to surface rights, thus leaving resource companies free to explor
and develop subsurface resources. Similarly, the multinationals woul
oppose any settlement that would give the native people any real power ove
resource production, pricing, or royalty decisions.

Multinationals want to avoid environmental damage both as a matter o
principle and because they know that a major environmental calamity coul
arouse public opinion against them and poison their relationship wit
Ottawa. At the same time they must pay the costs of environmenta
protection and frequently view the standards Ottawa sets as too restrictive
For example, Ottawa requires that the drilling season in the Beaufort Sea b
terminated before the point at which approaching ice actually forces th

rillships off their sites. This regulation is intended to ensure that should a lowout[58] occur, even in the last days of drilling, there will be time to drill a elief well to stop the flow before the winter ice moves in and forces an end to hipborne drilling operations. The drillers attempt to persuade Ottawa to nd the drilling season as late as possible in order to get as much information s they can from each season and to reduce the period of "wintering over" vhen their expensive ships and facilities are idle. The result may be a sacrifice f environmental values, even though they were recognized in principle.

Similarly, multinationals operating in the North recognize that their ctivities are likely to inflict some degree of social damage on nearby ommunities. However, they vary in the responsibility they are willing to ssume. Employment policies are the most prominent example. The older stablished mines tend not to have policies aimed at training native workers nd employing them. The trend in mines that have recently been established r are about to be created is toward achieving specified native-employment argets. The Nanisivik mine is supposed to have a 60 per cent native work orce, although for a variety of reasons, not all the fault of the company, the ate of native employment has not exceeded 24 per cent.[59]. The Polaris mine, cheduled to be opened by Cominco in 1982, is likely to achieve greater uccess because of an improved training program and more satisfactory cheduling of shift changes for native workers. Finally, the oil and gas xploration industry tends to attempt to employ substantial native work orces, while pipeline proponents have not all shown quite the same nthusiasm.[60]

However, industry attempts to deal with the community problems aused by the sudden influx of cash from wages, the absence of family nembers working away from the community, or the intergenerational lashes that employment can produce. While perhaps they ought not to bear ne primary responsibility, their statements on social impact tend to ninimize the social destruction that will follow in their wake.

The Government of Canada

)ttawa's goals for the North are enshrined in a statement entitled *Northern* ˈanada in the Seventies,[61] which lists them as follows:

1. To provide for a higher standard of living, equality of life and equality of opportunity for northern residents by methods which are compatible with their own preferences and aspirations.
2. To maintain and enhance the northern environment with due consideration to economic and social development.
3. To encourage viable economic development within regions of the northern territories so as to realize their potential contribution to the national economy and the material well-being of Canadians.
4. To realize the potential contribution of the northern territories to the social and cultural development of Canada.
5. To further the evolution of government in the northern territories.

Ottawas goals for the North [handwritten margin note]

6. To maintain Canadian sovereignty and security in the North.
7. To develop fully the leisure and recreation opportunities in the northern territories.

The goals identified in this statement are laudable, but they are al contradictory. They recognize, though only implicitly, that the governme of Canada bears a special constitutional responsibility for the wellbeing native people. Indeed, many federal civil servants have laboured with gre devotion to achieve this goal. However, they have gained little success: fir the problems facing northern natives are extremely complex and seven second, neither social science nor practical experience in the North h produced a formula that has gained a great deal of credibility in Ottawa f addressing the problems of northern natives.

This is not to say that such a formula does not exist. While this judgme does point to a weakness of theory and praxis, it also acknowledges a thi reason that implementing such a formula would conflict with the norther goals closest to Ottawa's heart. In other words, while the government Canada is officially committed to the wellbeing of northern native people and to the protection of the northern environment—and some feder officials sincerely seek these ends, the balance of power and opinion Ottawa favours non-renewable-resource development over providing f native people and the environment.[62] Departments more powerful than tl Inuit and Indian Affairs side of DIAND—departments such as the Treasu Board and Energy, Mines and Resources—find it too costly, either in dolla or in modification of their own programs, to accept the kinds of policies th might truly address the problems of native people and environment protection.

In deciding among the contending policy claims its various departmen and ministers press on it, the cabinet considers above all the interests southern Canada viewed in the context of southern assumptions about tl North. The first and foremost set of interests is economic. Canada has entere the 1980s as an economically troubled country. Inflation has been running; a painful rate, unemployment has been high, and the immediate futu promises little relief. Canadian capital has been turning to opportuniti abroad rather than in Canada. The country has been in an unfavourab balance-of-payments position caused at least in part by its reliance o substantial quantities of expensive imported oil. Finally, there has been gre concern about the future availability of secure stocks of crude oil and, i central Canada, about Ottawa's ability to direct the use of western oil and g; "for national purposes."

Northern megaprojects have seemed a promising response to several these problems. They appear likely to assist with the unemployme problem by stimulating economic growth. For example, Allan MacEache the leader of Ottawa's team negotiating the Alaska Highway Pipelir Agreement with the United States, promised that the project would provic

00 000 man-years of employment and pump as much as $4 billion into the anadian economy.[63] If the northern portion of the pipeline does proceed, flation will have raised this figure far above MacEachen's 1977 estimate. milarly, Dome Petroleum takes pains to emphasize that their plans involve lacing substantial orders with Canadian shipyards, for whom such contacts would be a great boon.

The economic activity that northern megaprojects stimulate in the outh provides opportunities for investment capital. Northern megaprojects use Canadian funds to stay in or foreign funds to enter Canada, thereby ountering the tendency of Canada to run a deficit on the capital flows into id out of the country. An even more significant pressure on Canada's lance of payments is the deficit resulting from the import of foreign crude l. If Canada could substitute frontier oil for some or all of this foreign oil, is drain on the national wealth would be eliminated. Also, supply would be ore certain because Canada would not depend on the vagaries of Middle-ast politics. In addition, the federal treasury would not be drained by the eed to subsidize foreign oil imports in order to keep the Canadian price as far elow world levels as Ottawa wants it to be. If Ottawa continues a policy of wer than world prices for oil and gas, it may have to subsidize the roduction of frontier oil, but at least a large portion of that subsidy will main in Canada and stimulate the Canadian economy. The extent of the enefit, of course, would depend on the oil industry's decisions and on ttawa's appetite for regulating the oil industry.

Northern energy production seems particularly attractive to Ottawa, in at the federal government alone enjoys the legal right to all of the royalties om that production and possesses complete regulatory authority over the roduction of the oil and gas. It will not have to face the negotiating and rolonged deadlock on these matters that have plagued its dealings with the ydrocarbon-producing provinces, particularly Alberta. In view of the retched history of this federal-provincial relationship since 1973, this rospect must seem tremendously attractive to Ottawa. Indeed, the aspects of e 1980 National Energy Program, which encourages northern hydrocarbon xploration, seem to reflect this reasoning.

Because energy has become such a critical issue, northern energy projects ave appeared to hold out particular promise for Ottawa. However, mining evelopments have also seemed likely to stimulate the southern-Canadian onomy by providing jobs and markets for industry, to assist Canada's lance of payments if the mines' output is shipped out of Canada, and to rovide royalty and tax revenues for Ottawa. In addition, mining develop-ents are smaller in scale than the proposed energy megaprojects and ccordingly will not cause the kind of economic dislocation anticipated for e megaprojects. For example, they will not swallow up such immense sums f capital nor monopolize certain types of tradespeople, thus obstructing rowth in other economic sectors. Finally, while northern mines may rely on

new forms of shipping to carry their ore or concentrate to market, they a
generally less technologically innovative than are the energy projects; aft
all, a mine is a mine. Costs are therefore less likely to soar above t
projections because of unforeseen problems associated with new technolog
Costly breakdowns are also less likely. For all of these reasons, Ottawa h
welcomed new mining activities in the North.

Northern mines and oil and gas operations also appeal to Ottaw
because they reinforce Canada's claim to sovereignty over its Arctic Islan
The most contentious issue of Arctic sovereignty today is Canada's right
regulate shipping traffic through the waters of the Canadian North
Canada's claim to control the islands is generally accepted, but policy make
fear that it may come into question if substantial resource discoveries a
made, particularly if the resources found are energy resources. The mo
effective method of countering such a claim is to conform to the tradition
international law that "effective occupation" is a fundamental method
demonstrating sovereignty. Effective occupation could be gained by statio
ing a substantial military establishment in the Arctic Islands, but th
solution would be extremely expensive. Far more preferable is to show t
flag in the form of mines and energy undertakings under Canadia
authority. Rather than costing anything, these projects could actually bene
Ottawa financially and the country economically. Thus, Ottawa has bo
economic and diplomatic interests in the North that lead it to promo
megaprojects.

The most damning view of Ottawa's behaviour in the North is that th
interest in large-scale economic development has led Ottawa to run interfe
ence for industry in some objectionable ways. One highly publicized examp
is the Banks Island episode of 1970 in which the federal government lied
the Bankslanders about seismic activities in the area in order to clear the w.
for industry to proceed with its plans.[65] A more recent example is t
Northern Pipeline Act, described in Chapter 4, which creates a regulato
regime so favourable to the builders of the Alaska Highway pipeline that
has been bitterly characterized by a spokesman for native people as a "W
Measures Act against Indians." Even more objectionable to native people
Bill C-48, the Canada Oil and Gas Act. This bill, which was introduced in th
House of Commons in December of 1980, has provoked an outcry of ange
particularly among northern leaders, native and non-native. Their particul
concerns include provisions in the bill that:

1. Direct all royalties on production in the North to Ottawa and
2. Appear to give the Minister of Energy, Mines and Resources exceeding
   broad discretion to decide on approval of oil and gas developme
   projects in the North without necessarily having to refer them to t
   regulatory process they must pass now.

The bill completely ignores the concept of aboriginal title and that nati claims remain outstanding throughout the lands in question. On the basis of such a record, it is not surprising that one allegation commonly heard in the North is that the federal government's interest in native claims is strictly to remove the encumbrance an unsettled claim places on the exploration and development efforts by companies at work in the North.

Without commenting on the validity of this view, Ottawa's policies can also partly be explained in terms of social philosophy and a particular interpretation of social realities of the North. The social philosophy of southern Canada leans heavily on materialism and individualism. Canadians tend to stress that individual and personal satisfaction is based on material attainments; the group and the gratifications of intangible relationships within it are less important. In the postwar period when the Canadian government began to pay attention to its northern native population, it could not help but be struck by the material poverty of that population. Yet northern natives did not consider themselves poor. Of course, the lot of northern natives was exceedingly hard, even to the point of occasional death by starvation. However, the native people tended to interpret their situation as richer and more satisfying than did Ottawa because they were accustomed to a hard life and because they were sustained by the support of extended family ties, other social relationships, and traditions and rituals associated with their ways of life.

Regardless, Ottawa's southern values led it to interpret the native lifestyle as so unrewarding as to be dead, incapable of resuscitation. Accordingly, the special characteristics that differentiated northern natives from other "poor Canadians" were ignored and it was decided that the northern native people should have applied to them the policies the welfare state generally applied to its less-advantaged members. This policy meant concentrating the native people in settlements where medical and educational programs could be economically provided. Ultimately, native people who were healthier and better educated (in white terms) would be able to assume a position alongside the other elements of the Canadian population. While this goal was assimilationist and highly judgmental, it was not necessarily malicious in its intent, for it was based on the individualistic and materialistic view that no alternative to "poverty" existed for northern natives.

Ottawa has clear interests in the North, which lead it to subordinate the evolution of northern native society to the needs of megadevelopment whenever the two principles come into conflict. It also operates on the basis of certain principles consistent with policies of accommodating northern natives to changes dictated by external factors rather than of accommodating northern development to the needs of the native people. If development has been the final goal, what political resources has the federal government in seeking it? The answer is that its formal powers are almost absolute. Parliament is sovereign over the North and need not negotiate its policies with any other government or with any group in northern society. Ever aboriginal title only exists at the pleasure of Ottawa, for Parliament has th legal authority to legislate aboriginal right out of existence.[66]

However, while Ottawa's formal powers are almost limitless, its actua power is limited. Ottawa needs the economic advantages that norther development might supply. If it is willing to go only a limited distance in th direction of state ownership, it must rely on private corporations as th vehicles for this development. This reliance leads to a relationship c dependence that the corporations can exploit if they wish by claiming tha they will not undertake a development unless they receive certain polic concessions. However, its growing enthusiasm for using crown corporation as a vehicle for northern development may be a major policy contrast betwee the 1970s and the 1980s. The National Energy Program of 1980 dealt Petro Canada a strong hand in general and in frontier exploration in particular. I Petro-Canada continues to enjoy strong governmental support, the politica leverage of multinationals operating in the North will decline.

Ottawa is also limited in using the power it has as a result of it dependence on information gathered by development proponents because i lacks the resources or, more correctly, has not allocated the resources to gathe the information itself. Because it depends on this information, it can be le toward certain decisions by the manipulation of the information it receives. Finally, Canada may be subject to pressure from the United States concernin some aspects of northern policy. For example, the United States will want t guarantee unhindered shipping through the Arctic Islands so that its tanker may freely use this route, should it become economical. In this and othe matters that will arise in the future, the United States is sure to bring i formidable political resources to bear against Ottawa, which is a mismatch. In this sense, while Ottawa is much more powerful than its colonies in th North, it is constrained in its use of that power by forces to which it may hav to defer.

The large, usually multinational corporations and Ottawa define th northern political context. Still, the local structure of northern society shape the political issues in the North as well as the North's response to issues thrus on it from outside. As the North gradually achieves greater legal authority the political dimensions of its social structure will become all the mor important in determining northern politics.

3. The Native People

In 1978, 9740 Indians and Métis and 14 485 Inuit lived in the Northwes Territories[69] and about 6000 Indians and Métis lived in the Yukon.[70] Th appearance, language, skills, politics, and goals of these people displa almost as much variety as does Canadian society all told. For example, th native people of the Yukon have been greatly affected by the white contac because a large proportion of Yukon natives have moved into communitie along the Alaska Highway. In contrast, the Inuit have had less direct contact with large numbers of whites and their contact has been much more recent. As a result, their culture retains more traditional, particularly religious, elements. The Yukon Indians face the most immediate threat of social and cultural dislocation from the Alaska Highway gas pipeline. The Inuit are not facing the pressure that the imminent prospect of such a huge undertaking creates, although the communities around the Beaufort Sea must address the prospects posed by the successful drilling in the area. Because of these and other variations from region to region and because natives are as individual as the members of any other social group, generalizations about them may hide more than they reveal. Still, while stereotyping must be avoided, it is possible to speak meaningfully about the native experience in northern Canada since "contact," the first exposure to non-natives. The importance of this experience is that it explains so much of the native peoples' situation today.

Native life before the arrival of whites was far from simple and static. Waves of native migration passed over the North and it was not uncommon for adjacent groups of native people to struggle for control of particular hunting and trapping areas.[71] (See Figures 1-3 and 1-4 for settlement areas.) Also, the economies of the native people varied from place to place, depending on the species and abundance of the animals available to be hunted. Northern natives lacked the technological sophistication of the Europeans with whom they came into contact, but they had a sophistication of their own that enabled them to survive in an environment overwhelming to the early European visitors. In addition, northern natives evolved cultures particularly suited to the stresses of living in close quarters and under constant threat from natural calamities such as prolonged inclement weather or the failure of the hunt because the animals did not appear when expected. To survive in such conditions, ethics of sharing and egalitarianism restricted wasteful competition. Similarly, self-control prevented outbursts that might embitter relations in a hunting camp and obstruct the cooperation on which all relied for their survival.[72] Even today, native people tend to keep feelings inside themselves.

Politics have been consensual rather than adversarial. Commands are not usually given. Instead, clues are given to indicate that some action should be taken, but without risking the indignation that might be aroused if someone presumed to be superior by giving a command. It would be improper, for example, to order someone to fill a lamp with more oil if it were running low. Rather, a person who was in a position to want a lamp to be filled without doing it himself would simply refer to the fact that it was running low and someone would accept the responsibility for filling it, without appearing to have been commanded to do so. In this way, which is particularly characteristic of Inuit culture, confrontation is avoided and harmony in the group is maintained.

Another very important element of native culture has been the unity the native people feel between themselves and the land. Non-natives view land as pieces of property that individuals buy, hold, and sell essentially for economic gain. While the land does provide an economic base for the native people of Canada's North, it also has a deep symbolic significance, in that natives see it and themselves as equal parts of the same larger system. Because they are a part of the land and it of them, they do not see themselves as "owning" it, and traditionally avoid exploiting or abusing it.[73] Many native customs and religious beliefs originate from their experiences on the land. Their success in living off the land and the patterning of their lives accordingly to the cycle of the seasons on the land have traditionally been profound sources of psychological meaning in their lives. Thus, for example, native trappers may not "make a profit" with their hunting and trapping activities; however, they continue their trapping activities—often financing them with income from the non-traditional economic sector—because "on the land" is where they want to be.

The native feeling for the land can be appreciated through the words of René Lamothe, speaking to the Berger Inquiry:

Figure 1-3
Distribution of Historic Inuit Groups
in the Northwest Territories

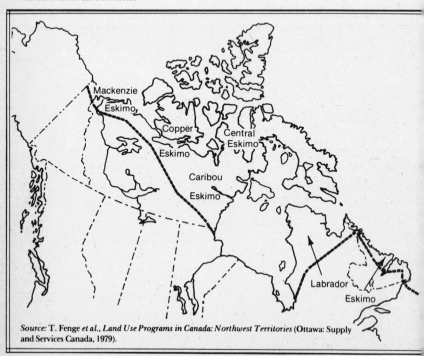

Source: T. Fenge et al., Land Use Programs in Canada: Northwest Territories (Ottawa: Supply and Services Canada, 1979).

The love of the Dene for the land is in their tone of voice, a touch, the care for plants, the life of the people, and their knowledge that life as a people stems directly from the land. The land is seen as mother because she gives life, because she is the provider, the protector, the comforter. . . . She is a teacher, a teacher who punishes swiftly when we err, yet a benefactress who blesses abundantly when we live with integrity, respect her, and love the life she gives. We cannot stand on her with integrity and respect and claim to love the life she gives and allow her to be ravaged.[74]

To summarize, northern native peoples at the time of the first appearance of white men had developed cultural systems that included technical mastery of their environment, religious belief and symbolism, and patterns of social organization that were well adapted to the hard realities of life in the North. Their lifestyles should not be romanticized: they were difficult and no more perfect than those of other societies. Still, their ways had coherence and internal unity. These cultures comprised a number of aspects—religious, economic, political, esthetic—that shared a unifying logic and reinforced one another in a powerful and psychologically satisfying way. Many of the elements of these cultures remain among northern native peoples; their image of themselves as peoples and their desire to grow as peoples are very

Figure 1-4
Distribution of Historic Indian Groups in the North

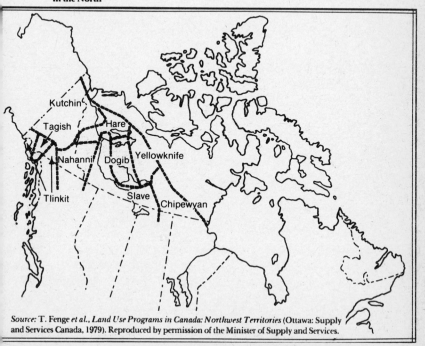

Source: T. Fenge *et al., Land Use Programs in Canada: Northwest Territories* (Ottawa: Supply and Services Canada, 1979). Reproduced by permission of the Minister of Supply and Services.

strong. However, what has changed is that contact with white society has destroyed the unifying logic that gave coherence to the old cultures. Contact has repudiated some of their elements, denied the moral authority of native ways, and created economic and social conditions that undermine the old culture without providing a viable substitute.

Several forces have contributed to this pattern. The first was the fur trade. This trade took a variety of forms across the Arctic, but its major significance was to introduce white trade goods such as guns, traps, and metal knives into the native economy. Over time, native people came to accept these and other items that made their lives easier and more pleasant, in most cases without drastically altering their traditional land-based economy. It is worth noting as evidence that "tradition" does not necessarily mean an unchanging life as a museum piece (a charge sometimes directed against native claims to prove the alleged impossibility of their achieving their goals) that native societies were at first generally able to adapt white technology to traditional purposes without great social disruption. It was not the fur trade itself that hurt the native people, but the collapse of fur prices that began in the 1930s and lasted until the mid-1950s. Native people found they could not afford the goods that the trade had made available to them and on which they had come to rely. The result was the creation of southern-style poverty in the North and the loss of native self-reliance and dignity.

The second force was Christianity—or, rather, the missionaries who carried it to the northern natives. The missionaries helped the native people by giving them as much medical aid as possible, by creating written forms of native languages, and by attempting to curb violence in native life. However, they demanded that the native people end practices the missionaries considered pagan, but whose traditional symbolism was a source of great emotional comfort and group identity—of "we-ness"—and thus of social cohesion for the native people. To the demoralization that resulted from the banning of drum dancing and the wearing of lip ornaments[75] was added the great sadness when native children, often at a very young age, were separated from their parents to attend mission-run schools. In the schools, the use of native languages was often harshly forbidden and the children were made to feel ashamed of their identities. When they returned to their parents, they were marginal people, not equipped to function in white society, yet incapable of rejoining native society in the fullest sense.[76] The impact of the missions was all the greater because they faced no regulation or competition that might have made them less aggressive. For decades the federal government had no great interest in the North other than to assert sovereignty over it. Like all colonial powers, Ottawa wanted to minimize its spending on its colony and was very happy to let the churches take on the responsibility for education and the provision of social assistance in the North. The missions had a free hand in the North. Though their intentions were undoubtedly good, they wrought havoc on native social and family values.

The loss of economic and religious integrity had an enervating impact on most native people, causing them to feel that for the first time they were encountering overpowering social forces. Formerly, they had a great deal of experience in their world to plan their actions. The coming of non-natives replaced this world with a new one in which unpredictable and inexplicable events regularly occurred. They found such a world most debilitating psychologically because they could not predict with confidence what the consequences of their actions might be. The resulting anxiety and frustration were reinforced by the imposition of a legal system that, while often sympathetically enforced, emphasized the native people's new subordination by casting aside—indeed, declaring illegal—traditional ways of dealing with social problems and wrong doing. Here again, native ways succumbed to the dictates of white society.[77]

The fourth factor occurred during the Second World War in the Yukon and during the 1950s in the N.W.T. This factor was the movement—often forced—of native people out of their scattered hunting camps and into towns. In the Yukon, the impetus came from the construction of the Alaska Highway. Many native people moved to crossroads on the Highway in the hope of gaining employment and in this way improving on their economic position, which had been hurt by falling fur prices. Others moved because they were ejected by government from the lands they had traditionally occupied.[78] This ejection remains a major source of Indian bitterness in the Yukon. An additional factor—which played a major part in the urbanizing of native people in the Mackenzie—was that government services were only provided in the villages. Many families in the Mackenzie moved into villages to be near their children who were attending schools, because the government applied a great deal of pressure to make the children attend. In some instances in the eastern Arctic, Inuit were simply forced to move to the communities.[79] The major economic result of this northern urbanization is that it created a situation in which the land surrounding each village could not possibly sustain the traditional pursuits of the people. Northern natives historically lived in a sparse pattern of settlement because it was the only way to avoid exhausting the fish, game, and marine mammals that the limited capacity of the land and water could provide. Clustering the people together meant that only a fraction of them could sustain themselves on the land.[80] The rest had only minimal prospects of employment and—to fill the needs that the very limited economies of the towns could not fill—welfare payments. In this way, the end product of urbanization has been the creation of a generation of native people who, because of no innate inferiority on their part, have fallen victim to the sense of failure and hopelessness that welfare dependence produces.

A survey of native social problems in the North demonstrates that they have good cause to feel demoralized. Native people tend to be poor. Together, the continuation of the traditional economy, wage employment and government transfer payments in the form of social assistance, family allowances, and payments to the elderly usually provide northern native people with only a marginal income and one far less than whites enjoy. For example, the 1976 per-capita income in Frobisher Bay, which has a 60 per cent white population, was $5040, whereas 1976 per-capita income in Pangnirtung, also on Baffin Island but with only a 10 per cent white population, was only $2206. Similar figures for Yellowknife, 87 per cent white, and nearby Rae Edzo, 9 per cent white, were $8027 and $1407.[81] Such figures must be handled carefully because they do not necessarily translate in terms of the quality of life or personal happiness in the communities, some of which depend much less on the dollar economy than others. For example, people in Pangnirtung obtain most of their food from the land and live in government housing with very low rent. However, even allowing for such differences in lifestyle, there can be no denying that most northern natives lack cash, particularly in comparison to the non-natives in their communities.

Northern natives suffer from a variety of social ills that reflect the terrible stress of uncontrolled, profound, and rapid change. Alcohol use is probably the most severe problem, in that it is so widespread and is so often a factor in family and other violence—which has increased significantly in the North in the last quarter-century.[82] Alcohol also contributes to a high incidence of accidents leading to death and injury. The problem of alcoholism has been widely recognized and has led some communities to either ban or restrict its import into the community. For example, in some cases, local committees judge applications by individuals to bring in liquor and decide on the basis of their assessment of the individual's ability to use the alcohol in a responsible fashion. Such experiments in local control have had substantial success but, overall, alcoholism remains a grave problem.

Native people also suffer from health problems far more than do other Canadians. The native infant mortality rate runs about three times that for non-native infants.[83] Suicide is becoming increasingly common, particularly among younger native people. In one particularly unhappy case, Frobisher Bay in 1978 experienced six suicides of young Inuit in a total Inuit population of under 1600.[84] Substantial numbers of native people suffer from a variety of psychological disorders that reflect the turmoil, anxiety, and frustration they feel.[85] Native nutrition is often deficient, for many native people have to some degree substituted foods with little nutritive value for high-protein native food. A serious problem has been the extremely high incidence of dental problems caused by the native people's appetite for sugared food products, such as candy and soft drinks. In one example, the 450 people of Coral Harbour consumed 100 000 candy bars and 4000 cases of pop in 1976.[86]

One aspect of the northern social picture that might offer some hope for the future is education. However, young native people are only beginning to receive the kind of educational experience that will provide them with a strong cultural background to help them face change with a more secure sense of themselves. The Northwest Territories has initiated a policy of permitting 40 per cent of class time to be devoted to native cultural education, the content of which is determined by each local community. In contrast, the Yukon government has done little in this regard other than to finance some curriculum development projects and one small native-run school, in Burwash Landing. A serious problem in both territories is the high dropout rate among native students. They leave school not only because of the gap between native culture and the curriculum, but also because they feel that academic preparation is unlikely to lead to employment and, accordingly, is not worthwhile. As a result, for example, of 1138 native students in Yukon elementary and secondary schools in 1978-79, only twelve were in Grade 12, the last year of high school.[87]

While these social problems form a grim enough catalogue on their own, their impact and their permanence are all the greater because they are interrelated. In a sense they resemble the pathology of poverty that all people at the lower end of the social ladder share. Children experience the failure and powerlessness of their parents and come to anticipate it for themselves. This expectation and ill health, often associated with poor housing and nutrition, contribute to lack of interest in their school performance. Dropping out of school reduces employment prospects and adds to the despair and dependence that promote psychological disorders and a continuation of the cycle. Worse, the racial factor intensifies the problem in the North, in that native people also experience the culture shock of facing the dominance of an alien culture whose unfamiliar ways make it all the more difficult for them to succeed according to its standards. They also feel the injustice of the imposition of white control over their lands and their lives. In addition, ethnic stereotyping often stands in the way of their succeeding in white society or of even trying to succeed. Finally, while the urban poor sometimes live in cities where there are employment opportunities or can in some instances move to these opportunities, northern natives often find it very difficult to face the move away from the North, yet they live in settlements in which enough jobs simply do not exist. They are truly trapped.

However, an increasingly assertive northern-native leadership argues that they need not always be trapped. These leaders, mostly young people, reflect a growing ethnic awareness and political energy among their people. As northern natives return to their cultural roots, they are coming to realize that the problems they face as peoples are more a comment on Canadian society than they are on the native people who have fallen victim to the larger society's policies. Interpreting their ethnic identity in terms of non-native legal concepts, they are coming to view themselves as nations and, as nations, entitled to self-determination. This view leads them to seek, while remaining within Canada, the legal authority to control the factors that will shape their futures, as much as it is possible for any government to control these forces. In

this way, they seek powers that generally resemble those of the provinces
With these powers, northern natives could redefine the economic choices the
face. For example, some native people receive welfare for part of the year and
use the money to obtain supplies and equipment for living on the land
Others combine some forms of wage labour with welfare, or rely totally or
wage labour to finance their activities on the land. With real economi
authority, the native people feel that they might be able to rationalize thi
haphazard arrangement by organizing some form of guaranteed annua
income for natives who hunt, fish, and trap.

While this type of program as well as the provision of jobs and trainin
for natives are important, even more important is the healing of the socia
and psychological wounds the native people have suffered during the las
century. This healing requires the rekindling of dignity and self-esteem tha
can only be achieved by regaining the ability to control their lives, an abilit
they lost with the coming of white men. Should this renaissance happen
through their recognition as self-determining nations, native people will b
in a much stronger position to apply their traditional values to the changin
world and to evolve a relationship with other Canadians that embodies thei
integrity and worth as native peoples.

Because a great deal of rhetoric has been spoken about this future, it
nature deserves some comment. Opponents of natives' aspirations ofter
condemn them as attempts to revert to a past that can never be revived. Thi
interpretation takes as its starting point the natives' emphasis on th
retention of traditional values. It then simply assumes that "traditiona
values" imply a static life and unchanging technology and argues th
impossibility of such a life, if only because almost all native people hav
come to rely to some degree on white technology and cash income, an
because the land simply cannot feed the present number of native people
While the facts these opponents use are correct, they do not lead to th
suggested conclusion because the natives' traditional values are no mor
static and unchanging than non-natives' traditional values are: a cultur
applies its time-tested ideas and forms of social organization to nev
situations. In this way the culture evolves new forms, yet retains a coherenc
because the old forms are adapted to the new.

What is most important in maintaining the viability of the culture i
that the people be in a position to decide themselves how their traditions wil
evolve under changed circumstances. They must have enough control ove
these circumstances to ensure that they are not so radically and suddenl
changed as to utterly distort the culture. For natives to obtain this control, th
status quo in the North would have to change substantially. Such a grea
social change is unlikely to occur as a result of a piecemeal and evolutionar
process. If native people are to break out of their trap, their place in norther
society must be redefined. The only opportunity on the horizon that seem
substantial enough to produce such a redefinition is the settlement of native

claims. This is why the claims have assumed such great symbolic as well as economic importance for northern native people.

The Appendix argues that the success of any group engaged in politics depends largely on its political resources. For the native people of Canada's North, these resources are modest, but not negligible. Electorally, northern natives count for almost nothing in determining the composition of the House of Commons. They have not figured prominently in shaping the Legislative Assembly of the Yukon, both because they form a minority of the Yukon electorate and because they have not organized to vote as a bloc. However, in the Northwest Territories, natives form a majority of the electorate and succeeded in 1979 in electing an Assembly with a native majority and a number of whites sympathetic to native interests. The high priority given by this Assembly to the native cause is a major political resource.

Northern natives also enjoy a substantial degree of sympathy from southern Canadians who feel disturbed by the treatment that native people have historically received in Canada. This feeling has an institutional base in the largely church-sponsored organizations such as Project North and the Committee for Justice and Liberty, which attempt to rally support for native people in their dealings with Ottawa. These groups successfully brought pressure to bear on Ottawa's northern-pipeline decision of 1977. The ethical question the natives' situation raises is increasingly receiving international exposure, which embarrasses the federal government. For example, in 1980, when Canadian natives appealed to the United Kingdom not to patriate the British North America Act until Ottawa adequately safeguarded their rights, northern natives made special appeals in support of their claims.

The concept of aboriginal right represents another political resource of northern natives. The exact nature of the guarantees in law that this concept gives native people has never been clearly determined by the Canadian judicial system. The constitutional proposals—which at the time of writing are still before Parliament—provide that "the aboriginal and treaty rights of Aboriginal Peoples of Canada are hereby recognized and affirmed." If the constitutional package becomes law, this affirmation will provide a great psychological lift for native people: the view of themselves will be entrenched in the constitution, a view they have struggled for decades to convince the federal government to accept. It would legitimize their continued participation as a people in Canadian society. However, this provision may not greatly strengthen aboriginal right as a political resource. As Chapter 2 discusses in detail, aboriginal title has been interpreted very narrowly by the courts. It only provides for native hunting, fishing, and trapping on traditional lands, but does not give ownership of them or of the resources underneath them. Moreover, aboriginal right can be extinguished unilaterally by an Act of Parliament. However, because Canada's political parties are reluctant to face the public outcry such a blunt action would arouse, claims based on aboriginal title will remain current and may intimidate the resource developers whom Ottawa wants to exploit northern resources. This ability to thwart Ottawa's wish for economic activity in the North can give native people a degree of leverage, particularly if a major project like the Alaska Highway gas pipeline is left hanging and in need of a slightly more favourable environment before it can be confirmed.

To date, native resources have proven no match for those of the natives' adversaries. The native people lack Ottawa's legal authority to approve drilling in the Beaufort Sea, uranium exploration in the Keewatin, or a pipeline through the Yukon. They lack the economic resources to carry out studies to match the work done by large resource-extraction firms to justify their proposals. Sympathetic groups such as the Canadian Arctic Resources Committee do study megaproject applications and produce testimony before regulatory agencies to support the native groups' positions, but their resources also are limited. Native people certainly lack the wealth to command any of the pressure points of the northern economy in a way that would enable them to bargain with governments from a position of strength. These factors and the fact that megaprojects promise to accomplish several of Ottawa's northern goals lead Ottawa to subordinate the interests of northern natives when considering megaproject applications.

Another deficiency of northern native groups is their fragmentation. Northern natives organize in regional groupings because of the huge size of the North and the differences in their ethnicity, history, and economic interests. This regionalism is unavoidable, but it divides their strength. The native groups also expend a great deal of energy in maintaining their links with their people and giving them real authority in the making of decisions. While this approach is true to the traditional grassroots emphasis of native politics, it complicates the task of the groups' leaders and drains their energies.

Finally, in the Yukon and particularly in the Mackenzie, the distinction between status Indians and native people who are not recognized as native people under the arbitrary definition by the Indian Act has created two groups of natives, one of which receives benefits under the Act and the other of which does not. The economic interests of the two in settling claims may differ and lead them to devote much energy to struggling with each other, rather than uniting against their common antagonist. This problem seems on its way to being resolved in the Yukon with the amalgamation of the Yukon Native Brotherhood and the Yukon Association of Non-Status Indians under the name of the Council of Yukon Indians (CYI). The CYI had existed since 1973 to handle the joint claim of the two groups, but in 1980 replaced them completely by taking over all of their other functions. In the Mackenzie, the Dene Nation and the Métis Association of the Northwest Territories, while not composed purely of status and non-status natives, respectively, have struggled with each other on grounds that owe a great deal to the distinction. This disunity has greatly impeded progress on native claims in the Mackenzie Valley.

The conclusion to be drawn from this sketch of the native people's resources is that the native people face the resource-development industry and the federal government at a substantial disadvantage. Ottawa's eagerness to promote northern development, particularly energy-related projects, is only rarely blocked by the mass sympathy of southern Canadians because they tend to be preoccupied with other political issues closer to home, if they are involved in politics at all. With this source of support neutralized, except in the most dramatic of confrontations, northern natives must rely on their own resources. In this type of struggle, perhaps the greatest resource is determination. So long as they remain committed to their goals, they may lose battles and see their position eroded, but they will at least not have accepted defeat.

4. The Non-native Population of the North[88]

The non-native population of the territories is as diverse as the native population. While some come to the North to settle and create a life for themselves and their families, others motivated strictly by economics intend only to stay in the North long enough to gain the income they are seeking or as long as they can stand the climate and the isolation. Non-natives vary greatly in the degree of sympathy they feel towards native claims and in the extent to which they involve themselves in northern politics. The following discussion will attempt to identify a few of the most prominent categories of northern non-natives, but, as with a description of the native peoples, generalizations must be handled very carefully to avoid stereotyping individuals.

The non-natives in the North can be divided into two basic groups, the long-term residents and the transients; persons of the latter group have not committed themselves to the North and are likely to leave within a few years of their arrival. The long-term residents usually fall into one of three categories. The first of these is the business and professional people and their families. While these people are esthetically attracted to the North and its particular lifestyle, they are primarily motivated by economic considerations and feel particularly acutely the economic stagnation that in recent years has afflicted those sectors of the northern economy dependent on the construction of a pipeline up the Mackenzie Valley and, more recently, on the construction of the Alaska Highway gas pipeline.[89] These business and professional people have anticipated increases in demand either in the form of the direct demand from the builders of these megaprojects or from the increased population anticipated in the wake of the projects. Not only have their expectations been dashed in the Mackenzie and delayed in the Yukon, but business and professional groups must also pay the costs of the inflation that occurred, particularly in real estate, in anticipation of the pipeline boom. In some instances, infrastructure such as hospital additions, water treatment facilities, and serviced land was created, but now is underused leaving a small number of ratepayers to carry an unnecessary burden.[90] This situation creates for the business and professional community a strong interest in a more active economy. Business and professional people tend to feel that, since manufacturing is unlikely to flourish in the North, the most probable source of economic growth is resource extraction. For this reason they tend to support megaprojects and candidates for the territorial assemblies who favour such developments.

While in a sense they depend on southern-Canadian and multinational business initiatives, they often feel estranged from the South. They recognize that the South's interest in them is either romantic or, more usually, based on short-term economic considerations that are unlikely to lead to economic stability in the North. They feel they are treated as colonials not only by corporate decision makers, but also by distant and often seemingly anonymous officials in Ottawa. Their dependence on unresponsive forces particularly offends their special sense of independence. The decision to move to the North without guaranteed employment or economic wellbeing and the will to stay in the North despite economic disappointments and the low level of amenities demand a particular personal energy and strength of will. People with such traits dislike being confined. They resent what they consider to be excessive regulation by government and undue governmental concern for the native claims.

This frustration, amplified by an independence of mind, is the dominant trait of the northern nonnative business and professional community. Its members may enjoy the highest standard of living and social status in northern society, but they feel marginal in terms of the larger forces shaping that society and determining the success they achieve.

The federal and territorial governments employ about 8500 workers in the North.[91] Of these employees, most at the management and professional levels are not native; these people and their families comprise the second group of long-term non-native northerners. Territorial employees favour increased power for the territorial governments and tend to feel anxious about changes, such as the settlements of the claims, that would give native people political powers at the expense of the territorial governments. The federal employees tend not to be unduly concerned about the prospect of increased territorial-government powers, in that such a change would simply mean their transfer from the employment of one government to that of another. In general, both groups of public servants tend not to be active in partisan politics because of the longstanding Canadian tradition separating the roles of public servants and elected politicians.

A third group of long-term non-native northerners includes those who have come to the North primarily to seek relief from the hectic pace and aggressive quality of life in the South. This heterogeneous group consists of some people who have decided to live in the bush and others who approach their wage income or their business activities with a less development-centred philosophy than that of many other non-natives. This group tends not to figure prominently in territorial politics. However, its members can be vocal from time to time and can sometimes be quite effective in reminding inquiries and regulatory panels of the special beauty of the North and the fragility of its social relations.[92]

The short-term non-native residents of the North are also heterogeneous. Many are public servants engaged in the actual delivery of services, such as teachers and nurses, who stay for only a year or two before returning to the South. A number of workers migrate in and out of the territories, depending on the labour needs of the mines and on expectations that rise and fall with each announcement and postponement of megaprojects such as the Alaska Highway pipeline. The most significant such group in the 1980s may well be the gold miners who are returning to the Yukon to work the old goldfields because of the great increase in the price of gold in recent years. A final group of short-term non-native residents in the North are the workers in mines and exploration activities who are flown directly from southern Canada to their shift camps, remain there for a few weeks or months, then return south on rotation.

By and large the short-term non-native residents of the North influence politics very little. Most of them have come north either as public servants— in which case their political activities must be confined—or to make money, a goal the newcomer is hardly likely to attain by becoming active in northern politics. The very fact of their being short-term residents also discourages them from politics, for they tend not to stay in the North long enough to become very interested in social issues. The few who do become interested are likely to be gone long before any effort they might make to seek change through politics will actually achieve results.

The generally apolitical stance of the short-term non-native residents of the North reduces the support base the long-term residents can count on when seeking to press their various claims on Ottawa and reduces the value of their numbers as a political resource. Only in the Yukon can non-natives count on a numerical advantage producing any results on election day. The wealth they can bring to bear on politics is greater than natives can apply to electoral politics, but in the realm of regulatory hearings and interest-group activities in Ottawa, the native groups' funding from Ottawa and occasionally from sympathetic southern groups is on a par with the resources that members of the non-native community can bring to bear. Probably the greatest political resource enjoyed by the non-natives is the way their interests complement those of Ottawa and the corporations; all share the strategy of using non-renewable-resource projects as the cutting edge of economic growth. However, this political resource is an unstable one that permits only intermittent gains, which is what the business and professional community

of the North has been able to manage for itself to date. Long-term non-nativ
residents may form the elite of northern society, but they are very much
colonial elite. Their resources are weak in comparison with the major actor
in northern politics (Ottawa and the corporations) and their best hope lies in
trying to gain the sympathy of these southern powers, a colonial tactic if eve
there was one.

While the non-native population of the North has been politically wea
and dependent vis-à-vis Ottawa, it has been powerful in the small Inui
communities of the eastern Arctic. Until recently in these communities, th
settlement manager was in a position to grant or withhold a variety c
benefits and came to be seen as the agent of the authority of the distant an
powerful government for which he worked. He and the few other non-native
who might reside in the community—the members of the RCMP detachmen
the manager of the Hudson Bay store, the nurse, the teacher, and possibly th
missionary—formed a small elite who ran everything of substance in th
community and thus denied to the Inuit any authority in white institution
The strength of the non-natives in the communities was the weakness of th
Inuit. While most of the non-natives in the communities carried out thei
duties with the best of intentions, the inequalities in the relations betwee
themselves and the Inuit could not help but produce misunderstanding an
bitterness.[93] The growing sophistication in southern ways among the Inu
and changes in local government structures have reduced the politica
inequalities between non-natives and Inuit in the communities to som
degree, but many Inuit still feel subordinated and alienated from the politica
institutions they feel have been imposed upon them.[94]

Conclusion

Despite the diversity within each group, it is valid to generalize that nor
natives and natives in the North face each other across the gulf of the
different cultures and values, a gulf that has been widened by the history o
their contact with one another. Because their relations have not been based o
equality, the difficulty of working constructively together has been con
pounded. When they come together, the legitimacy of institutions, th
firmness of alliances, and basic trust are always in question. The splits i
northern society are to some extent bridged by sympathetic non-natives o
the one hand and acculturated native people on the other: efforts are bein
made, particularly in the Northwest Territories, to build on the communi
of interests that non-natives and natives share as northerners. Still, at the sta
of the 1980s, the jury is still out on the question of the future of th
cooperation. Each of the groups has tended to fasten its hopes onto a formul
for the political and economic future of the North that does not exclude th
other group, but that has come to be interpreted as based on ethnic interes
These two formulae, native claims and "political development," are th
subject of the next two chapters.

Notes

[1] This is Louis St. Laurent's apt description of the policy approach to the North taken by the government of Canada until the 1950s. House of Commons, *Debates*, 22nd Parliament, First Session, Vol. I (Ottawa: Queen's Printer, 1953), p. 698.

[2] Louis-Edmond Hamelin, *Canadian Nordicity*, William Barr (trans.) (Montreal: Harvest House, 1978), pp. 15-46.

[3] K.J. Rea, *The Political Economy of Northern Development*, Background Study No. 36 (Ottawa: Science Council of Canada, 1976), includes much information on the northern parts of the provinces in its analysis.

[4] A fuller discussion of the northern climate may be found in F.K. Hare, "The Atmospheric Environment of the Canadian North," in Douglas H. Pimlott, Kitson M. Vincent, and Christine E. McKnight, *Arctic Alternatives* (Ottawa: Canadian Arctic Resources Committee, 1973).

[5] The phenomenon of permafrost and the engineering problems it creates are the subject of Peter Williams, *Pipelines and Permafrost* (London: Longman Inc., 1979).

[6] Thomas R. Berger, *The Report of the Mackenzie Valley Pipeline Inquiry*, 2 vols. (Ottawa: Supply and Services Canada, 1977), Vol. I, pp. 18-21, and Vol. II, pp. 132-36.

[7] The environmental dangers of offshore drilling are detailed in D. Pimlott, D. Brown, and K. Sam, *Oil under the Ice: Offshore Drilling in the Canadian Arctic* (Ottawa: Canadian Arctic Resources Committee, 1976), Ch. 8.

[8] The policy issues raised by the prospect of this type of shipping are examined in Janet B. Wright (ed.), *Marine Transportation and High Arctic Development: Policy Framework and Priorities* (Ottawa: Canadian Arctic Resources Committee, 1979). Further information can be located in M.J. Dunbar, *Marine Transportation and High Arctic Development: A Bibliography* (Ottawa: Canadian Arctic Resources Institute, 1980). Background issues and a detailed description of the proposed Arctic Marine Locomotive are to be found in Robert F. Keith and Janet B. Wright (eds.), *Northern Transitions*, 2 vols. (Ottawa: Canadian Arctic Resources Committee, 1978), Vol. II, pp. 348-80. The history of Canadian Arctic shipping technology is sketched in T.C. Pullen, "The Development of Arctic Ships," a paper presented to the Royal Society of Canada Symposium, "A Century of Canada's Arctic Islands, 1880-1980" (Yellowknife, August 1980). The paper is excerpted in *Arctic Seas Bulletin*, Vol. 2, no. 9 (September 1980).

[9] Berger, *op. cit.*, Vol. I., p. 68.

[10] H.J.F. Gerein, *Community Planning and Development in Canada's Northwest Territories* (Yellowknife: Government of the Northwest Territories, 1980), p. 20.

[11] See, for example, J.D. Acheson, "Problems of Mental Health in the Canadian Arctic," *Canada's Mental Health*, xx:1 (1972).

[12] Berger, *op. cit.*, Vol. I, p. 25.

[13] Gerein, *op. cit.*, p. 18.

[14] The particular problems of oil pollution in the frigid waters of the North are noted in John B. Sprague, "Aquatic Resources in the Canadian North: Knowledge, Dangers and Research Needs," in Pimlott, Vincent, McKnight, *op. cit.*, pp. 175-76. See also note 7 above.

[15] S.L. Ross, "Countermeasures for Oil Spills in Canadian Arctic Waters: The Arctic Marine Oil Spill Program," a paper presented to the AMOP Technical Seminar (Edmonton, June 1980), excerpted in *Arctic Seas Bulletin*, Vol. 2., no. 7 (July 1980).

[16] Gerein, *op. cit.*, p. 15.

[17] D.M. Dickinson, "Northern Resources: A Study of Constraints, Conflicts and Alternatives," in Keith and Wright, *op. cit.*, Vol. I, p. 271.

[18] Aspects of this economy as practised by the Dene are described in Scott Rushforth, "Country Food," in Mel Watkins (ed.), *Dene Nation: The Colony Within* (Toronto: University of Toronto Press, 1977). The extent of the Inuit dependence on the land is described in Milton Freeman, *Inuit Land Use and Occupancy Study*, 3 vols. (Ottawa: Department of Indian Affairs and Northern Development, 1976).

[19]This theme is elaborated later in this chapter on pp. 32-33.

[20]Berger. *op. cit.*, Vol. II p. 15, See also Frank J. Toster, "And the First Shall Be Last: Some Social Implications of the Baker Lake Decision." *Northern Perspectives*, Vol. III, no. 3 (1980), p. 10.

[21]*Ibid.*, p. 10.

[22]Richard F. Salisbury, "The North as a Developing Nation," in the *Proceedings* of the Eighth National Northern Development Conference (Edmonton, November 1979), p. 76.

[23]In almost all cases, these projects seek non-renewable resources such as oil, gas, or minerals. However, this is not universally the case, as in the case of hydroelectricity projects. For this reason, this book will use the term "megaprojects," rather than the less accurate though more common term, "non-renewable-resource sector."

[24]The scholarly literature on staples is reviewed from a marxist perspective and major pieces (including some with specifically northern content) are identified in the footnotes to Mel Watkins, "The Staples Theory Revisited," *Journal of Canadian Studies*, 12:5 (Winter 1977).

[25]As used here, the term "multinational corporation" includes Canadian firms whose operations extend outside Canada. In other words, the emphasis is not on the nationality of the interests that own and control the firm: one need only look at the cases of Inco to realize that Canadian multinationals behave in ways very similar to foreign firms. What is important about multinationals is their resources and the special advantages their multinational activities give them when they deal with government.

[26]See Chapter 4, pp. 154 and 162. It should be noted that the large energy multinationals are less active in the North than they were in the mid-1970s because some curtailed their exploration programs after the Arctic Gas pipeline was rejected in 1977.

[27]C.M. Drury, *Constitutional Development in the Northwest Territories: Report of the Special Representative* (Ottawa: Supply and Services Canada, 1979), p. 113.

[28]Government of the Yukon, Department of Tourism and Economic Development, *Yukon Economic Review* (2nd qtr. 1980), p. 2.

[29]These concerns were raised several times at the Eighth National Northern Development Conference, as reported in its *Proceedings*, pp. 19, 31, and 142.

[30]Farley Mowat, *Canada North Now* (Toronto: McClelland and Stewart, 1976), p. 152.

[31]Robert B. Gibson, *The Strathcona Sound Mining Project*, Background Study No. 42 (Ottawa: Science Council of Canada, 1978), pp. 17-19.

[32]National Energy Board, *Reasons for Decision: Northern Pipelines*, 3 vols. (Ottawa: Supply and Services Canada, 1977), Vol. II, Ch. 5.

[33]This is not to deny that these benefits would be even greater were it not for the fact that the Canadian economy all told is itself a colonial economy.

[34]Gerein, *op. cit.*, p. 43.

[35]Advisory Committee on Northern Development, *Annual Northern Expenditure Plan* (Ottawa: Department of Indian Affairs and Northern Development, 1978), p. 11.

[36]Gordon R. Cameron, "The North-Canadian Myths," in *Proceedings of the Eighth National Northern Development Conference*, p. 36.

[37]*Ibid.*, p. 10. This figure includes all spending by the federal and both territorial governments.

[38]John Ridsdel, "Dome's Big Gamble," *Calgary Herald* (August 22, 1979).

[39]K.J. Rea, *The Political Economy of Northern Development*, Background Study No. 36 (Ottawa: Science Council of Canada, 1976), p. 68.

[40]Gibson, *op. cit.*, p. 46.

[41]The potential social disruption associated with megaproject development is explored in telling fashion in the context of a specific project—the Nanisivik Mine in *ibid.*, pp. 56-66.

[42]Mel Watkins, "From Underdevelopment to Development," in Watkins, *op. cit.*, p. 92.

[43]This line of argument is pursued in D.M. Dickinson, "Northern Resources: A Study of Constraints, Conflicts and Alternatives," in E.B. Peterson and J.B. Wright (eds.), *Northern Transitions*, Vol. I: *Northern Resource and Land Use Policy Study* (Ottawa: Canadian Arctic Resources Committee, 1978).

[44]For example, during the 1977-78 trapping season, fourteen trappers earned more than $8000 apiece in the Inuvik administrative region. This does not compare particularly favourably with incomes in southern Canada, but it represents income from what is only a seasonal activity. Government of the N.W.T., Department of Economic Development and Tourism, *Northwest Territories Statistical Profile* (Yellowknife: interim publication, n.d.), p. 54.

[45]Figure supplied in interview with staff of the Department of Economic Development and Tourism, Government of the N.W.T. (August, 1980).

[46]Personal interview (July 1980).

[47]Dan Westman, "N.W.T. Demography and Labour Force Activity" (Yellowknife: Government of the N.W.T., Department of Economic Development and Tourism, 1980), p. 3.

[48]*Ibid.*, p. 13.

[49]*Ibid.*, pp. 12 and 15.

[50]For example, in testimony before the National Energy Board, the President of Interprovincial Pipe Line indicated that his firm had no intention of giving any kind of special preference to hiring native people, other than that given to northern people in general. *Edmonton Journal* (October 16, 1980), p. C9.

[51]The Government of the Northwest Territories' Outpost Camp Program assists native people wishing to carry out traditional activities on the land. This program is discussed in Gerein, *op. cit.*, p. 76.

[52]*Edmonton Journal* (August 30, 1980), p. G13. This figure refers to the potential, rather than the active, labour force.

[53]Westman, *op. cit.*, p. 12.

[54]*Edmonton Journal* (September 27, 1980), p. B2.

[55]Advisory Committee on Northern Development, *Government Activities in the North* (Ottawa: Queen's Printer, 1969), p. 293, and Drury, *op. cit.*, p. 109.

[56]Advisory Committee on Northern Development, *op. cit.*, p. 293, and Commissioner of Yukon, *Annual Report*, 1978-79, p. 54.

[57]It is very difficult to assess the likelihood of violence. Three factors can be noted, however. First, native leaders from time to time predict and even threaten violence in the context of proposed megaprojects. Second, the means are at hand: dynamite and heavy equipment needed to damage, say, a pipeline are widely available in the North. Third, a pipeline is an inviting target because of the impossibility of protecting its entire length.

Native people have not engaged in politically motivated violence in the North, but it is not impossible that their growing political consciousness may lead them in this direction if they become increasingly frustrated. One source of this frustration could well be the very megaprojects whose planners must consider the consequences of violence on the cash flow of projects, the economics of which may be so tight that they are particularly sensitive to disruptions of any kind.

[58]A blowout is an uncontrolled flow of oil or gas from a well. A gas blowout would not produce grave environmental damage because the gas would simply rise to the water's surface and dissipate. However, an oil blowout could be an ecological disaster.

[59]Personal interview, Department of Economic Development and Tourism, Government of the Northwest Territories (August 1980).

[60]Note 50 above is relevant here, as are the plans of Foothills Pipelines for hiring native workers for both the construction and operation phases of the Alaska Highway pipeline.

[61]*Northern Canada in the Seventies*, A Statement to the Standing Committee on Indian Affairs and Northern Development on the Government's Northern Objectives, Priorities and Strategies for the 1970s (Ottawa: mimeo, 1972).

[62]Edgar J. Dosman, *The National Interest* (Toronto: McClelland and Stewart, 1975), attacks this policy statement for its failure to acknowledge the unresolved native claims in the North. It also argues that the federal government was remiss in publishing it only after announcing the Northern Pipeline Guidelines (1970), which favoured development.

[63]Francois Bregha, *Bob Blair's Pipeline* (Toronto: Lorimer, 1979), p. 157.

64The question of northern sovereignty is examined by Edgar J. Dosman (ed.), *The Arctic in Question* (Toronto: Oxford University Press, 1976), Franklyn Griffiths, *A Northern Foreign Policy*, Wellesley Papers (July 1979) (Toronto: Canadian Institute of International Affairs, 1979), and Donat Pharand, *The Law of the Sea of the Arctic* (Ottawa: University of Ottawa Press, 1973). Northern strategic issues are discussed in W. Harriet Critchley, "Canadian Security Policy in the Arctic: The Context for the Future," in Janet B. Wright (ed.), *Marine Transportation and High Arctic Development: Policy Framework and Priorities* (Ottawa: Canadian Arctic Resources Institute, 1980).

65The Banks Island affair is described in Peter J. Usher and Gail Noble, "New Directions in Northern Policy-Making: Reality or Myth?" in *Proceedings* of the Mackenzie Delta: Priorities and Alternatives Conference (December 3 and 4, 1975) (Ottawa: Canadian Arctic Resources Committee, 1977).

66Chapter 2 contains a discussion of the legal status of aboriginal title.

67Personal interview, Department of Indian Affairs and Northern Development (Yellowknife, August 1980). A variation of this problem occurs when government officials are too few in number or lack the expertise to effectively monitor non-renewable-resource operations. An example of this type of situation is provided in *Northern Perspectives*, Vol. VIII, no. 6 (1980), p. 12.

68See, for example, Bregha, *op. cit.*, p. 162, assessing the outcome of the Canada-U.S. negotiations on the Alaska Highway gas pipeline.

69Gerein, *op. cit.*, p. 40.

70D.K. Redpath, *Land Use Programs in Canada: Yukon Territory* (Ottawa: Supply and Services Canada, 1979), p. 16.

71Keith Crowe, *A History of the Original Peoples of Northern Canada* (Montreal: McGill-Queen's University Press, 1974), Chs. 1-3, discusses the precontact period of northern-native history and culture.

72Jean Briggs, *Never in Anger* (Cambridge, Mass.: Harvard University Press, 1970), and O. Schaefer and M. Metayen, "Eskimo Personality and Society—Yesterday and Today," in Roy J. Shepherd and S. Itoh, *Circumpolar Health: Proceedings of the Third International Symposium—Yellowknife N.W.T.* (Toronto: University of Toronto Press, 1976), provide incisive discussions of Inuit culture. See also, Hamelin, *op. cit.*, p. 236, for a statement of basic elements of Amerindian culture.

73Contemporary cases can be cited where native people have hunted wastefully and acted in ways that have irresponsibly damaged the environment. It is not possible to fully understand these instances without examining the specifics of each of them. However, at least part of the explanation is that the native people behaved as they did because they felt that the stewardship of the land and its resources had been taken from them. The tie between themselves and the land having been broken, they may have lost their traditional sense of responsibility for the land. Part of the purpose of the various claims is to reunite the native people and their land in a variant of the traditional relationship.

74M. Watkins, *Dene Nation: The Colony Within* (University of Toronto Press, 1977), p. 11. Justice Berger's views on the relationship of the Dene and the land may be found in Vol. I, pp. 93-95, of his *Report*. This subject is also discussed in P.J. Usher, "The Significance of the Land to Native Northerners," *Canadian Association in Support of Native Peoples Bulletin*, Vol. 17, no. 1 (March 1976). The actual extent of native land use has been documented in several studies related to native claims. See, for example, Milton Freeman, *Inuit Land Use and Occupancy Project*, 3 vols. (Ottawa: Department of Indian Affairs and Northern Development, 1976).

75Keith Crowe, *A History of the Original Peoples of Northern Canada* (Montreal: McGill-Queen's University Press, 1974), p. 148.

76This phenomenon is described and examples of relevant testimony from native people are provided in Berger, *op. cit.*, Vol. I, p. 92.

[77]Hugh Brody suggests the impact of the RCMP in imposing southern norms in *The People's Land* (Harmondsworth: Penguin, 1975), pp. 28-29. The contrasts between Inuit social practices and white laws are described in Jack Sissons, *Judge of the Far North* (Toronto: McClelland and Stewart, 1973), particularly Chs. 27 and 28.

[78]Kenneth M. Lysyk, Edith E. Bohmer, and Willard L. Phelps, *Alaska Highway Pipeline Inquiry* (Ottawa: Supply and Services Canada, 1977), p. 15.

[79]This problem is becoming less severe as new methods of travelling, particularly the snowmobile, have greatly increased the area throughout which town-based hunters can operate.

[80]It is difficult to fault the government in most of these instances, for the native people in question were at the time (the mid-1950s) in dire circumstances, even to the point of starvation because of problems with the hunt. It was thought that their basic needs, at least, could be served in the towns and accordingly they were relocated. In this way, the government's motivation was not malicious, but it clearly did not understand the social and psychological consequence of its policy of relocation.

[31]*Northwest Territories Statistical Profile* (Yellowknife: interim publication, n.d.), pp. 12, 14, and 22.

[32]Hugh Brody, "Alcohol, Change and the Industrial Frontier," *Etudes Inuit Studies*, Vol. I, no. 2 (1977), pp. 31-46.

[83]Government of the Northwest Territories, *1979 Annual Report*, p. 27, and Yukon Region, Medical Services Branch, Health and Welfare Canada, "A Report on Health Conditions in the Yukon: 1979" (mimeo), p. 63.

[84]*Edmonton Journal* (January 25, 1979), p. F12.

[85]See for example, J.M. Lubart, *Psychodynamic Problems of Adaptation—Mackenzie Delta Eskimos* (Ottawa: Information Canada, 1971), and Allan Seltzer, "Acculturation and Mental Disorder in the Inuit," *Canadian Journal of Psychiatry*, Vol. 25, no. 2 (1980). Mental-health problems in one eastern Arctic community are described in "Modernity, Social Structure and Mental Health of Eskimos in the Canadian Eastern Arctic," in Shepherd and Itoh, *op. cit.*

[36]*Yukon Indian News* (September 11, 1980), p. 8.

[87]Figure supplied by the Council for Yukon Indians (October 1980).

[38]While most of this population is caucasian, non-caucasians do live in the North and make it impossible to use the term "white" when describing the northern non-native population.

[39]Examples of this feeling are the presentations of Rolf Hougen and Barry Ashton printed in the *Proceedings* of the Eighth National Northern Development Conference.

[90]Ashton, *op. cit.*, p. 18.

[91]Advisory Committee on Northern Development, *op. cit.*, p. 42.

[92]Julie Cruikshank, "Myths and Futures in the Yukon Territory: The Inquiry as a Social Dragnet," *Canadian Issues*, Vol. II, no. 2.

[93]This subject is discussed in Hugh Brody, *The People's Land* (Harmondsworth: Penguin, 1975), and in Robert Paine (ed.), *The White Arctic: Anthropological Essays on Tutelage and Ethnicity* (St. John's: Institute of Social and Economic Research, Memorial University, 1977).

[94]Peter Usher, "Geographers and Northern Development: Some Social and Political Considerations," *Alternatives* (Autumn 1974), and "The Class System, Metropolitan Dominance and Northern Development," *Antipode*, Vol. 8, no. 3 (September 1976).

2/Native Claims: Negotiating Social Contracts for the North

Nowhere do the conflicts within northern society and between North and South make themselves more acutely felt than in the issue of native claims. Because of the comprehensive nature of these claims, their settlements will determine the extent to which the North will make the contribution to the Canadian economy that many people have long anticipated. In the North itself, the claims have for two reasons taken on a profound symbolic status. The first is that their settlements will determine the future evolution of the North and with it the future wellbeing of natives and non-natives. The second and more immediate reason is that, so long as the claims remain unsettled, the North will be uncertain of the direction of its development and unable to apply its energies to the task of creating a new northern society. For their part, many non-native northerners are frustrated by the freezes on land use[1] and delays in gaining fuller self-government,[2] pending settlement of the claims. Native people resent the delays in negotiating claims settlements, delays which they feel reflect governmental indifference. While history and other irritants set natives and non-natives apart in the North, the claims symbolize most dramatically the difficulties of their relationship. To understand why, it is necessary to understand the logic of the claims that have been presented.

The Logic of the Claims

The native peoples of the North see their claims as a final, once-and-for-all opportunity to fashion a satisfactory relationship between themselves and the rest of Canadian society. They want to create a set of social contracts, not in the sense of an agreement among individuals, but a compact between groups. Their goal is so fundamental and comprehensive because it follows from their interpretation of themselves and their place in Canadian society. In their view, each of the various native groups represents a people whose members share a common culture, religion, and history. Most important, they share a commitment to one another and to the future of their people that transcends the primarily individualistic quality of relations among most other Canadians. The deep sense of community in traditional native life has been eroded by contact with a dominant society that does not share the basic logic of native life. However, that logic and the feelings of community are far

50

from dead. To the contrary, traditional ways still provide not only an enduring economic base,[3] but also an important part of many natives' sense of identity and an important source of meaning in their lives.[4] Many native people are determined to preserve and enhance these feelings. For these people, assimilation into Canadian society promises cultural poverty. It also promises continued poverty in an economic sense; the experiences of their past contacts with white society and their current social problems suggest that, were they to assimilate, they would be consigned to the backwaters rather than admitted to the mainstream of Canadian society.

For most native people, a claims settlement has a better chance of succeeding if it gives them a measure of meaningful control over the many features of their lives that influence their self-definitions and their collective life as a people. They believe that, to succeed in the evolving modern society of Canada's North, they must build on the sense of identity as native people that gives meaning to their lives; the denial of this sense of identity by white society has degraded them as a group. To appreciate all that this means, it is crucial to remember that this identity is multidimensional and touches on most aspects of their lives—religious, economic, political, esthetic, familial.

Fostering this identity requires claims settlements that will provide a total cultural support system. A comprehensive set of supporting structures is needed to give native cultures a reasonable chance of adapting with integrity to the new realities of the North.[5] The native people also recognize that, to succeed, this adaptation will require an economic base. Economic success requires sufficient capital to finance it. Moreover, a significant portion of this capital must belong to the native people themselves if they are to avoid continued dependence on nonnatives. While they may borrow from nonnatives, the natives' capital supply must be sufficient to enable them to make decisions that emphasize their own needs rather than the priorities of others. Claim settlements present the obvious—indeed, the only—source of this supply of capital.

Land

The first and most important concern of the native people is for the land. Indeed, most people refer to the native claims as "land claims." This usage is misleading because it incorrectly suggests that the claims are about land and nothing else. Still, land is the native peoples' basic concern because of the special relationship they feel with it. Based on this feeling for the land and the economic benefits it provides, the various claims would require the federal government to confirm native ownership of enough land to enable native people who wish to pursue the traditional economy on the land to do so—either full time or as a supplement to other economic activities.

The usual wording of Indian treaties and more recent settlements is that the native people "cede, release, surrender and yield up all their native claims, rights, titles and privileges whatsoever."[6] In contrast to this approach of

Figure 2-1
Native Claims Boundaries

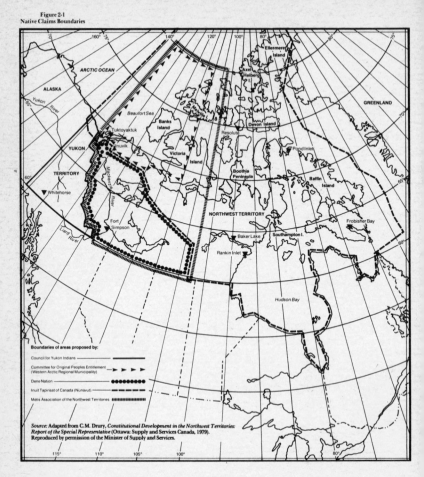

Boundaries of areas proposed by:

Council for Yukon Indians ──────────

Committee for Original Peoples Entitlement ➤ ➤ ➤ ➤
(Western Arctic Regional Municipality)

Dene Nation ●●●●●●●●

Inuit Tapirisat of Canada (Nunavut) ── ── ──

Metis Association of the Northwest Territories ▮▮▮▮▮▮▮▮▮

Source: Adapted from C.M. Drury, *Constitutional Development in the Northwest Territories:
Report of the Special Representative* (Ottawa: Supply and Services Canada, 1979).
Reproduced by permission of the Minister of Supply and Services.

"extinguishing" their title, the Council for Yukon Indians and the Committee for Original Peoples Entitlement are seeking recognition of their ownership of a fraction of the total area to which they claim aboriginal title—in other words, to "consolidate" their title. The Dene and the Inuit Tapirisat have gone a step farther, in wanting all lands to which they lay claim to be ruled by governments that are in effect native controlled. Non-natives could own land,[7] but the native legislative control over it would ensure that it would serve the purposes the native people intended for it.

It should be emphasized that land owned by the native group would be shared by all its members, not owned individually by them. The land could be leased, but it could not be sold, except to the crown. In this way, native ownership of the land could be guaranteed for all time. This would provide for the sense of security in their relationship with the land traditionally at the heart of native culture. Ideally, in order to fully safeguard this security, the native groups would like Ottawa to renounce its powers of expropriation over the lands allocated to native people under the settlements. However, they recognize that this is a demand that Ottawa will not accept. Accordingly, they are pressing for a special status for their lands that would make it very difficult but not impossible for Ottawa to expropriate native land.

In making their claims, the native groups recognize to varying degrees that ownership of land is of little use without having control over what takes place on that land. Because the traditional use of the land involves the harvesting of renewable resources, the native people want to control the policies affecting the health and abundance of these resources. In practical terms this means policies concerning fish, game, and marine mammals. In a broader sense it can be interpreted to include all of the development activities in the North. Mining operations, petroleum exploration, or pipeline building all affect the environment and thus have the potential to harm the wildlife the native peoples harvest. Because the wildlife wander freely across the boundaries that would divide native and non-native land (where such a division is proposed) and because it is obviously nonsense to apply two different wildlife-management schemes to the same animals, the natives argue that they should govern wildlife not only on their own lands, but throughout the North, because their interest in the wildlife is more fundamental than that of non-natives.

Financial Terms

The native people recognize that they will require large sums of money if they are to resolve their social problems and have a meaningful opportunity to determine their futures. Moreover, they believe that they are entitled to receive these sums in exchange for the ownership of those northern lands they relinquish. Generally, the financial transfers the native groups are seeking fall into the following categories, not all of which are being sought by each group:

Compensation for profits realized in the past by non-natives on native lands. The native groups argue that the resources of their lands—particularly mineral resources—have been extracted without their permission or their being paid for them. They believe that the federal government must compensate them for the wrongful use of their land by non-natives. Compensation for social and cultural damage. The native groups argue that the costs of repairing the damage to native society in the North since the coming of the white man should be paid for by the government, under whose authority the vast majority of these white men arrived in the North. This calls for a lump-sum payment or a government commitment to continue a variety of social services well into the future to compensate for and repair the social damage already done.
A share in future resource revenues, on the grounds that the native people

are the rightful owners of the resources. Just as non-renewable-resource development has harmed native society and necessitated expensive remedial programs, so too will future development. Hence, royalties will also be needed to meet new social needs.

4. Exemption from taxation. Some native groups argue that northern natives and the corporations they will form to administer their joint business affairs should be exempt from any taxes because the land the settlements will allocate to the crown represents, in effect, a prepayment forever of taxes.[8]

5. Access to funding for specific social, economic, and cultural development that is made available under general programs of the Department of Indian Affairs and Northern Development.

Of course, the native groups realize that Ottawa will not accept unlimited financial claims. They also recognize that the different sources or justifications for funding are not all equally attractive to them. For example, revenues from royalties depend on development's actually occurring. If a native group decides to rely heavily on royalty income to fund its programs, it may find itself in the awkward position of being tempted to approve a development project it would not otherwise favour, but feels it must approve in order to obtain the royalty income. In this way, royalty income could become a trap. The Agreement in Principle between the Government of Canada and the Committee for Original Peoples Entitlement puts the Inuvialuit of the western Arctic in very much this position. Not only does it give them royalties, but it also makes these royalties tax free for a period of 25 years, a provision that puts great pressure on the Inuvialuit to support quick development in order to reap the tax benefit. Another possible problem is that program funding can vary from year to year, depending on government priorities. In general the task facing the native groups is to find the type of financial terms that maximizes their revenues but minimizes the potential for such future problems.

It should be noted that, just as there are tradeoffs among the various forms or justifications for funding, so too there is a tradeoff between the land and the money parts of any claim settlement. If a settlement leaves the native people with relatively little land, the social and psychological disruption caused by the loss of the land will likely be greater and require more money to compensate. The economic base of the people would also be limited, requiring money to direct the people towards other economic pursuits. If, on the other hand, the settlement accords large amounts of land to the native people, presumably less money needs to be transferred. The best tradeoff between land and money is a matter each native group will decide itself. However, there appears to be some feeling that land is to be sought more actively than is money, in that money can disappear but the land cannot. In view of the place of the land in native culture, this preference should come as no surprise.

Political Powers

Northern natives have suffered in the past from their powerlessness. They have had to adjust to developments decided elsewhere and to programs imposed on them by outsiders, however well intended. They have been free to decide how to respond to these influences, but because they could not control the influences themselves, they lost the power to make the most fundamental decisions. Frequently, the choice that remained was simply a choice among undesirable alternatives. For example, Indians in the Mackenzie were posed with the choice of either sending their children to schools that separated them from their families and disrupted their life on the land or going to jail.[9] In order to do away with situations in which they are presented with a set of alternatives that erode their culture, most of the native groups believe that they need to take over at least some of the responsibilities of government that affect their integrity as a group and the viability of their culture. In the words of the Dene:

> Culture, if it is alive, is not the worship of a dead past, but the celebration of the present by a people who refuse to be defined by others. . . . To encourage "cultural diversity" requires not separation of culture and politics, but their marriage and to insist on that separation is to destroy, or attempt to destroy culture.[10]

The governmental responsibilities fall into two general categories. The first responsibility sought relates to programs that directly affect socialization—that is, the learning of cultural values. Into this category fall educational, cultural, and social-welfare programs. The second responsibility relates to powers to control economic development because, as was noted in Chapter 1, megaprojects may undermine the traditional economy and prevent native people from pursuing it. Alternatively, wage employment may encourage native people to leave stable, predominantly traditional ways of earning a living in favour of jobs in the modern economy that may be more comfortable and better paying, but that may be only temporary. When the job ends, the native person faces either welfare or the difficulties of reequipping himself to return to a life on the land. In addition, wage labour itself may upset relationships in native society so severely that its social desirability may be dubious in some instances.[11]

The various native groups have approached their needs for political authority from a variety of angles, falling into three broad categories. The first category of approach, which the Métis Association of the Northwest Territories has adopted, relies for its cultural protection on a restructuring of the Territorial Assembly that would make it more sensitive to native needs. Thus, no specifically native government would promote and protect native values. The second type of approach, adopted by the Dene Nation, the Inuit Tapirisat, and (with an important qualification) the Committee for Original Peoples Entitlement (COPE), involves designating a particular region as a governmental unit and giving to that government the power over selected matters of particular importance to the native people. The Dene and the Inuit Tapirisat have not suggested that Ottawa could veto the action of the governments of these proposed regions. In contrast, the COPE claim would permit such a veto and in this sense represents a weaker position than that of the other two.[12]

The Dene proposal, which rests on a forceful assertion of the native right to self-determination in the N.W.T., advocates a metropolitan or United Nations model for political structures in the N.W.T. along the following lines:

1 That the present N.W.T. be divided into three separate geographical boundary territories—one where the Dene are a majority, one where the Inuit are a majority, and finally one where the nonnative people are in the majority.

2 Each territory would recognize the political rights of all its citizens, regardless of race.

3 Each new territory would have a government with a direct relationship with the Federal Government, as the provinces have a direct relationship.

4 The powers of each new territory would resemble the present federal/ provincial division of powers in the South.

5 Each territory would set up a legislature according to the democratic decision of its respective populace. [A reasonable assumption would be that the nonnative territory government would continue along the lines of the Territorial Council, and the Dene and Inuit would institute traditional forms of government.]

6 There would be no more single governing structure like the N.W.T. Council surviving the recognition of self-determination of northern people.

7 Instead of the N.W.T. Council, we would propose that a form of government could still exist for the whole of the North. We would propose that a Metro, or United Nations model, of government be organized by the three new governments to deal with matters, issues, and programmes of common concern. Like the U.N., each new government would send representatives to negotiate with representatives from the other two governments, meet as equals and negotiate with each other until an agreement was reached on any joint activity.

8 Possibly a joint civil service could deal with the resulting programmes, etc. This could be decided by the representative of the governments.[13]

For its part, the Inuit Tapirisat of Canada (ITC) is energetically pursuing its proposal to create a separate territory North of the treeline called Nunavut. The ITC proposes that this territory achieve full provincial status fifteen years after the date of its formally coming into existence and that it would not itself represent a settlement of the aboriginal claims of the Inuit. However, it would greatly simplify the negotiation of the claim by limiting it primarily to questions of the nature of land and resource ownership.

The concept of a defined region of jurisdiction could give these groups meaningful control over their affairs because the populations of the region

iat their proposals define are predominantly native. Accordingly, it is
asonable to assume that the electoral process will guarantee natives power.
1 contrast, the Council for Yukon Indians (CYI) is the only member of the
iird category; the CYI must face the fact that native people are not a majority
f the Yukon population. They can never hope to gain control of the
erritorial Assembly through the ballot box unless voting is restricted to
eople who have resided in the Yukon for a long time, a provision that would
iminate many white voters. For this reason the CYI has opted for a func-
onal definition of government, arguing that a native government should
ontrol certain government functions throughout the Yukon, such as game
ianagement, while the Yukon Territorial Government would control
thers or would have the same jurisdiction over non-natives in matters such
education and social welfare that the native government would have over
ative Yukoners.[14]

ligibility

ecause intermarriage between natives and non-natives has produced large
umbers of people of mixed ancestry in the North, it is not obvious who the
eneficiaries of the claims settlements are to be. The question, particularly in
ie Mackenzie area and the Yukon where most interracial mingling has
ccurred, is very simply how much native ancestry a person must have in
rder to be eligible to benefit from a claims settlement.

This question is important but difficult. It is important because its
iswer will confer potentially substantial benefits on some and deny them to
hers. Depending on how the lines are drawn, resentments may be created
iat will embitter northern native communities for generations. That this
ossibility is not exaggerated can be appreciated if it is kept in mind that the
igibility question relating to native claims is precisely the same question
ie Indian Act attempts to handle in defining who is an Indian. The Indian
ct, and before it the treaties, have for a century divided the native
ommunity in Canada into status Indians, who have a right to receive
enefits from Ottawa, and non-status Indians, who do not. This division
eates an obvious conflict between the haves and havenots and has greatly
eakened the native voice in Canada.

The eligibility question is difficult precisely because of this traditional
vision. Southern-Canadian status-Indian organizations believe that they
ive an interest in having the beneficiaries of the settlements limited to status
dians, and have attempted to persuade status Indians in the North of the
rrectness of their point of view.[15] While it is not possible to be sure of their
asoning, it is at least possible to guess that they fear that a recognition of
n-status people in the North as equally deserving as status people will lead
n-status people in southern Canada to demand similar treatment, citing
e northern precedent. Assuming that Ottawa's funding for native people is
latively fixed for any year, a gain by the non-status people would mean a

loss for the status people. The status-Indian groups may also fear a dilutic
of the meaning of "Indianness," possibly accelerating the total loss of th
identity.

Obviously thorny problems confront the eligibility question. The Der
and the Métis Association of the Northwest Territories have skirted tl
question in their formal statements by asserting, in the words of the Den
"The definition of the Dene is the right of the Dene. The Dene know wl
they are."[16] The COPE, ITC, and CYI claims are more specific in identifying
beneficiaries of the anticipated settlements those people with one-quart
native blood and the descendents of such people.[17] This formula has the gre
advantage of avoiding the present injustice that occurs when Indian wome
lose their legal status as Indians when they marry non-Indians. The feder
government has endorsed the one-quarter principle in the COPE Agreemei
in Principle and for the Yukon.[18] Thus, it may appear that this one questic
about the claims has, indeed, been settled. However, the importance of tl
question guarantees that the advocates of the various answers will return to
until the ink is actually dry on the settlements.

Entrenchment

Ottawa has the authority to overturn any provision of a claim settlemen
This power derives from the fundamental principle of the parliamenta
system of government, that of "parliamentary sovereignty," according
which no legal restraint exists that can limit the authority of Parliament
act.[19] Parliamentary sovereignty means that, after settling a claim, nativ
people will have given up a variety of advantages in exchange for the benefi
of a settlement. However, they may discover that when Ottawa wish
something they oppose, it might simply legislate its wishes into reality. F
example, it might force their participation in a national health-ca
insurance plan, even if the settlement confers control over health care to tl
native people. Obviously, the political backlash from such an arbitra
action would stay the government's hand in most instances, but it is not
guarantee, should the government feel that it has a strong interest i
overriding a provision of a settlement. Clearly the native people wish
formulate the claims settlements in such a way as to prevent this type (
government action. To accomplish this goal, they have turned to the onl
possible vehicle, the British North America Act itself, and have asked th;
their settlement be "entrenched" in the Act by actually becoming part of
and subject to change only with the permission of the native peop
themselves.

The start of the 1980s has pointed up this aspect of the claims. Prin
Minister Trudeau's commitment to patriate the BNA Act quickly h;
jeopardized the natives' ability to appeal to Great Britain for entrenchment (
any settlement reached in the future. For this reason, the leaders of th
northern claims groups have taken an active role in the efforts of Canadia
native people in general to persuade the British Parliament that an
patriation of the BNA Act must adequately safeguard native interests.

he Politics of the Claims

he implications of the land, financial, and political aspects of the claims
ake the settlements potentially the biggest thing to happen to the North
nce the gold rush. Quite understandably, with the stakes so high, the
olitics of the claims are intense. With a large number of affected parties
hose interests form a patchwork of community and conflict, the politics are
so complex and subtle. The following discussion will attempt to sketch
ome of the patterns in the quilt of native-claims politics.

Implications of the Claims for Non-renewable-Resource Development

ny settlement of the COPE, CYI, and Dene claims that accepts their basic
ositions would enable the native people to regulate non-renewable-resource
velopment. They would have the power to issue or withhold the land-use
ermits that must be obtained by any firm planning an exploration program
a significant size. Moreover, they would be able to determine the terms and
nditions such operators must abide by. Sufficiently rigorous conditions
ight make exploration appear so costly as to cause the level of exploration
decrease. Once minerals were found, it would again fall to the native
ople to decide whether they should be extracted and what methods should
used for their extraction and transportation. For example, the native
uthority might decide that a pipeline across its territory would cause
nacceptable disruption of the renewable-resource base or the native
uthority might make certain stipulations about environmental protection
about the hiring of native workers. Native policy on these questions might
pear sufficiently unattractive to deter the investment needed to translate
onomically viable finds into actual production. This is a plausible
ospect, given the economic marginality of many northern projects
sulting from the high cost of operation.

The native people tend not to approach non-renewable-resource de-
lopment with the same sense of urgency as do non-native northerners.
owever, they do not oppose development in principle. Many of the native
ople would be quite happy to work on non-renewable-resource projects,
ring both the construction and the subsequent operating phases. Some are
ready employed on megaprojects.[20] Provided that the mine or drilling
erator permits them long enough periods at home between their shifts to
aintain their sense of security in their family life and to pursue their wildlife
rvesting, they are very happy to have this employment, in part because it
lps pay the cost of equipping themselves with the snowmobiles, fuel, and
her essentials of what is becoming an increasingly capital-intensive life on
e land. This type of employment means that communities in the Arctic
ands and on the coast of the Arctic Ocean are not now facing the
employment encountered in the Keewatin, Mackenzie, and Yukon regions
the North and are likely to suffer less from the anticipated growth in
employment in the 1980s.

At least one native organization, the Inuit Development Corporation

(IDC), has shown its willingness to participate directly in non-renewab
resource development by becoming a partner in the proposed Cullaton La
gold mine in the Keewatin.[21] While not all Inuit applaud this initiative, t
IDC and the interest of native workers generally in seeking employment in t
non-renewable sector show that it is false to allege that native people oppo
non-renewable-resource development. Rather, they oppose projects th
would jeopardize the renewable-resource base and they tend to oppose t
undertaking of new projects before the settlement of native claims. Th
accept non-renewable-resource projects, but only when the time and t
project are right.

In this sense they differ from non-natives: natives tend to consider a set
factors—the viability of the renewable-resource base—to which non-nativ
have given lip service but, for the most part, little policy recognition
Moreover, while natives might like to work on northern projects, they tend
doubt that these projects will offer many secure jobs to native northern
because such projects in the past have provided little employment to native
and future projects are unlikely to be markedly different.[24] Finally, many
the factors that have prompted the growth in mineral exploration in t
North emanate from the South and do not concern the native people as mu
as they concern Ottawa and the corporate sector. Thus, a native authority
charge of land-use policy would be unlikely to enact policies as favourable
the development of mining and petroleum as are current governme
policies.

This point should not be overstated. To the extent that the native peop
will share in the royalty revenues from such projects, they will have
incentive to encourage them. The hope of native employment will also ser
as an incentive. Thus, the view that any claim settlement favourable to t
native position will "shut down the North" is wildly overstated. Still, it c
be expected that such a settlement will to some extent slow the pace
economic activity. For this reason, Ottawa, the Yukon Territorial Gover
ment, most non-native northerners, and corporations involved in the hu
for northern minerals all oppose those portions of the claims that would gi
exclusive jurisdiction over land-use policy to the native people.[25] The she
strength of this alliance guarantees that this component of the claim has t
least chance of being implemented without some drastic changes.

2. The Position of the Government of Canada

The federal government's 1969 White Paper on Indian Policy[26] express
stated that Ottawa no longer intended to recognize native land rights.
taking this position, Ottawa wished to do away with what it viewed as :
obstacle to its undertaking a variety of activities, in the South as well as t
North. It also wished to end any uncertainties in the way of priva
developers' plans and to avoid potentially costly financial settlemen

However, after the Calder decision in 1973[27] suggested that aboriginal title might be a valid legal concept, Ottawa admitted that aboriginal claims "might" exist.[28] In July 1974, it established the Office of Native Claims within the Department of Indian Affairs and Northern Development (DIAND) to prepare the government to negotiate claims. Late in 1980, in response to strong pressure from native organizations, it amended the proposed Charter of Rights to recognize aboriginal and treaty rights. However, as will be discussed later, it would be a mistake to read too much into this change of heart. In general since 1973, Ottawa has been eager to have the claims negotiated because it wants to dispel the atmosphere of uncertainty about the outcome of the claims that has dampened northern development. However, because it has wanted settlements that promote development and conform to its philosophy, it has conceded very little to the native people. Its position is apparent from a variety of federal-government documents[29] and from a review of the Agreement in Principle it negotiated with COPE, the only northern agreement in principle it has reached to date. It did take part in the discussions that led to the James Bay and northern Quebec settlement,[30] but its views cannot be demonstrated by reference to this settlement, for the province of Quebec was the primary government negotiating the claim because the claim covered land in the province, which falls under provincial jurisdiction.

Ottawa has approached the land question by distinguishing between several different categories of land, of which two are particularly important. The first is land designated for the exclusive use of the native people. To guarantee their undisturbed tenure of this land, subsurface rights—that is, ownership of all oil and minerals beneath the surface of the ground—would be given to the native people. They would be able to refuse permission to development companies to enter these lands to undertake exploratory work that could disturb the wildlife population. The second category of land is land to which the native people hold surface rights, but not subsurface rights. These lands are available for hunting, fishing, and trapping, exclusively by natives, but are also open to non-renewable-resource development that may jeopardize the biological resource on which the hunting, fishing, and trapping are based. Obviously, Ottawa is willing to confirm native ownership of substantially more Category 2 land than Category 1 land. The COPE Agreement involves 95 800 km² of the former, but only 13 000 km² of the latter, none of which is to be selected from areas with known oil or gas reserves.

Regarding both types of land, Ottawa has been willing to offer only "fee simple absolute" title. The practical consequence of this legal concept is that the rights of the native peoples to such land are those of any Canadian holding property, but not more. Thus, this title does not give to the native people the power to legislate over their land. Similarly, it does not prevent expropriation of native land by a government. Both of these aspects of this title would weaken the confidence the native people want to feel in their tenure of their land.

Ottawa is willing to include financial compensation as part of the claims-settlement packages. However, it is determined to limit the amount of such funding. It also seeks to avoid unexpectedly large outlays in the future: it is unwilling to pay a portion of future years' budgets or programs for Indian organizations if they are set by the native people for fear that the budgets might grow to unacceptably large amounts. Ottawa is willing to share royalty revenues with the native people, particularly because this revenue is an incentive to the native people to accept rather than obstruct non-renewable-resource exploitation on their lands. In the COPE Agreement in Principle, the sum total of Ottawa's financial compensation to the native people amounts to $45 million as a lump sum, plus a share of royalty revenue gained on native land.

This settlement will definitely not guarantee the economic future of the native people involved. Indeed, it is a relatively low price to pay to dispel any legal uncertainties about the government's right to promote oil and gas exploration in the area. The settlement represents a particularly good deal for Ottawa, in that Ottawa anticipates—as it does regarding all of the northern settlements—that the funding given under the claim settlement will reduce the amount of money it has to allocate to ongoing services to native people. Moreover, while the money received by native groups from the settlement will not be subject to taxation, Ottawa has totally rejected any native claims for future exemption from taxation.

Ottawa has reacted to the natives' claims for political institutions by baldly rejecting any form of government structured along racial lines.[31] Instead, it has argued that northern natives should be involved in political structures that govern all northerners regardless of race. For example, Hugh Faulkner, the then-Minister of Indian Affairs and Northern Development, instructed the new Commissioner of the Yukon at the time of her appointment:

> The most important aspect of this relationship [among the federal government, Yukon territorial government, and native groups] will be to increase native participation in the political, economic and social evolution of Yukon society. Yukon Indians must be adequately represented and effectively involved in government at both territorial and community levels; they must be assured of appointments and effective participation in subsidiary bodies of government ... and in the public service of the Yukon.[32]

Clearly Ottawa's preferences are for what is commonly called the "one government system" in the North rather than the "two-government system" involving separate native and non-native political institutions. To enhance the attractiveness of the one-government system, Ottawa has suggested that it is open to proposals for modifying the residence requirement for voting to reduce the political weight of the transient population, but it is not willing to consider the ten- to fifteen-year requirements that native leaders have suggested. It is also willing to give some special recognition of the natives' interest in the North and their unfamiliarity with white political ways by guaranteeing them a measure of representation in the governments of the territories. However, the representation suggested has either been a minority of the assembly or agency in question or of an advisory nature only.[33] Neither of these two stances in any way provides the native people with the needed guarantees for their future.

The extent of Ottawa's hostility to the political component of native claims can only be fully appreciated by noting that it does not view native claims as having a constitutional component. The federal government views the claims as basically a real-estate transaction involving property owners rather than a social contract between peoples. For this reason it did not hesitate to entrust the task of advising on the constitutional future of the N.W.T. to the Prime Minister's Special Representative, the Hon. C.M. Drury. He considered the native view as one of many in the North, but was not obligated to meet the native people in the only arena in which they have any bargaining power, the claims forum.[34]

Moreover, Ottawa chose to misconstrue several of the native claims by claiming that they are racially structured, when in fact they represent a strict application of democratic principles to all of the people residing in particular regions of the North. Thus, for example, the Liberals rejected the Dene "metro proposal" to divide the N.W.T. into several regions, one with a majority of Dene voters, despite the fact that the non-Dene residents would be given the vote and all rights and privileges of citizenship in the proposed area and in Canada in general. The Liberals rejected such an idea as racially motivated, but did not recognize that its own rejection was itself racially motivated, in that it very strongly implies an unwillingness to permit a situation to develop in which non-natives may be governed by a native majority.

Many considerations affect Ottawa's reaction to the northern natives' claims. The first of these is the philosophy of individualism that rules both the Liberal and the Progressive Conservative parties.[35] This philosophy makes Ottawa not merely hostile to native claims but also suspicious of their sincerity. This misunderstanding occurs because the philosophy elevates the individual to the status of the ultimate social and political entity. According to this view, the purpose of the state is to organize a basically individualistic and self-serving mass of people into a coherent whole. The state receives allegiance, but the basic attribute of society is the individualism of its members. Because each individual is as worthy as the next, the state is loath to legally recognize any differentiation among them. Individuals may organize themselves into a variety of groups, but the ties they feel to these groups should be clearly subordinated to their identifications as Canadians. This view is held for both normative and empirical reasons. In other words, it believes as a matter of social prescription that society functions better if people behave individualistically and it takes as a matter of fact that Canadians are individualists. Thus, it approaches native claims with substantial skepticism because it cannot bring itself to believe that group identity is a central fact of life for native people and not merely some public-relations device.

For this reason, Ottawa is willing to apply to northern natives the accommodation typical of the brokerage form of politics in Canada. Thus, without particularly accepting the natives' views of themselves, it is willing to grant them concessions consistent with its other goals in the North. This policy resembles its willingness to promote multiculturalism in the rest of Canada, so long as it does not threaten ethnic-group members' allegiance to Canada or cost too much financially. Basically Ottawa treats northern native groups as merely another type of interest group.

If Ottawa is unwilling to accept the native peoples' view of themselves, what considerations do underlie its response to native claims? Certainly economics ranks high on the list. Since the northern vision of John Diefenbaker, Canadian politicians have actively pursued the economic development of the North in order to bolster the southern economy. In doing so, they have hoped to create jobs, investment opportunities, markets for Canadian manufacturers, and exports of minerals to improve Canada's balance-of-payments position; to produce taxation and royalty revenues for the federal government; and to reduce the bleeding of the Treasury to pay for Ottawa's deficit on its northern activities.[36] What must be kept in mind is that Ottawa has a strong interest in rejecting proposed settlements that could dampen non-renewable-resource development in the ways suggested previously. To accept such settlements would be to jeopardize its long-cherished economic hopes for the North. It also is eager to increase the physical presence of Canadians in the North in order to meet anticipated challenges to Canada's sovereignty there.

Federal politicians may also see an analogy between the aspirations of the native claims and the logic of independentism in Quebec, in that both seek political institutions to express ethnic identity. To concede anything to northern natives might be argued to create a precedent, weakening Ottawa's position in dealing with Quebec. Ottawa clearly is loath to appear to accept arguments based on ethnicity for fear that this acceptance would cause independentists to think that Ottawa might be becoming more sympathetic in principle or less determined in its resolve to oppose nationalism in general and Quebec nationalism in particular.

Ottawa in recent years has been engaged in discussions with Canada's Indians concerning the possibility of amending the Indian Act. The increased militance and organization of Canada's Indians and general dissatisfaction with the restrictive and outdated nature of the Act are likely to lead to relatively substantial revisions to it. However, Ottawa is unwilling to give the Indian people all of the substantial changes they seek. The process of revising the Act has involved and will continue to involve hard bargaining. In anticipating this bargaining, Ottawa is most reluctant to grant to northern natives the concessions that might be appropriate to the northern situation and manageable when granted to a relatively small number of people, but which would be too costly or politically difficult to grant in the South. For example, Ottawa resolutely opposes such elements of northern claims as the desire for exemption from income tax for native people. It does not want the Indians in southern Canada to be able to press such a claim by pointing out that it has already been granted in the North, and arguing that this proves that Ottawa has no objection in principle to such a provision appearing in the new Indian Act. If this happened, Ottawa would have to argue on the basis of expediency, not principle, a position it hardly wishes to manoeuvre itself into.

However, analogies between the northern hinterland and the South can work to the advantage of the northern claims. In recent years DIAND has begun to evolve a policy of transferring to Indian reserves the authority to operate the programs and to provide the services formerly provided by DIAND itself. The area of Indian education has probably shown the most progress, but some reserves are also involved in law-enforcement activities, economic-development programs, and social-assistance administration. These developments seem to be meeting with native approval and DIAND is likely to rely on them more and more. If it does, it will be hard pressed to deny these powers to the northern native-claims groups. While they can thus point to the South for justification for the new social contract they wish to create between themselves and Ottawa, they will have to move very carefully because the continuation of the southern programs tends to be subject to the approval of Ottawa rather than entrenched as a constitutional right. For this reason the new policy direction of DIAND does not involve the sovereign control over culturally fundamental areas of jurisdiction that the northern native claims seek. Still, it does offer a new precedent on which to base an argument during negotiations.

The government's position on claims is basically the position of the Liberal party. However, in maintaining this position, the Liberals encounter relatively little effective opposition from the other political parties in the House of Commons. For their part, the NDP tend to be sympathetic to the cause of the native groups, but the NDP's electoral strength does not make it a formidable opponent in the House nor a likely challenger at the polls. However, in a minority government, the NDP can assist the native cause. It did this in promoting the appointment in 1974 of Justice Berger, known to be a strong friend of the native people, to conduct the Mackenzie Valley Pipeline Inquiry.

The Progressive Conservatives are the official opposition and could put pressure on the Liberals to modify their position on the claims. However, aside from the rhetoric that opposition status compels the Conservatives to offer, they do not press the Liberals to modify their stance because the PCs are, if anything, even more firmly set against the claims than are the Liberals. During their brief tenure in office, the Conservatives did approach negotiations in a more flexible fashion than the Liberals had. They began the practice of assigning non-bureaucrats to head their negotiation teams, a practice sought by the claims groups to avoid the problems of dealing with people who tended not to have a direct access to the Minister and to have very little discretion to bargain. The Conservatives also agreed that questions of political institutions could be discussed during negotiations, a concession the Liberals steadfastly refused. However, while making these concessions, the Progressive Conservatives ignored the claims altogether in granting the Yukon responsible government, thus removing many of the protections Ottawa afforded to the native people of the Yukon and much of the incentive for the Yukon Territorial Government to adopt a conciliatory position toward the CYI.

At least the Liberals, for all their unwillingness to offer concessions at the negotiating table, took care to avoid actions that would repudiate the underlying rationale of the claims. Thus, for example, they refused to transfer lands to the control of the territorial governments or to move the territorial governments precipitously in the direction of responsible government and provincial status out of deference to the unresolved status of the claims. In doing this, they maintained the validity of the claims in a fashion that implicitly legitimated the native groups and held out some promise to their activists. In failing to continue this policy, the Conservatives' action in the Yukon infuriated the CYI. The same result followed when the Conservatives reopened negotiations of the COPE settlement, in part because they felt that this settlement unduly restricted development opportunities in the western Arctic. In addition, Jake Epp, the Conservative Minister of DIAND, consistently took a position in his public speeches that informed observers viewed as much more favourable to non-renewable-resource development, regardless of native claims, than the Liberals had been. All told, the Conservatives' record in office suggests that they have no interest in persuading the Liberals to make concessions to the native claims. This fact substantially increases the Liberals' freedom to choose among the alternative possible outcomes to the claims discussed at the end of this chapter.

3. The Response of the Non-native Population of the North

Ottawa has a strong interest in seeing the claims greatly modified before they are actually settled. Moreover, Ottawa's resolve is stiffened by the position that most of the non-native population of the North has taken against the claims.

This position reflects the social philosophy of the non-native population as well as their fears for their economic, social, and political wellbeing. Non-native northerners share the philosophy of individualism of anglophone Canada and of the federal government. They tend to be unable to appreciate the significance to native people of the psychological bond that links them. Moreover, they tend not to think that the state ought to recognize any such bond. In their opinion, ethnic ties are fine, but the government is and ought to be a government of individuals, not of groups. If social problems exist, even problems that tend most frequently to afflict a particular group, they feel that they should be addressed with programs available to all individuals equally as individuals, rather than to them as members of certain groups. This basic outlook makes it difficult for many non-native northerners to take the native claims seriously. Assuming, as people everywhere tend to do, that others bring to political and social questions the same set of values, non-natives suspect that the motivation behind the native claims is basically individualistic self-interest seeking an economic payoff rather than a primordial, cultural concern. Because they tend not to appreciate the cultural differences between themselves and native people, they reject native claims based on these differences.

Their philosophical predisposition against claims based on ethnicity is strongly reinforced by considerations of their personal self-interest. As noted, aside from income derived from tourism and government services, the wellbeing of non-native northerners depends ultimately on non-renewable-resource development. Claims potentially jeopardize this development by placing control over land uses in the hands of people who are unlikely to have as great an interest in seeing such development proceed as does the federal government, the present holder of this power. In addition, the uncertainties surrounding the implementation of native claim settlements—if these settlements reflected native wishes to any significant degree—would disturb investor confidence and the flow of capital to the North, perhaps precipitating a slowdown in the non-native northern economy. If opportunities for non-renewable-resource exploration and development are limited, particularly in the mining sector,[37] the spinoff benefits to northern businesses will also be limited. Many businessmen also fear that the economic-development corporations that may be established as part of the various claims settlements will harm them.[38] They fear that the corporations may well have more capital or create native businesses that have more capital than the non-native businesses and accordingly will be able to compete with them at a substantial advantage. They also fear that the native corporations may favour native businesses when deciding on contracts. Hence, they may freeze the non-native businesses out of enough of the market for their services to jeopardize their already often-tenuous situation. Thus, for most non-native northern businessmen, settlements of the claims in favour—to any substantial degree—of the native position would threaten the businessmen with economic marginality and would perpetuate a no-growth situation for their enterprises. For this reason, they may endorse the settlement of native claims, but only for the purpose of extinguishing any special position in northern society for native people as native people.

While these views reflect the thinking of most non-natives, some white northerners interpret the economic potential of the claims more positively and even view them as a more attractive base for northern development than is the nonrenewable sector. In the words of Ione Christensen:

> Once settled, [the claim] will have the greatest single economic impact on Yukon that it has ever seen or perhaps will see for sometime to come. It will have all of the positive attributes that one could wish for in development— no immigration of short-term residents, no environmental damage, all revenues invested in and used by Yukon, while nothing is being removed as a result.[39]

The extent of this feeling among non-native northerners is not clear. However, the idea itself is significant, in that it could serve as the basis of an alliance between native and non-natives that might overcome the opposition to the claims of the bulk of the non-native community.

Most non-native northerners, whether businessmen or not, feel some anxieties about how they would fare at the hands of governments controlled by well organized and politically self-conscious native people. For example, the curriculum currently taught in the North devotes more attention to the particular needs of native children than used to be the case but is basically modelled after southern-Canadian curricula. It is likely that any native curriculum will reflect an awareness that native children need to be prepared to relate to the North American milieu. However, a native-oriented curriculum could accomplish this task and still look very different from the ones currently in place. It is the differences that unsettle northern non-native parents. They fear that an emphasis on native culture and skills would suggest to their children that their background is deficient or at least not the officially recognized one. They also worry that their children would be at a disadvantage in the school system in comparison with children whose home backgrounds would give them more familiarity with the skills and concepts being taught. Finally, the skills emphasized in such a curriculum would not be skills the non-native parents deem to be useful. In other words, their situation would be very much like that of native parents in the North today. Conflicting interests could also arise in terms of wildlife-management policies, an intensification of government-employment practices favouring native candidates, and a preference for native businesses in the granting of contracts.

The point should not be exaggerated; non-native northerners hardly wake up every day with the cold clutch of fear gripping their innards. They recognize that Ottawa is unlikely to accept claims settlements that would give native people *as native people* control over northern policy. However, their economic concerns are quite real and, to the extent that social and political concerns are felt, their basis lies in the fear of powerlessness. This fear has traditionally focused on the two territorial legislative assemblies whose powers would be gutted by the political component of the claims settlements of the CYI, the Dene, and the ITC.[40] Not surprisingly, both assemblies have in the past rejected the political portion of the claims. The Eighth N.W.T. Legislative Assembly's statement of principles concerning the settlements of native claims stated categorically:

1. The Government of the Northwest Territories . . . is the senior government in the Northwest Territories and represents all Northwest Territories residents. Canada, through the settlement of native claims, shall not erode any constitutional authority of the Government of the Northwest Territories.
2. The Government of Canada shall not give, through the settlement of native claims in the Northwest Territories, to any group or groups of peoples any constitutional authority or responsibility which has not yet been delegated to the Government of the Northwest Territories.[41]

The Yukon Territorial Government's position is less firmly stated, but generally reflects the views found in a document prepared by the Commissioner of the Yukon, entitled "Meaningful Government for all Yukoners." This document asserts that the Yukon government "would like to discourage a separate and independent native government" and that the proper response to native political aspirations is "to assess and describe how native people could be encouraged and given opportunities to participate at all levels of the Yukon Territorial Government."[42] The proposed opportunities give the native people either a minority position on bodies such as the Assembly or Executive Committee that enjoy some real power, or equal status with non-natives on advisory boards that lack power.

Moreover, in order to be in the best possible position to press their views on the claims negotiations, both territorial governments have in the past sought full participation in the negotiations and a veto power over the outcome. The native groups oppose such participation on the principle that their claims relate to Ottawa's obligation to them and that no other party should interfere. The practical side of the matter, in the Yukon at least, is that any tripartite process of negotiation would pit them against two opponents rather than just one. Ottawa's position on this issue is not completely clear. Regarding the N.W.T., it has asserted:

The continuing involvement of the N.W.T. Government in claims negotiations is essential . . . because of the role that the Territorial Government will have in the implementation of any settlement. It is also a means of assuring that the views of the N.W.T. residents . . . are taken into account.[43]

In the Yukon, territorial officials have not participated as territorial officials in negotiations, but have been temporarily assigned to work on Ottawa's negotiating team. Ottawa's position is that if it and the CYI reach an agreement, it will take effect even if the Territorial Government objects. However, it is quite unlikely that Ottawa will agree to something that Whitehorse opposes because their interests are so complementary. As a result, the question of the Territorial Government's veto power is unlikely to arise formally because it will be able to exercise its veto informally.

The preceding description is half contemporary and half historical. It was once true that both territorial governments were dominated by the non-native population of the North, whose interests they strongly promoted, particularly with regard to native claims. However, the balance shifted in the Northwest Territories with the election in October 1979 of the Ninth Legislative Assembly. A majority of the members of the new Assembly are native people who support native claims. Some of them, such as Nellie Cournoyea, James Wah-Shee, Richard Nereysoo, and Tagak Curley have been leaders of claims groups. In addition, several non-native MLAs are sympathetic to the claims. One of the first actions taken by the Ninth Assembly was to repudiate the former Assembly's policy hostile to the claims. During its second session, held in February 1980 at Baker Lake, the Assembly considered a Sessional Paper entitled "Aboriginal Rights and Constitutional Development in the Northwest Territories." This document recognizes aboriginal rights as valid and commits the government of the Northwest Territories to promote prompt resolution of the claims. It thus indicates that for the foreseeable future, the native people of the N.W.T. can expect to find an ally in the Assembly on most claims questions.

4. The Legal Basis of the Claims

The claims of the aboriginal peoples rest on economic, anthropological, social and political arguments. They also gain much of their popular support from their ethical premises. However, their ultimate success will depend on their legal strength: the resources of the claims' opponents are so much greater than those of the claims' backers that legal action may be the only way to redress the balance. For this reason, it is important to appreciate the weight of the legal case for the claims.

The basic legal argument supporting the claims is that of aboriginal right. This doctrine argues that native people enjoy rights to the lands they have occupied since time immemorial and thus that "the customary law of native people . . . [must] . . . be protected and recognized."[44] Aboriginal right does not rest on any specific piece of legislation because it is customary and predates legislation on the matter. Thus, the Royal Proclamation of 1763, which is often thought to have created aboriginal right in North America, did not actually do so. However, for two centuries it has performed the important function of putting aboriginal title on a firm legal footing.[45] This position is strengthened in the case of the North, as well as in certain of the provinces, by the fact that in 1867 the government of Canada, in asking the United Kingdom to transfer control of Rupert's Land to it, promised that:

... upon the transference of the territories in question to the Canadian government, the claims of the Indian tribes to compensation for lands required for the purposes of settlement will be considered and settled in conformity with the equitable principles which have uniformly governed the British Crown in its dealings with the aborigines.[46]

The British Order in Council transferring Rupert's Land incorporated this commitment as a condition of transfer, which has received some judicial recognition in Canada as binding on the Canadian government.[47]

Overriding all of these historical bases of aboriginal title is its formal recognition in Section 33 of the amended Charter of Rights, which proclaims:

(1) The aboriginal rights and treaty rights of the Aboriginal Peoples of Canada are hereby recognized and affirmed.
(2) In this Act, "Aboriginal Peoples of Canada" includes the Indian, Inuit and Métis peoples of Canada.

In addition, Section 24 as amended reads:

The guarantee in this charter of certain rights and freedoms shall not be construed so as to abrogate or derogate from any aboriginal, treaty or other rights and freedoms that pertain to the Aboriginal Peoples of Canada including

(a) any rights and freedoms that have been recognized by Royal Proclamation of October 7, 1763, and

(b) any rights and freedoms that may be acquired by the Aboriginal Peoples of Canada by way of land claims settlements.

Particularly after the Charter of Rights becomes law, aboriginal title may seem to provide a strong basis for native claims. However, its power is limited by three considerations.

The first consideration is that, in the words of the Judicial Committee of the Privy Council, aboriginal title is "dependent upon the good will of the Sovereign." In other words, it is within the power of the Parliament of Canada to legislate aboriginal rights out of existence whenever it wishes to do so. Also Parliament, in passing a piece of legislation, may extinguish by implication aboriginal title in the area covered by the legislation if the substance of the legislation is incompatible with aboriginal rights. Judicial interpretation of the Charter may conclusively end this possibility. However, it is also possible that the courts may decide that what the Charter guaranteed was an aboriginal right, one of whose basic features was its subordination to the will of the sovereign. In the provinces, an act abrogating aboriginal title might require the concurrence of both the relevant provincial government and Ottawa. (North of the sixtieth parallel the federal government would still be the sovereign; hence, no such mitigating negotiations would be required.) If it felt that the need was sufficiently pressing, the federal government might insist in court that it had the power to terminate aboriginal title, possibly offering natives compensation for that title. In other words, the concept of aboriginal title may contain a fatal flaw, despite entrenchment in the Charter of Rights.

This speculation may remain untested for the same reason that has led Ottawa not to explicitly extinguish native title in the past. This reason is that Ottawa has not felt any compelling need to do so: the native interest in northern lands has not yet sufficiently jeopardized any of Ottawa's plans. While the bases of this calculation may be changing, it is undoubtedly still the case that parliamentary action stripping the native people of their rights would be unpopular and that any government in Ottawa would hesitate before unilaterally extinguishing native title. Still, it must be remembered that this is a possibility.[48]

② The second consideration is that, in the words of Mr. Justice Mahoney of the Federal Court of Canada, "Canadian courts have successfully avoided the necessity of defining just what an aboriginal title is."[49] The Baker Lake case, which Justice Mahoney decided in November 1979, provides the most recent, but still incomplete, judicial statement on the subject.[50] Justice Mahoney asserted that the Inuit of Baker Lake still enjoyed aboriginal title to a substantial area of land around their community because Parliament had neither explicitly nor implicitly extinguished it, although some pieces of federal legislation had eroded it. In this sense, the decision was a victory for the Inuit, for it endorsed the concept of aboriginal title, whose legal status had been uncertain since the ambiguous outcome of the Calder case in 1973.

Since Calder, Ottawa has hedged on the question of aboriginal title by only acknowledging that this title might exist. Presumably, the Baker Lake case has put pressure on Ottawa to face the issue of aboriginal title, and may have contributed to Ottawa's acceptance of it in the amended Charter of Rights.

But what is the nature of the title that Justice Mahoney confirmed? It has been generally agreed that the title involved is one of "usufructuary right," which means the ability to use the land and benefit from it, but not to sell it to any party other than the Crown itself. In other words, aboriginal rights are not property rights and they do not seem to provide a basis for the political rights in the native claims, but aboriginal rights do offer certain guarantees. In Justice Mahoney's opinion these guarantees amount to protection against situations that would threaten wildlife hunted by native people. He concluded that it was not enough to prove that hunting, fishing, or trapping had diminished. Instead, he required proof that non-renewable-resource-related activities such as seismic operations, drilling, or surveying altered the behaviour of the wildlife, a much more difficult point to demonstrate. Because the Inuit could not prove to his satisfaction that the caribou on which they relied were being harassed by mineral exploration, he refused to grant an injunction preventing the federal government from giving land-use permits to mineral developers in the Baker Lake area.

This decision left substantial confusion and unhappiness. Ottawa, which argued vigorously that aboriginal right did not exist in the Baker Lake area, and the mineral companies themselves are concerned because the decision did not definitively reject the concept of aboriginal title. Also, it did not clearly define the types of non-renewable-resource activities that would be viewed in a subsequent court case as in conflict with aboriginal title. For example, a mineral-development company wishing to invest large sums in an exploration program might be afraid to commit that money if it was possible that the native people could argue successfully at some time in the future that the mine the company developed as a result of its exploration did in fact harass wildlife and accordingly violated aboriginal title. The Baker Lake decision leaves open this kind of uncertainty and in this way still enables native groups to use aboriginal title as a credible, although unwieldy, weapon in their arsenal.

For their part, the Inuit of Baker Lake are unhappy that a threat to their major economic and cultural resource has been approved by the courts. Native people in general are dismayed by the narrowness of the grounds on which the decision declared a case of aboriginal title could be based and the difficulty of proving that the grounds did in fact exist.

Over and above this problem is the difficulty of cost, the third limit on the usefulness of aboriginal title. In order for the Inuit in the Baker Lake case to prove that they had aboriginal title, they had to hire anthropologists to prepare detailed testimony. To prove a case of harassment of wildlife, they had to hire zoologists and, of course, their case required a great deal of work by legal counsel. All of this high-priced labour produced a staggering bill. Legal costs alone for the Inuit Tapirisat were $74 000.[51] Clearly, native groups cannot afford to go to the courts frequently to press claims based on aboriginal title. Their bills would be equally high for each case because the existence of aboriginal title and the fact of harassment of wildlife would have to be proven for each area concerning which native people wished to argue a case.

What conclusions can be drawn from this unsatisfactory legal situation? Peter Cumming has argued that, in any case:

> It seems obvious that these issues are best determined and resolved by legislation rather than by litigation. The questions involved cannot easily be answered on a yes or no basis, which is the only approach a court can take. The issues are such that they can only really be resolved to the satisfaction of all through a negotiated, fair settlement which requires a political and legislative approach and solution.[52]

Viewed in this context, aboriginal right becomes another factor in the complex equation leading to a settlement of the northern native claims. For example, the threat of court action based on it could sufficiently intimidate potential participants or investors in proposed northern developments to frighten them off. Such an attack of nerves could jeopardize projects, particularly if substantial uncertainties of other sorts surround them. The end result might be the blighting of Ottawa's hopes for northern development. It might well be that the wish to avoid this scenario could lead to a compromise. The native people might be willing to trade the potentially great but also insecure benefits of aboriginal title for a narrower set of entrenched rights. Ottawa, for its part might be persuaded to "consolidate" rather than extinguish native rights and in this way end the costly uncertainty in the way of promoting its northern-development plans.

Aboriginal right clearly cannot determine the outcome of the native claims; even entrenched in the Charter of Rights it is far from definitive in any legal sense. Rather, it may be an incentive for the parties to the native claims negotiations to deal seriously with each other.

While the recognition of aboriginal rights in the Charter of Rights may not strengthen the native position greatly, the reference to treaty rights may substantially benefit those northern native peoples who have entered into treaties with the federal government, in that it may give them a much stronger recourse through the courts than before. Of all the native people north of the sixtieth parallel, the only ones in a position to take advantage of this possibility are the Dene, whose lands are covered by Treaties Eight and Eleven, the only ones in force in the North. The Dene might be able to challenge Ottawa's right to authorize major development projects in the Mackenzie Valley on the grounds that Ottawa has not lived up to its obligations under the two treaties, hence has abrogated them and in this way permitted its authority to lapse. While this line of argument is highly speculative, it could obstruct proposed developments in the Mackenzie, such as the Norman Wells pipeline, which Ottawa would like to see proceed. This prospect suggests that Ottawa may seek to avoid legal challenges by giving the Dene claim a much higher priority than it has received since the demise of the Canadian Arctic Gas pipeline application in 1977. If Ottawa did behave in this fashion, it would be repeating its century-old pattern of dealing seriously with native claims only when they are seen to jeopardize the immediate economic-development plans of the federal government.

It is sometimes argued that the native peoples of the North are nations in the sense recognized by international law and that international law stipulates that they have a right to self-determination, which Canada is compelled to accept.[53] Those who argue that international law provides a basis for the claims point to the United Nations Declaration on the Granting of Independence to Colonial Countries and Peoples[54] and the UN Declaration on Principles of International Law Concerning Friendly Relations and Co-operation among States in Accordance with the Charter of the United Nations,[55] both of which assert a right of self-determination for all peoples.

While strong social and moral arguments do underlie the claims, these proponents are incorrect in turning to international law for support. A close reading of these declarations reveals that they place declaring the territorial integrity of a member state of the United Nations above the principle of self-determination. They are only intended to apply to the residents of legally designated colonies. Many of the relationships of the North to southern Canada may be colonial, but the North is not legally speaking a colony; hence, these declarations are not relevant to the North. Even if they were relevant, resolutions of the General Assembly are "devoid of legal obligatory effect."[56] There is no court to which the native people could take the government of Canada in an attempt to impose the declarations' provisions on Canada. In short, whatever the other merits of the claims, there is no case in international law to support them.

5. The Rhetoric of Native Claims

When contrasting cultures approach an issue of great material and symbolic importance, it should come as no surprise that they encounter difficulty in communicating. They comprehend such issues differently. The tragedy of their mutual unintelligibility is that they are unlikely to achieve any satisfactory compromise until they do understand each other. The parties in such conflict often use rhetoric as a weapon to undercut the other side, with the usual result that onlookers—and most Canadians are onlookers to the northern-claims debates—are confused. Despairing of understanding, they are likely to turn their attention to other issues.

Nation and Self-Determination

The rhetorical skirmishing surrounding northern native claims has at times reached the pitch of open warfare. At issue are differences over the basic meaning of the claims and their implications for the future of northern Canada. These differences particularly focus on the terms "nation" and "self-determination." The difficulties English Canadians suffer over the meanings of the word "nation" have been obvious since the debates on the use of the term by Québécois in the 1960s. The debate in the North assumes an almost identical form because there are two meanings of the term "nation." As Peter Russell states them:

> The oldest and most continuous usage associates the concept of nation or nationality with what is basically a cultural entity.... "a multitude of humans characterized by common and unique cultural factors. This multitude shares in a common historical past and is linked by an awareness of its uniqueness."

In the second sense:

> ... the nation is the sovereign legal entity which participates as an individual and independent member in the international community of nations, and nationality is a legal capacity bestowed by the sovereign nation on all of its citizens regardless of their cultural characteristics.[57]

These two senses are quite different and suggest quite different implications. The claims assume the first interpretation of nationhood and infer from it right to "self-determination", implying:

1. The recognition that the culture and values of those making the claim are worthy of being preserved.
2. That it is a primary goal of any claim settlement to ensure the preservation and growth of this culture.
3. That a culture can only evolve in a healthy fashion if the people who hold it control the factors affecting its viability.
4. That this requires that those people have a meaningful legislative authority over certain of the powers that usually accrue to governments in Canada, either provincial or federal.

Thus, the concept of self-determination implies some form of government effectively controlled by native people. The exact nature of the jurisdictional authority of such a government varies from claim to claim but is roughly what has been suggested on page 55.

   The opponents of the native claims seethe whenever claims advocates use the word "nation" because they assume that the second interpretation of the word is what really lies at the base of the claims. From this they deduce that self-determination is equivalent to the creation of independent native countries as autonomous members of the international community. In this interpretation they are occasionally encouraged by some loose usage among claims advocates. However, the official record is quite clear. The document produced by the Inuit Tapirisat of Canada, entitled "Political Development in Nunavut," consistently assumes that the proposed Nunavut will remain in Confederation and specifies as the ITC's goal that Nunavut ". . . take its rightful place within Confederation"[58] and for greater certainty explicitly considers and firmly rejects any form of looser link between Canada and Nunavut than that currently existing between Ottawa and the provinces. The Claims Proposal of the Council for Yukon Indians expresses a wish to "exercise self-determination in our homeland and yet be an intrinsic part of Canadian society" and to achieve a "rightful place [for] Native People in Canadian society."[59] Even the Dene Nation, popularly assumed to be the most radical northern native group, argues that the basis of their settlement must be "our right to self-determination *within the Confederation of Canada. . . .*"[60] Thus, the northern natives are not pursuing any "separatist" cause and are not seeking to dismember Canada.

Racial Government

Sceptics of the claims proposals often attack them as involving racial governments. For example, the Prime Minister's Office, in a definitive statement on the subject, declared:

In the North, as in the South, the Government supports cultural diversity as a necessary characteristic of Canada. However, political structure is something quite different. Legislative authority and governmental jurisdiction are not allocated in Canada on grounds that differentiate between the people on the basis of race.[61]

Undoubtedly the governments that the Dene and ITC proposals envision will be controlled by native people because of the way the boundaries of the territories they will govern have been drawn and because of the extended residence requirements for voters.[62] However, the two proposals do not establish racially defined governments; to the contrary, they go out of their way to affirm the political—and other—rights of all residents of the respective areas.[63] The only way such a situation may be considerd one of ethnic government is to suggest that the domination of the present-day Yukon Legislative Assembly and the Eighth N.W.T. Assembly by non-natives are examples of ethnic government. Those who attack the natives' proposals would never accept this description and, hence, there seems little reason to accept it as an interpretation of what is proposed by native claims.

Because native people constitute a minority of the population of the Yukon, they will accordingly be unable to dominate elections to any geographically defined legislature—unless a rigorous residence requirement is imposed. Thus, to assure a degree of native self-determination in the future, the CYI is forced to seek a government in which participation will be determined by ethnicity. The CYI has justified such a government by arguing that the current thrust of political development in the Yukon is "outmoded" and "unworkable"[64] and thus that no viable alternative exists other than the Indian government they seek. In all likelihood, the actual negotiations over their claim will see their accepting fewer responsibilities for the Indian government than are usually associated with provincial governments. This accommodation will mollify opponents somewhat by ensuring that some of the powers that they fear might particularly affect non-natives detrimentally—for example, administration of the courts and the education of non-native children—are still controlled by an all-Yukon rather than an Indian government.

Segregation

We have seen that, contrary to the attacks of their critics, the native claims are emphatically not separatist. With the exception of the Yukon claim, they do not attempt to establish racially defined governments. However, their critics level another charge that southern Canadians find particularly persuasive— the indictment that the claims are segregationist. The term "segregation" conjures up memories among liberal Canadians of the legally permitted injustices suffered by blacks in the United States. These fairminded Canadians are revolted at the thought that their government would permit similar institutions to be established in Canada. They are no less troubled by the suggestion that such institutions can also be seen as analogous to the traditional Indian reserves in Canada south of the sixtieth parallel and, worse yet, to the system of apartheid in the Union of South Africa. Thus, for example, Lyle Stewart, speaking during a debate of the N.W.T. Legislative Assembly, asserted:

> I was raised next to a reservation and never felt that the reservation concept worked at all. . . . The Inuit proposal is in the sense of the word a reserve, it is segregation in the matter of race. This has not worked, it will not work here.[65]

In a similar vein, the Eighth Legislative Assembly of the N.W.T. argued:

> Frankly, support [converting the N.W.T. into racial states] and you have to support South Africa and its policy of apartheid. . . . The fanciful name for it is "positive" racism. And it's well-known what the free world thinks of South Africa for it.[66]

It is true that native claims rest on an assumption of racial difference and that segregation in the United States, the Indian-reserve system, and apartheid rest on assumptions of racial difference. However, does this apparent similarity mean that all of these institutions are cut from the same cloth? Obviously this is a very contentious question—particularly as one side approaches it from the individualistic suspicion against any distinctions among groups of peoples, while the other assumes the primacy of the group and its need for self-determination. The claims differ from the suggested analysis, in that:

1. The structures sought by the claims are being sought by the subordinate ethnic groups for their own protection rather than being imposed on them, and
2. It is the indigenous people who will govern the institutions.

Thus, the whole intent of the claims is to create structures to protect the native peoples. In contrast, segregation and apartheid were created to exploit and control the subordinate races. The reserve system was established to clear the native people off lands sought by immigrants and to assimilate the native people.[67] It is surely a misinterpretation to lump the proposed claims settlements together with institutions of such obviously different intentions.

Integration and Assimilation

Much of the rhetorical confusion rests on a confusion over the future place of native people in northern Canadian society. The uncertainty and politicization of the terms "integration" and "assimilation" illustrate this latter confusion and the philosophical distance between the two contending visions of the northern future. Federal and Yukon policy is that native people should become integrated into northern society by obtaining the skills that would enable them to take up wage employment. Also, natives ought to be trained to participate in the institutions of the dominant society in which they live and on the same basis as other Canadians. Their doing so would satisfy the democratic principle that all citizens should bear the same relationship to the state and to society. At the same time, they can retain their sense of belonging to a native people, in exactly the same way that ethnic Canadians are permitted and indeed assisted to remember their own ethnic roots.

The governments take this to be an integrationist position, in that it does not legislate any bias against a group nor does it declare ethnic feelings and organization illegal. However, to the proponents of the native claims, it is highly assimilationist. They view it this way because their sense of the relationship between individuals and their society and their understanding of the organization of culture diverge greatly from those of non-natives. These differences lead them to believe that assimilation—and assimilation at the bottom of society—is inevitable if native people are treated as individuals rather than members of ethnic groups. They anticipate this outcome because of their fear, which has already been discussed, that individuals cannot resist the pressures of the economic and social choices presented to them. In this way they fear that, if the choices are structured by non-native factors, the native worker may very well find himself choosing between his economic and his cultural wellbeing.

This choice poses little problem to non-natives who are primarily interested in their personal wellbeing and who find the various aspects of lives to be relatively independent. One aspect can be disrupted without the others' being affected. Thus, for example, Ottawa's multicultural policies assume that people can move from their homelands and adopt different forms of dress, language, and economic activities while retaining viable cultures. The native people view what remains after such dislocations as merely folklore, and prefer to reserve the use of the word "culture" in a more complete sense: that which is imbedded in the realities of their everyday lives rather than in memories of some distant past. For them the multicultural dancers on Canada Day are symbols of an assimilation they do not wish to share.

What place, then, do they wish to occupy? What is their definition of integration? Their definition involves their forming a part of Canadian society on the basis of group equality with non-native Canadians, on the assumption that the maintenance and growth of their group as a group is a value that public policy must seek. They reject the concept of treating all individuals alike as ultimately destructive of true ethnic culture, particularly since the dominant assumptions of present northern society are not native assumptions. Instead, they wish to control enough of the determinants of culture to keep their cultures from becoming museum pieces. On the basis of cultural security, they then wish to take part in Canadian society and to participate in the development of the North.

Likely Outcomes of the Claims

The possible outcomes of the northern native claims can be described as lying along a continuum. Claims settlements towards one end of the continuum would go a long way to providing the cultural safeguards through political institutions that the claims seek. The recognition by some non-native northerners that the claims may foster rather than retard northern development and the philosophical difficulty of opposing the democratic aspects of the Nunavut proposal suggest that a sympathetic evolution of Ottawa's policies cannot be ruled out completely. However, for all of the philosophical and economic reasons already suggested, this outcome is unlikely. Still, Ottawa may be willing to compromise somewhat to achieve claims settlements. For example, it might find that its principles and self-interest lead it to offer native people authority over programs currently administered by DIAND or by the territories under contract from DIAND. In this way, the native people might control native education and social-assistance programs, which they want to direct, yet the territorial governments will not have any powers taken from them. Still, this is substantially less than the native-claims groups have been seeking and they may not find this compromise acceptable.

However, it is also possible that they may come to see themselves not merely as weak but also as weakening while Ottawa remains strong. They may see their cultures eroding day by day, come to the conclusion that half a loaf is better than none at all, and accept a settlement more in the middle of the continuum, a settlement such as that pressed on the native people of northern Quebec. The Inuit, Dene, and Yukon native leaders have asserted their resistance to such a development, but undoubtedly they must have some second thoughts. It is equally likely that some of their people challenge their adoption of strong claim positions. Whether native people maintain their determination in the future cannot be predicted, but we can note that many of the factors determining their commitment are at present beyond their control.

All of the outcomes suggested so far are instances in which an actual agreement is reached. Even if some formal agreement can be reached on claims, it would be naive to think that agreement would represent a final settlement of the claim. Even after the formal signing of a settlement, many questions of interpretation will have to be negotiated as it turns out that the two sides did not have the same understanding of particular items in the legal document. Similarly, situations that were not anticipated when the settlement was reached are sure to arise and require negotiation. Finally, the experience of the Alaska Highway and northern Quebec settlements suggests that governments may drag their feet in fulfilling their obligations under the agreements, or at least will be perceived as "chiselling" by native people. Here again, more negotiation will be required. For these reasons, the claims settlements will turn out to be processes rather than events. This should not be seen as any weakness in the concept of the native claims. Rather, it follows as an inevitable consequence of the fact that the claims settlements the natives seek are, as has been noted before, social contracts, in effect constitutional statements of relationships between groups of people. Because the relationships change, the social contracts must be equally flexible. For this reason, ongoing negotiation leading to adjustments is both unavoidable and desirable.

The continuum of outcomes includes some where no formal settlement is made. At the extreme end is the possibility that some or all of the claims may be formally extinguished by an Act of Parliament. We have seen that there is no doubt among legal scholars that Ottawa has possessed the legal authority to do this, but that the situation is less clear in view of the recognition of aboriginal title in the proposed Charter of Rights. Ottawa might wish to extinguish unilaterally native title if a situation ever developed in which the future of a non-renewable-resource development were seriously jeopardized by the continued pressing of a native claim and if Ottawa thought that unilateral extinguishment could rescue the proposal. For example, if natives threatened a lengthy lawsuit, extinguishment might appear to be an attractive response. However, if they threatened violence, the extinguishment would only incite their more militant members, exactly the opposite of the desired result. In any event, it is likely that such an act by Ottawa would be repudiated by most Canadians who, while they lack much interest in the North, do cherish a national self-image of fair play that would be violated by such an action.

It is far more likely that, if Ottawa felt that it had to expedite a proposed megaproject, it would repeat the tactic it used in passing the Northern Pipeline Act in 1978.[68] In this instance, Ottawa did not explicitly extinguish aboriginal title and indeed paid lip service to the principle. However, the legislation it passed approved the construction of a pipeline across land on which there was still an unresolved native claim. The act denied the native people any control over the activities associated with the construction of the pipeline on their land and gave them only the most minimal opportunities to appeal to the courts. Ottawa does not have to move more aggressively than this: it has no pressing practical need to settle the question of aboriginal rights in the abstract, because it has no specific plans for most of the area of the North. However, when aboriginal rights obstruct particular projects, Ottawa can apply the tactic of legislating in disregard of aboriginal title, all the while claiming to be sympathetic to it. This ploy sufficiently muddies the waters that Ottawa can exercise its overwhelming power, yet minimize the resulting controversy.

A recent variant of this device suggests that Ottawa may even be losing its concern about controversy surrounding its handling of the North. The Charter of Rights recognizes aboriginal title, but Bill C-48 ignores it completely in putting into place a process for administering northern oil and gas activities that places their promotion very much above other national and northern concerns. In effect, this stratagem would be the cutting edge of a design to settle the more intractable claims by default.[69] Ottawa may decide that the native organizations will not agree to terms acceptable to it and accordingly may decide to pay no more than lip service to the claims process, if that. This implies different political strategies in each of the two territories. In the Yukon, Ottawa may attempt to satisfy some native desires by granting greater self-government to the local Indian communities. It will also work to increase the attractiveness of native participation in the Territorial Government. In doing this, it may try to attract potential new native leaders, thus bleeding the Council for Yukon Indians of talent and energy. It will also urge the Territorial Government to be more responsive to native needs. This would increase its legitimacy in the eyes of the native people and undercut the support for the Council for Yukon Indians.

The present hostility between Yukon Indians and the Territorial Government does not recommend this approach as a promising strategy in the short run, but it might achieve Ottawa's goal of conceding nothing fundamental over the long term.

Ottawa's response to the components of the claims in the N.W.T. dealing with political institutions and native self-determination is more complicated and less predictable. Because the Ninth Assembly supports the native claims, Ottawa cannot use it as an ally against the claims groups. It is also difficult for Ottawa to present the Assembly as an alternative to the governmental institutions sought in the claims, because the Assembly may reach decisions on specific issues that might be the types of decisions Ottawa fears giving the native people the power to make. Thus, for example, if the Assembly were given some authority over megaproject development, it might delay the approval of projects until certain needs of the native people were met. To avoid such a situation, Ottawa can be anticipated to drag its feet on devolving further power to the Assembly of the N.W.T., particularly power to influence non-renewable-resource development. At the same time, it will look favourably on efforts to increase the role of local governments because it recognizes that this is a change that native people want very much, yet one that can be granted without diminishing Ottawa's sovereignty in the North.[70]

The N.W.T. situation becomes more complex because, should Nunavut become a separate territory, the majority of the population in the remaining part of the Northwest Territories will be white. This development could well lead to the election of a future Assembly whose views on native claims and northern development closely resemble those of the Yukon Assembly and the Eighth Assembly of the N.W.T. If such a development comes to pass, Ottawa might apply the same strategy suggested for the Yukon. It would also be likelier to devolve additional power to the Assembly of the Northwest Territories than it might if the Assembly continued to be chosen by a majority native electorate.

While the two sides jockey on the political front, the continual emphasis on the development of the non-renewable-resource sector of the northern economy means the further entrenchment of the logic of that system and a resulting weakening in the ability of the native cause to oppose it. Bill C-48 is the perfect case in point. The tactic of recognizing aboriginal rights in principle while in practice legislating as if it did not exist is certain to demoralize native people. So too is the government's lack of faith in seeking to reopen for negotiation aspects of the Agreement in Principle that it reached with COPE.[71] The native people may hold fast to their beliefs or they may be drawn more fully into the wage economy and turn their backs on their land-claims proponents. Whichever outcome turns out to be the case—and the outcome may vary from claim to claim—Ottawa may find itself less and less forced to consider the native claims as a factor in its policy making. Bill C-48 and the apparent reneging on the COPE Agreement in Principle suggest that Ottawa has already decided that heightened southern interest in northern development, particularly regarding energy, reduces the need for it to deal seriously with native claims. Quite conceivably, this development will result in less and less being heard of the claims as most natives lapse into political lethargy while a few strive to rise through non-native political institutions. In other words, the native people may very well come to approach politics as do Canadians in general.

However, while they may enjoy formal equality with other Canadians—that is, equality under the laws of Canada—no one should hold the illusion that the native people of the North will enjoy the same opportunities Canadians like to believe all of their fellow citizens share. To the contrary, the coming of non-natives and more recently the domination of the non-renewable-resource-based economy have devastated native society. Northern native people have become marginal to the society developing in the North. As marginal people they are ill equipped to succeed in this society. They are ill educated in the skills and values it prizes, lack the capital necessary to establish themselves in it, and bear the burden of social problems resulting from their frustrations in trying to relate to it. Without going to the extreme of complete native control over the North, it might be possible to fashion land-claim settlements that could reintegrate native society in a way that might give native people more confidence and a fuller measure of resources with which to join in Canadian society. If *de facto* extinguishment comes to pass, this opportunity for social creativity will have been lost.

The significance of this development for all Canadians is that it would condemn Canada to repeat the century-old mistakes that have tended to confine the country's native population to the lower rungs of the social ladder. A century after the major Indian treaties were signed, Canada's Indians tend neither to assimilate nor to succeed on their own terms. Some promising developments can be seen, but the total picture is not one of which Canadians should be proud. It is a picture that certainly ought not to be duplicated in the frontier regions of Canada. However, the logic of past federal-government policies toward Canada's northern natives and their aboriginal claims is precisely the logic that underlay the making of the treaties. This is not necessarily to suggest that these policies are being promoted with any ill will against the native people. It is, rather, simply a reflection of the fact that northern native societies have suffered disintegration as a result of contact with non-Indians, that the non-settlement of the claims or very watered-down settlements of the claims will produce similar consequences for northern natives as the treaties did for southern natives, and that subsequent remedial policies cannot help but be partial and at best marginally successful. This is the ultimate challenge of the land claims—and the ultimate ethical problem they pose for Canadians. After a century, are we any better able—or more willing—to meet the needs of our indigenous people than we were in Victorian times?

Notes

[1] These restrictions on development are discussed in Chapter 5. An example of this sentiment is the view of Robert Catho, a Whitehorse mining consultant. Speaking to the Sixth Northern Resources Conference, he argued that land claims have become a serious problem for mining development "because they are at the centre of government land policies which are in conflict with a rational mining strategy." *Edmonton Journal* (October 19, 1978), p. E1.

[2] Louis-Edmond Hamelin, *Canadian Nordicity* (Montreal: Harvest House, 1978), pp. 122-23.

[3] Mr. Justice Thomas Berger, *The Report of the Mackenzie Valley Pipeline Inquiry* (Ottawa: Supply and Services Canada 1977), Vol. II, pp. 14-34.

[4] *Ibid.*, Vol. I, p. 85.

[5] Council for Yukon Indians, "Yukon Indian Position, 1979," *Northern Perspectives*, Vol. VII, no. 4 (1979), pp. 7-8.

[6] Treaty Number Eleven, reprinted in D.G. Smith, *Canadian Indians and the Law: Selected Documents, 1663-1972* (Toronto: McClelland and Stewart, 1975), p. 208. See also Treaty Number One, reprinted in *ibid.*, p. 205.

[7] Dene Nation, "Agreement in Principle between the Dene Nation and Her Majesty the Queen, in right of Canada: A Proposal presented to the government and people of Canada on 25 October 1976," Section 16, reprinted in M. Watkins, *Dene Nation: The Colony Within* (Toronto: University of Toronto Press, 1977), p. 187.

[8] Individual Indians on reserves in southern Canada are presently exempt from provincial and federal income tax on income earned on the reserve. However, Indian corporations are not. See Richard H. Bartlett, *Indians and Taxation in Canada* (Saskatoon: University of Saskatchewan Native Law Centre, 1980).

[9] Michael Asch, "The Dene Economy," in Watkins, *op. cit.*, p. 53.

[10] Indian Brotherhood of the N.W.T. (Dene Nation), "Self-Determination for Aboriginal Nations in Independent Countries," prepared for the International NGO Conference on Discrimination against Indigenous Populations (Geneva, Switzerland: September 1977).

[11] Dene Nation, "Metro Proposal," reprinted in R.F. Keith and J.B. Wright, *Northern Transitions* 2 vol. (Ottawa: Canadian Arctic Resources Committee, 1978).

[12] Asch, *op. cit.*, p. 56.

[13] Committee for Original Peoples Entitlement, *Inuvialuit Nunangat* (1977), p. 19.

[14] Ray Unger, "The Land Claims Package: An Assessment," *Yukon Indian News* (June 20, 1978), pp. 6 and 7.

[15]This view was expressed quite clearly in the National Indian Brotherhood's reaction to the release of a draft of the CYI Claim. This reaction is reported in the *Yukon Indian News* (June 6, 1978), pp. 4-6.

[16]*Dene Declaration*, in Watkins, *op. cit.*

[17]COPE, *op. cit.*, pp. 13-15; Inuit Tapirisat of Canada, *Nunavut Proposal* (1976), Section 301, reprinted in *Musk-Ox*, No. 18 (1976), p. 6; K.M. Lysyk, *Alaska Highway Pipeline Inquiry* (Ottawa: Supply and Services Canada, 1977), p. 111.

[18]*Ibid.*, p. 111.

[19]In the case of Canada, of course, the existence of a federal system of government requires that the definition have added to it the words "within the sphere of its powers as set out in the British North America Act."

[20]For example, the Inuit Development Corporation agreed in 1980 to supply labour for the construction of the Polaris mine (*News/North* [October 10, 1980], p. B3) and several native communities in the Yukon entered into contracts to clean brush on the right of way of the Alaska Highway gas pipeline, despite the CYI's position that no pipeline should be built before a claims settlement.

[21]*News/North* (February 20, 1981), p. A10.

[22]See, for example, D. Pimlott, "Offshore Drilling in the Canadian North: Elements of a Case History," in *Mackenzie Delta: Priorities and Alternatives* (Ottawa: Canadian Arctic Resources Committee, 1976).

[23]R.F. Keith *et al.*, *Northern Development and Technology Assessment Systems*, Background Study No. 34, (Ottawa: Science Council of Canada, 1976), p. 125.

[24]Berger, *op. cit.*, Vol. I, pp. 135-36. See also National Energy Board, *Reasons For Decision: Northern Pipelines* (Ottawa: Supply and Serivces Canada, 1977), pp. 5-203, 5-204.

[5]However, this does not mean that alliances on some aspects of the claims are impossible. Some pipeline companies have supported native claims in order to encourage their settlement and thus eliminate a source of uncertainty concerning their proposed projects.

[6]Government of Canada, "Statement of the Government of Canada on Indian Policy" (Ottawa: DIAND, 1969).

[7]In this case, the Nishga Indians of the Nass River Valley in British Columbia sought a court declaration that their aboriginal title had never been extinguished. Ultimately, the Supreme Court of Canada rejected their position, but in a fashion that left the question of aboriginal title still very much unresolved. Three of the judges supported the concept, three opposed it and the seventh and tie-breaking judge decided against the Indians, but on a legal technicality, not on the merit of their case. *Calder* v. *Attorney General* [1973] S.C.R. 313. See also, K. Lysyk, "The Indian Title Question in Canada: An Appraisal in the Light of Calder (1973)," 51 *Canadian Bar Review* 450.

[8]Although the 1973 DIAND "Statement on Claims of Indian and Inuit People" appears to say more, a close reading of the document reveals that it does not clearly endorse the concept of aboriginal right. Similarly, Ottawa's Agreement in Principle with COPE specifically asserts that Ottawa does not necessarily accept the concept. The COPE/Government Working Group, "Joint Position Paper on the Inuvialuit Land Rights Claim" (1978), p. 16.

[9]DIAND, "Statement on Claims of Indian and Inuit People" (Ottawa: Queen's Printer, 1973); K. Penner, "Dene and Métis Claims in the Mackenzie Valley: Proposals for Discussion" (Ottawa: DIAND, January 24, 1978); Prime Minister's Office, "Political Development in the Northwest Territories" (August 3, 1977), reprinted in R.F. Keith and J.B. Wright, *op. cit.*; Office of Native Claims, DIAND, "Native Claims: Policy, Processes and Perspectives," reprinted in *Ibid.*

[)]*The James Bay and Northern Quebec Agreement* (Quebec: Editeur Officiel du Quebec, 1976). While the JBNQ Agreement, strictly speaking, does not represent Ottawa's policies on native claims, it does provide many lessons on the forces affecting claims and the problems in negotiating them. Early statements respectively proclaiming and attacking the James Bay power project are Robert Bourassa, *James Bay* (Montreal: Harvest House, 1973), and Boyce Richardson, *James Bay: The Plot to Drown the North Woods*, A Sierra Club Battlebook

(Toronto: Clark, Irwin and Co., 1972). Negotiating and implementing the settlement are the subjects of Ignatius LaRusic *et al.*, *Negotiating a Way of Life* (Montreal: ssDccInc, 1979).

[31] Prime Minister's Office, *op. cit.*

[32] Letter from Hugh Faulkner, Minister of Indian Affairs and Northern Development, to Ione Christensen, Commissioner of the Yukon (January 1979).

[33] Prime Minister's Office *op. cit.*, pp. 280-81.

[34] P.H. Russell, "An Analysis of Prime Minister Trudeau's Paper on Political Development in the Northwest Territories," in Keith and Wright, *op. cit.*, p. 295.

[35] This subject is incisively treated in J. Rick Ponting and Roger Gibbins, *Out of Irrelevance: A Socio-Political Introduction to Indian Affairs in Canada* (Scarborough: Butterworth, 1980) pp. 327-31.

[36] On this point, see "Economic Structures" in Chapter 1.

[37] As noted in Chapter 1, oil and gas exploration tends to contribute little to the northern economy, because firms supply much of their needs directly from the South.

[38] See, for example, the comments of John Steen, Legislative Assembly of the N.W.T., *Debates* 66th Session (October 27, 1978), p. 447.

[39] Ione Christensen, "Presentation to the Eighth National Northern Development Conference (Edmonton, November 15, 1979), p. 7.

[40] The views of the 7th Council and 8th Assembly of the N.W.T. are reported in Wayne Haimila "Directions and Tendencies of the Council of the Northwest Territories with Regard to Native Claims: January 1972 to May 1977," in Keith and Wright, *op cit.*

[41] Legislative Assembly of the N.W.T., *Debates*, 8th Assembly, 66th Session (October 27, 1978) p. 443.

[42] Office of the Commissioner of the Yukon, "Meaningful Government for all Yukoners (Whitehorse: 1975), p. 3.

[43] Penner, *op. cit.*, p. 6.

[44] Peter A. Cumming, "Canada: Native Land Rights and Northern Development," *Alberta Law Review*, Vol. XII, no. 1 (1974) p. 23.

[45] Peter A. Cumming and Neil H. Mickenberg (eds.), *Native Rights in Canada*, 2nd ed (Toronto: General Publishing, 1972), p. 26.

[46] Address to Her Majesty the Queen from the Senate and House of Commons of the Dominion of Canada (December 16 and 17, 1867), reproduced in R.S.C. 1970, Appendices, 8.

[47] David W. Elliott, *The Development of Greater Self-Government in the Yukon Territory, Legal and Constitutional Provisions Affecting Yukon Indian People* (Whitehorse: Government of Yukon, 1979), pp. 22-23.

[48] Cumming and Mickenberg, *op.cit.*, p. 166.

[49] Quoted in H. Herchmer, " 'Caribou Eskimos' v. The Canadian Legal System," *Northern Perspectives*, Vol. VIII, no. 3 (1980), p. 2.

[50] Mr. Justice Patrick Mahoney, *Reasons for Judgement* between the Hamlet of Baker Lake and the Minister of Indian Affairs and Northern Development, Federal Court of Canada, T. 1628-78.

[51] *Musk-Ox*, No. 25 (1970), p. 104.

[52] Cumming, *Alberta Law Review*, p. 58.

[53] See, for example, the comments of Michael Jackson reported in Keith and Wright, *op. cit.*, p 257.

[54] General Assembly Resolution 1514 (xv).

[55] General Assembly Resolution 2625 (xxv).

[56] L.C. Green, "Human Rights and Canada's Indians," *Israeli Yearbook of Human Rights*, Vol 1 (1971), pp. 157-58.

[57] P. Russell, "The Dene Nation and Confederation," in Watkins, *op. cit.*, pp. 163-64.

[58] Inuit Tapirisat of Canada (September 1979), p. 6.

[59] Council for Yukon Indians, *op. cit.*, p. 8.

[60] Dene Nation, "Proposed Agreement in Principle . . ." reprinted in Watkins, *op. cit.*, p. 182.

[1]Keith and Wright, *op. cit.*, p. 280.

[2]This latter question is a subject of much debate, in that the majority of the transient population to be denied the vote will be non-native. However, the argument that transients do not have as much of a stake in the decisions of northern legislatures as do the permanent residents has a great deal of plausibility. It has been recognized by Ottawa in the N.W.T. Political Development paper, although not to the extent of the ten-year residence requirement suggested by some native groups.

[3]See, for example, The Dene Nation, "Recognition of the Dene Nation through Dene Government," pp. 2-3, and ITC, "Nunavut Proposal," reprinted in *Musk-Ox*, No. 18 (1976).

[4]Council for Yukon Indians, *op. cit.*, p. 8.

[5]Legislative Assembly of the N.W.T., *Debates*, 59th Session (May 28, 1976), p. 537.

[6]Legislative Assembly of the N.W.T., "You've heard from the Radical Few about Canada's North . . . Now hear from the moderate many" (Yellowknife: 1977), p. 6.

[7]Treaties and Historical Research Centre, DIAND, "The Historical Development of the Indian Act," 2nd ed. (Ottawa: DIAND, 1978), p. 53.

[8]Bill C-25, Third Session, 30th Parliament, 26-27 Elizabeth II, 1977-78.

[9]A fuller statement of this argument can be found in Gurston Dacks, "Northern Native Claims: Will Ottawa Default?" *Canadian Forum*, Vol. LVIII, no. 687 (March 1979).

[10]Ottawa has identified this as a possibility toward which it is sympathetic. Prime Minister's Office, "Political Development in the Northwest Territories," in Keith and Wright, *op. cit.*, p. 281. C.M. Drury, the Prime Minister's Special Representative for Constitutional Development in the Northwest Territories, has also endorsed such a devolution. His views are contained in "Notes for Remarks to the N.W.T. Council" (Yellowknife: October 20, 1978), p. 15.

[1]*News/North* (February 20, 1981), pp. A9, A12.

3/The Political Evolution of the Canadian North

The 1970s saw the first substantial erosion of colonialism in the North. Th
1980s will be in large measure a period of adjustment to the changes of th
1970s. In addition, they will see substantial strain as the various interests i
the North try to proceed with their often incompatible agendas. The first an
foremost of the actors is Ottawa, whose power in the last analysis is virtuall
absolute. Northern factors may influence northern politics, but souther
factors will decide it. This hard colonial fact must never be forgotten whe
assessing the political prospects for the North. In the North, those who see
more self-determination will find that colonialism dies slowly because i
reflects the interests of both those who created it and those who have come t
benefit from it. They will also find to their dismay that the patterns o
thinking and behaviour formed in the context of colonial political structure
may themselves obstruct efforts to erase colonialism. Where a degree of unit
can be achieved among northerners, political colonialism may well continu
to fade. However, where consensus cannot be reached, pressing social an
economic problems are likely to persist; conflict is likely to intensify. Th
factors influencing this choice of political futures in the North are the subjec
of this chapter.

The Interplay of Agendas

During most of the 1970s, the politics of the two northern territorie
fundamentally resembled each other. Each was defined by three majo
political actors that had the same agenda in both territories. The first set o
actors was the native-claims group, which sought to guarantee their cultura
viability through claims settlements that would create native politica
institutions. The second set of actors was the territorial assemblies, bot
dominated by long-term non-native northerners[1] who wanted to ensure tha
future northern political institutions would:

1. Not obstruct the large-scale resource projects they considered essential fo
   ending the long and frustrating wait for real economic growth in th
   North and
2. Not give natives advantages that non-natives did not enjoy, advantage
   such as tax exemption, political power disproportionate to their numbers
   or privileged access to the use of northern lands.

The third and by far the most powerful actor, Ottawa, faced an agenda complicated by the contradictory goals it was seeking in the North. Ottawa's 1972 statement of its northern goals, "Canada's North, 1970-80," emphasized northern interests and particularly those of northern natives. However, it is hard to avoid the judgment that in the 1970s Ottawa based its most significant northern decisions less on its commitment to northerners than on its hopes that the North would contribute to the country's economic health generally and energy supply particularly.[2] This approach complemented the territorial assemblies' goals, although they wished that Ottawa would promote the goal even more actively. However, Ottawa also recognized moral and legal obligations to the native people of the North. Both out of ethical concern and to extinguish aboriginal title so that development would proceed unimpeded, Ottawa funded native groups to prepare their claims for negotiations. In this way it contributed to native political awareness. However, it did not satisfy the demands this awareness prompted because the demands would have taken control of resource development out of its hands. At the same time, until the very end of the decade it resisted the territorial assemblies' desires for more power and autonomy, in part out of deference to political aspects of the native claims and in part out of a determination to maintain control of the natural resources of the North to avoid the type of conflict it was encountering with the oil-and-gas-producing provinces.

By the end of the 1970s, this conflict of agendas had produced, particularly in the Yukon, a virtual stalemate that was proving to be an insurmountable obstacle to political development in the North. The blockage seemed insurmountable because it was both based on conflict in northern society and sustained by Ottawa's self-interest. It was costly because it prevented northerners from addressing their urgent problems. While movement is now visible in the N.W.T., just how costly the blockage was for both territories—and is likely to remain in the Yukon—can be appreciated by measuring the politics of the North against the yardstick of political development.

Political Development

Political development is the ability to perform the political function. It is the ability of the members of a society to make and implement effective binding decisions on goals accepted as legitimate by the members of the society. There no particular type of political institution to best accomplish this task. Rather, political institutions and processes can be considered developed if they can generally bridge the gaps in society, contain conflict, and produce a consensus. On the basis of this consensus, government can make decisions reasonably promptly rather than avoid thorny issues. Its decisions will distribute burdens and benefits among the groups within society in a fashion that at least ensures that none are systematically disadvantaged; these decisions will represent reasonably relevant responses to the challenges posed

by the issues.[3] For all of these reasons, even if specific decisions provok
unhappiness, they at least will tend to be accepted as legitimately arrived a
Over the long run, the processes and institutions that produce legitima
decisions—in other words, the political system—will come to be seen a
legitimate and valuable in and of itself. However, to define politica
development is not at all to suggest that societies necessarily accomplis
higher and higher levels of it. Indeed, history contains countless cases in
which social divisions have been too deep to permit the attainment of hig
levels of political development, with usually unfortunate consequences. Th
question facing the North is whether it can avoid this fate.

Political development is not synonymous with institutional develop
ment. A political system is not necessarily highly developed simply becaus
its government is structured along the complex, highly specialized, repre
sentative democratic lines that work reasonably well in many moder
societies. Such a structure tends to promote political development, but only i
it fits the society it is intended to govern. The governments of both norther
territories are cases in point. During the 1970s they grew substantially, bu
this growth did not produce an equivalent growth in political developmen
To appreciate why, it is important to understand their structural evolution i
the 1970s. Because the details differ so significantly, the two territories will b
examined separately.

The Yukon[4]

In 1898, the Yukon was set apart from the rest of the Northwest Territories.
Commissioner was appointed to exercise executive power and an appointe
council of up to six members shared legislative authority with the Commi
sioner over most of the areas of jurisdiction possessed by the provinces. I
1908, a fully elected council of ten members was created. The Commissione
did not sit on the Council, but remained as the head of the executive of th
territory, acting on behalf of his employer, the federal Minister of Resource
and Development.

This chain of command differs greatly from the pattern of responsib
government in which the executive remains in office only so long as it enjoy
the support of the majority of the elected legislators. Because the head c
government was a federal civil servant, the Yukon's government was coloni
and dependent upon Ottawa. This dependence was reinforced by the feder
cabinet's authority to disallow any territorial legislation. This and Ottawa
power to unilaterally amend the Yukon Act, the "constitution" of th
territory, denied to the Yukon the *de facto* supreme law-making ability of th
provinces.

The day-to-day operation of government in the Yukon reinforced th
colonial relationship. The councils tended to be weak: the bulk of polic
making was done by the civil servants of either the territorial or feder
government, working within a policy framework or set of assumption

basically created in Ottawa. This situation has affected profoundly the political culture of the Yukon.

The most obvious consequence has been the wish of many non-native Yukoners to end or at least reduce their powerlessness. They have felt this need particularly strongly because the economy of the Yukon has been generally stagnant since the gold rush, yet until very recently Yukoners have not controlled any governmental structure that could work to improve the economic plight of their territory. Instead, their economic fate has been decided by a distant and often apparently indifferent government. It has been only natural for these Yukoners to seek change and in recent years to demand provincial status as the means of ensuring their independence from the unsympathetic colonialism of Ottawa.

Provincial status has not yet been granted, for reasons discussed below, but the Yukon's government has changed substantially. The change has taken two forms.

The first form of change has been the growth of the structure of the Yukon government itself. In 1969, an executive committee was created with a majority of appointed officials led by the Commissioner and a minority of elected members of the legislature. The legislators were responsible for the management of departments of the territorial government, the first two being (1) Health and Human Resources and (2) Education. In 1977, the elected members became a majority of the executive committee. The size of the Territorial Legislative Council was increased to 12 in 1974 and 16 in 1978. The growth increased the likelihood of at least some native members being elected to the legislature as it permitted the drawing of electoral boundaries to create some constituencies with very large native majorities. It also promoted party politics and the election of 1978 saw the Progressive Conservatives win a majority comprising 11 of the 16 seats. The party leader, Chris Pearson, then selected the members of the Executive Committee from his party's members in the Council. In this way, a major element in responsible government was intitiated in the Yukon and the party system was further strengthened.[5]

Throughout the 1970s, the members of the territorial legislature pressed for a second form of institutional growth—more political autonomy from Ottawa.[6] Their efforts won some success in January 1979 when the Minister of Indian Affairs and Northern Development, Hugh Faulkner, instructed the incoming Commissioner to follow decisions of the elected members of the Executive Committee within their jurisdiction, except for some matters of special concern to Ottawa.[7] In October 1979, Mr. Faulkner's Conservative successor, Jake Epp, went substantially farther by transferring ultimate executive responsibility from the Commissioner to the Territorial Legislative Assembly acting through what was now called its Executive Council. The Commissioner was no longer to sit on the Executive Council, whose members were not only individually responsible for their departments but also collectively for the territorial budget.⁸ This was a crucial grant of power given that the budget is the basic device used by governments to determine their priorities.

At the start of the 1980s, the Yukon Legislative Assembly was still limited by:

1. Narrower legislative jurisdiction than the provinces enjoy, particularly concerning land and non-renewable and most renewable resources.
2. The inability to amend its own constitution without federal legislation.
3. The possibility—in effect rarely realized—of federal disallowance of its legislation.
4. The fact that, while the Yukon gained in 1980 the power to levy its own income tax, Ottawa must still approve its plans for borrowing, lending, or investing funds.
5. The continuing need to negotiate the amount of funding it receives from Ottawa to compensate for the fact that its expenditures substantially exceeed the amount of revenue it can raise on its own.

Still, the structures of responsible government had largely come into being and were being seen by some as the basis from which provincial status might easily evolve.

The Northwest Territories⁹

While both remain colonial governments, the structure of the government of the Northwest Territories has evolved quite differently from that of the Yukon. Generally, institutional developments in the N.W.T. have lagged behind those in the Yukon. For example, the first N.W.T. residents were not elected to the territorial Council until 1951. The Council did not become fully elected until 1975, as contrasted with 1908 in the Yukon. Similarly, the administration of the N.W.T. only began to be based in Yellowknife, rather than Ottawa, in 1967, when a government of the N.W.T. distinct from DIAND was created as a result of the Carrothers Commission Report.¹⁰

The N.W.T. situation also contrasts with that of the Yukon, in that it has not achieved the same degree of responsible government. In the N.W.T. the members of the Assembly as a group rather than the leader of any particular party determine who among them will serve on the Executive Committee. While elected members constitute a majority of the Executive Committee, both the Commissioner and the Deputy Commissioner sit on it and the Commissioner acts as the chairman. The Commissioner has not yet been formally instructed by the Minister to accept the decisions of the Executive Committee.

If the formal details of the Northwest Territories' government suggest a less mature set of institutions, the actual practice brings the two territories much closer together. Following the election of the Ninth Legislative Assembly in October 1979, the elected members of the Executive Committee chose George Braden as their leader. While his position does not correspond as closely to that of a provincial premier as does that of the government Leader of the Yukon, it still provides a focus for territorial politics and could easily evolve into a government-leadership role with the growth of responsible government. Indeed, the willingness of the current Commissioner, John Parker, to accept the views of the elected members of the Executive Committee has virtually brought this about. Of course, it must be remembered that the sympathy of one official is not as secure a guarantee for the future as a constitutionally entrenched grant of power would be, but it does create a precedent that would prove awkward to reverse. Responsible government has also increased since the election of the Ninth Assembly, because the elected members of the Executive Committee have been responsible for all the departments of the territorial government that provide services directly to the public, leaving the Commissioner and Deputy Commissioner only responsible for administrative departments.

The first institutional priority of the new Executive Committee has been to develop a coherent public-policy process, a mechanism for ensuring that decision making meets two criteria. First, decisions must be made on the basis of adequate information, careful analysis, and full consideration of their implications for the whole range of governmental departments potentially involved. Second, the process must proceed reasonably quickly. Only with the creation of such a system will the Executive Committee be able to exercise its growing powers efficiently and in this way prove itself worthy of additional powers. To accomplish this goal, a policy secretariat was initiated in 1980 to provide the Executive Committee with the type of services the cabinet in Ottawa receives from the Privy Council Office. With the policy secretariat in operation, the N.W.T. government has become more administratively advanced than the Yukon territorial government, a fact that will undoubtedly improve its ability to seek additional grants of authority from Ottawa.

Political institutions in the Northwest Territories are also more advanced than in the Yukon, in that local government is well established in a large number of settlements in the N.W.T. Local government has become the training ground for developing political skills on a widespread scale. As will be explained later in this chapter, this program has aroused controversy and undergone major changes since its inception. However, regardless of its problems, it at least represents an attempt to bring large numbers of territorial residents and particularly native peoples into the territorial political system, a goal that has not been seriously pursued in the Yukon.

Summary

For all their other differences, the two territories have received roughly the same grant of powers from Ottawa. As in the Yukon, the N.W.T. Assembly does not enjoy the control the provinces hold over land, non-renewable and most renewable resources, labour relations, and certain aspects of criminal law. In addition, its decisions are subject to the possibility of federal disallowance and its financial plans require Ottawa's specific approval. However, both territories are evolving financial relations with Ottawa that more and more resemble those of the provinces. For example, in 1978 the N.W.T gained the authority to set its own income-tax rate instead of receiving a grant in lieu of income tax.

At the start of the 1980s, then, the Yukon enjoyed more responsible government than did the Northwest Territories, but the N.W.T. had advanced further in establishing a coherent policy process within government and training its citizens for political roles. In both territories colonialism had weakened, but was still a major political fact.

Obstacles to Political Development in the North

1. Colonial Political Culture

While the governments in the North have matured substantially in the past decade, popular attitudes toward them have been shaped by the decades of frustration that northerners have felt when contemplating their political weakness. The almost daily repetition of events that emphasized their dependence on a distant and often apparently uncaring government has produced a colonial political culture. Of course, not all people in the North hold this set of beliefs and values. Rather, it touches individuals to the extent that they conceive of themselves as being in the northern political system. In practice, this means that long-term non-native residents of the North tend to display the colonial political culture most clearly.

This mentality comprises several mutually reinforcing orientations The first is the low legitimacy of the territorial governments. Because they have been so weak, they have come to be viewed popularly as mere talk shops This view has been reinforced by the second cultural element, the North's— and particularly the councillors'—definition of what the Councils' major roles have been. Ideally, legislatures are supposed to produce a coherent and socially responsible set of policies based on a consideration of the needs of the various groups in society and a desire to attach priorities to these needs and reconcile conflicts among them. Until recently, northern politicians were not compelled to develop self-discipline and skills as legislators because, being powerless, they felt less responsible for the quality of their output then legislators normally feel. They also lacked the access to the public service that governments in power find essential for creating legislative programs. In this way the northern councillors, as contrasted to the two commissioners, lacked the means to be legislators in the fullest sense. This encouraged some councillors, particularly in the N.W.T., to express far more than the usual concerns of legislators for their constituents. They felt that their primary responsibility was to view issues in terms of the immediate needs of their communities rather than to consider longer-term policies or the shape of policy for the whole territory. In addition, some devoted more time to expressing needs and wants than to working out priorities.

Particularly in the Yukon, territorial legislators lavished their time and energy on attacking Ottawa. This oppositional mentality results understandably from the alienation they felt because of their dependence on their distant rulers. However, it does not train politicians in the arts of persuasion and compromise, which are essential to effective government, and it does not produce a comprehensive and consistent legislative program. If territorial legislation met the needs of people, it was largely on the basis of the commissioners' priorities and their instructions from Ottawa, not the political process within the councils. The result of these colonial aspects of legislative behaviour in the North was that the councils were not a particularly satisfactory training ground for more self-government in the future, nor did they command the respect in the North or the credibility in Ottawa that would have supported their claims for greater autonomy.

One further aspect of the colonial political culture of the N.W.T. deserves mention because of its influence on the legitimacy of political institutions. This aspect has been the creation of unreasonable expectations by northerners and particularly native northerners. Because they have not until recently had the opportunity to exercise a meaningful degree of political power, northerners have not had to learn that political structures have limitations, that budgets are finite, and that political activity must be approached in a disciplined fashion. This discipline means both exerting the effort necessary to get out of the political system what can be gotten and recognizing what is simply unreasonable to seek. Many times, communities in the Northwest Territories have had the experience of having their wish for a new dock, generator, or schoolhouse granted immediately on or very soon after making their request to the Commissioner. They take such experiences as a standard of what is possible, even though the decisions were made in a process that has passed from the northern scene. When communities seek something from Yellowknife now and find that it is delayed, denied, or requires more justification from them, they may feel cheated out of what they have come to expect is rightfully theirs. In this sense, they have been spoiled like children, making it all the more difficult for the elected politicians in Yellowknife to command the public support they need to press their case for more autonomy from Ottawa.

2. Profound Social Divisions

The traditional weakness of northern political institutions has inhibited political development in the North. However, even if these institutions wielded much more power, they would still face the daunting task of bridging the kind of profound social divisions that inevitably arise when two societies meet in a colonial setting that defines one as dominant and the other as inferior. Undoubtedly, the northern native people have suffered from contact with non-native society in the ways described in Chapter 1.

The inequalities in the relationships and contrasts between them have produced in the North a climate of resentment on the one hand and indifference or judging on the other. Their differences in political perception seriously obstruct the attainment of consensus and cooperation. For example, politically sensitive native people, including virtually all of the leaders of the native organizations pursuing claims settlements, view the history of white rule over native people as coercive, assimilationist, and paternalistic—if not downright exploitative.[11] Whites tend not to notice the patterns of exploitation in white-native relations. They emphasize the efforts of governments to assist native people through providing housing, medical, and education services, among others. For example, whites point to Ottawa's funding of the native claims as proof of its benevolence. However, natives argue that Ottawa is less interested in justice than in defining native claims in order to extinguish them and in creating native organizations so that some native body with authority can sign the documents extinguishing the claims.

White and native interpretations of social change in the North also diverge. The white view tends to consider the fate of northern natives as an inevitable consequence of the meeting of cultures, one of which cannot compete technologically with the other. In this view, the inevitable consequences of technological inferiority are cultural destruction and then assimilation in order to benefit from the natural advantages of southern forms of economic organization. However, native leaders see the fate of their peoples as determined not so much by technology as by federal policies that wrested their land base from them and imposed alien religion, schooling, medicine, and culture on them. They see the breakdown of northern native society as far from natural and inevitable, but rather as the result of governmental manipulation. Of course, if life can be manipulated in certain directions, it can be redirected and assimilation avoided—hence the political component of the native claims. As has been noted, this whole line of reasoning tends not to make sense for white northerners. In this breakdown of communication lies a great potential for misunderstanding and conflict.

This tension is particularly severe in the Yukon, but, as will be discussed later in this chapter, is showing signs of easing in the Northwest Territories. To the extent that the tension remains, however, northern politics will display a fundamental incoherence, in that it will not be interpreted in the same fashion by all those who are active in it. Adding to the problem is that, as discussed in this chapter, the participants do not share a common political vocabulary. They do not fully appreciate the extent of the divergence of interpretations of northern politics and they can have difficulty communicating with one another on certain crucial issues. Because they do not adequately understand the assumptions on which the other side is operating or, sometimes, because they cannot appreciate the depth of feeling the other side brings to certain political questions, they fail to take the other side's positions nearly as seriously as it does. This lack of mutual respect in the bargaining process—particularly in the Yukon—tends to discourage the sides from trying to solve their problems together, embitters the negotiations which do occur, and gets in the way of their succeeding.

When whites and natives come together in political settings, they burden the negotiating table not only with their hostility and mutual incomprehension, but also—and equally troublesome—with very different goals and values, as noted in Chapter 1. It should be remembered that these different goals result from a substantial divergence in fundamental values.[2] Values vary greatly from one group of northern natives to another, but all display the four basic elements: attachment to the land, the sharing ethic, adapting to nature, and emphasizing the communal over the individual. In contrast, non-natives tend to hold the individualistic view of nature as something to be adapted for their purposes. They tend to view the society to which they belong and the land around them more as means to personal ends rather than as values in themselves.

In native societies, the need for unity shapes politics as a consensual process involving all of the adult members of the group. As a result, all tend to view decisions, once taken, as mutual agreements reflecting the wishes or best interests of the group rather than the imposition of the will of the strongest party. In contrast, the non-native political process tends to be structured along lines that emphasize conflict. For example, the logic of elections and of formal votes in legislatures defines some people as winners and others as losers. While the processes may be accepted as legitimate, they tend to emphasize division rather than unity.

Non-native politics also differs from native politics, in that it proceeds through specialized structures of government involving a relatively small proportion of the population, while the rest contribute only intermittently to politics, usually electing people to represent them in the specialized forums of government. The native approach tends to involve all adults actively in politics in several ways. Decisions are usually seen as properly made by the total group, not by some specialized organization. Thus, for example, the Dene Nation assemblies attract large numbers of Dene people. Also because native traditions were formed in the context of much smaller groups than the native claims groups or the territorial governments of today, there is a strong wish among native people of both territories to increase the power of the local governments, mainly to make decision making by the people feasible again. To the extent that power is not held locally or regionally, native people tend to see the people they elect to distant legislatures more as envoys than as representatives. Thus, they do not want these politicians to make decisions on their behalf, but wish them to return to them, to inform them of the issue at hand, and to seek their instructions. Clearly, this is a very different approach to legislating from the one most legislators bring to their jobs.

What are the consequences of these differences both in values and in approaches to politics? The first is the mutual incomprehension discussed above. A second is that the legitimacy of the territorial institutions is very much in question among northern natives, since these institutions embody unfamiliar and even hostile values and practices. As a consequence of this contrast and because the legislatures have been until recently (and the Yukon legislature still is) viewed as part of the unresponsive system that has degraded native life, native people have tended not to involve themselves with the territorial political institutions. For example, it was not until 1978 that the first native people were elected to the Legislative Assembly of the Yukon. The Dene Nation boycotted the Eighth Assembly of the Northwest Territories precisely because they felt it to be illegitimate. Despite their reversal on this stand and the election of a native majority sympathetic to native claims to the Ninth Assembly, the native members from the eastern Arctic waited a year before accepting two seats reserved for them on the Executive Committee. A variety of factors influenced their decision, but among them were their uncertainties concerning the legitimacy of the Assembly for people in their part of the Arctic.

These, then, are the obstacles to political development in the North:

1. Governmental structures, while maturing, are still colonial, dependent on Ottawa's sympathies and viewed as not completely legitimate by northerners.
2. An extremely complex society is characterized by mistrust and misunderstanding between natives and non-natives, contrasting goals by the members of the two groups, different approaches to politics, and quite substantial differences from one region of the Northwest Territories to another.
3. An overloaded agenda. Particularly in the N.W.T., the internal logic of northern society is evolving at a faster and faster rate, leaving little opportunity for the adjustments all societies must make when fundamental changes occur. The imposition of the needs of southern Canada both accelerates the rate of change and distracts the North from its own agenda, thus intensifying the stress of change and complicating the task of building coherent northern political systems.

Directions for Political Development in the 1980s

These political problems facing the North seem to guarantee frustration and incoherence for the foreseeable future. However, that prediction paints a bleaker picture than the evolution of the North in fact warrants. Some changes already in place give cause for hope and a variety of approaches can be identified that could contribute to the political growth of either or both of the territories.

Probably the most important change is that non-natives no longer monopolize northern political processes. At the start of the 1970s the native groups of the North were either unborn or in their infancy. During the 1970s, the native groups have undergone many birth and growing pains, but they have generally matured into capable bodies. Some are stronger in certain respects than others, but by and large they have the support of their people, means of maintaining the close contact with them that native culture demands, and good relations with sympathetic interest groups in southern Canada. They also have access to specialized expertise to enable them to come to grips with challenges presented by the dominant nonnative society of Canada, even if they do not always succeed in conquering those challenges. For example, the Council for Yukon Indians in recent years has developed areas of expertise in social and educational policies, economic development, and resource mapping that enhance its credibility greatly. Bodies as well established as this are difficult to ignore. They also command attention because, while the regulatory processes of the federal government have tended to favour southern-initiated large-scale developments, the processes themselves have raised the sensitivity of industry and northern nonnatives to native concerns. Moreover, the political atmosphere of the North is still charged with the memory of the rejection of the Canadian Arctic Gas pipeline application, at least in part out of deference to pressure mounted by and on behalf of native people. The lesson of that experience is that a strategy opposing the wishes of native people can never again be seen as a guarantee for success. As the 1980s begin, the native people of the North are no longer on the outside of politics.

One of the great developments of the 1970s was the closing of the power gap between natives and non-natives in the North. The coming of this greater degree of political equality may lead to an intensity of interracial political competition formerly unknown in the North, but it can also lead to a situation in which, for the first time, natives and non-natives will come to take each other seriously, simply because they are forced to. Put differently, the 1980s may be the decade in which the North realizes that it will only mature if its people are united. This process of maturation may well take several forms.

1. Unity: The Shape of the Future in the Northwest Territories?

A handful of events stands out as landmarks in the political evolution of the Northwest Territories. One of these was the transfer of the administration of the N.W.T. from Ottawa to Yellowknife late in the 1960s. This creation of a government of the N.W.T. brought a flood of public servants to the North and changed the face of Yellowknife. Another landmark was not merely the report released by Justice Thomas Berger in 1977, but more importantly the process of his inquiry. His hearings focused the developing political awareness of the native people of the Mackenzie Valley and created a solidarity among them and a divisiveness between native and non-native in the Valley that might never otherwise have come about.

An equally important event was the election of the Ninth Legislative Assembly on October 1, 1979. This election marked the end of the boycott of the Assembly by the Dene Nation, the most politically assertive native group in the N.W.T. The Dene had spurned the Eighth Assembly, calling it a colonial body. Without strong pro-native voices among its members, the Assembly took a hard line against the claims. Thus, instead of forcing Ottawa to the negotiating table, the Dene boycott simply turned the Assembly into a weapon in the hands of the Dene Nation's opponents. Despite their reluctance to act in a way that implied they viewed the Assembly as legitimate, the Dene were forced to recognize that they could not continue to ignore the Assembly. Moreover, the numerical majority of native people in the territorial electorate meant that it might be possible to turn the Assembly into a vehicle for native claims. With this hope in mind, a number of people active in the Dene Nation ran as candidates in the election. Two of them, James Wah-Shee, the former president, and Richard Nerysoo, vice-president of the Dene Nation, were elected. In addition, Nellie Cournoyea and Tagak Curley, who had been very active in the COPE and ITC claims groups, respectively, were elected.

The election of these candidates and of several others sympathetic to the native cause completely changed the complexion of the Assembly. One of its first acts was to repudiate the former Assembly's hostile position on the claims. It also quickly created a "Committee on Unity" to seek means of working cooperatively with the native groups in promoting the attainment of just settlements for the claims. The Assembly at its second session in February 1980 approved a position paper acknowledging the fundamental relationship between the claims and political development in the N.W.T. and committing the government of the N.W.T. to assist the claims groups.[13] This policy was implemented almost immediately when the Assembly actively supported the Dene in arguing that a proposed expansion of production at the Imperial Oil field at Norman Wells and construction of a pipeline in the Mackenzie Valley be delayed until after the native claims in the Valley are settled. At the third session of the Assembly, James Wah-Shee, the local government minister, announced that the Executive Committee had decided to give the hamlet of Baker Lake $30 000 to help it pay the legal fees it incurred in attempting to argue before the Federal Court of Canada that it should recognize the aboriginal rights of the people of Baker Lake and forbid mineral companies from carrying on exploration activities felt to disrupt the wildlife on which the hunters of Baker Lake depended.[14] In these and other ways, the Assembly has tangibly placed itself on the side of the native-claims cause.

The long-term consequence of this development may be the formation of a consensus in the Northwest Territories. The two foci of political activity in the N.W.T.—the Assembly and the native groups—are now working together: the interests of the majority of the population are now recognized by the Assembly. This new state of affairs will undoubtedly concern non-renewable-resource developers and non-native businessmen in the N.W.T.; in this sense, it is not completely accurate to define the evolving situation as one of unity. Still, there is ample evidence that the native people are quite willing to accept non-traditional forms of economic development, once they achieve the security of claims settlements. With this assurance and the recognition of the inevitability of a majority in the Assembly sympathetic to the native claims, the tone of territorial politics is changing. It is no longer fashionable to openly attack the claims. Rather, most people are attempting to come to terms with the philosophy and to work out the details of the claims. So long as no provocative event occurs to deflect this process, the N.W.T. for the first time in its history will be able to address the real political question, which is its relationship with the South. Whatever the outcome of this struggle, at least it can be said that the N.W.T. will approach it much more united than at any time in its history.

2. Division of the Northwest Territories

A society whose politics are ill developed because profound differences set apart various groups within it can attempt to bridge those gaps and to build a consensus. However, another approach may reduce division within a society if its different groups cluster in different geographic regions. This approach is to split the society into several components, each of which is more homogeneous than the original, larger society. This option of division has long been debated in the Northwest Territories because it reflects one of the most fundamental social facts of the N.W.T.—regional differences.

The immense expanse of the North and the differences in the cultures, economic activities, and histories of the peoples of the various regions of the N.W.T. have created a strong sense of regionalism. This regionalism is not merely an awareness of differences among regions, but also a feeling that the differences make it unlikely that a single body can effectively govern all of them together. Put more bluntly, regionalism is a belief that one's interests would be better served by a regional government than by the status quo.

As a partial response to this feeling, the government of the Northwest Territories embarked in 1976 on a program of placing substantial administrative authority in the hands of the officials in its regional offices.[15] However, this move only devolves administrative activities, while legislative authority remains in Yellowknife. If this continuing monopoly of law-making power is to end, one likely mechanism will be the evolution of regional councils. The Baffin Regional Council and the Central Arctic Area Council at present enjoy only advisory powers. However, they may come to hold program and financial authority in the future, as may the proposed South Mackenzie Area Council. The COPE claim proposes a Western Arctic Regional Municipality that will hold some governmental powers. Finally, it may be noted that the Drury Report advocates the establishment of regional councils depending on the willingness of the communities in each area of the N.W.T. to devolve or delegate some of their authority to such a council.[16]

These responses satisfy regional feeling to some extent. However, they are not a substitute for the most dramatic reflection of regionalism, proposals to divide the Northwest Territories. The pursuit of division has evolved through two distinct stages. In the first stage, at its height in the 1960s, non-native business and community leaders in the Mackenzie Valley argued that Ottawa recognize the greater economic development and political sophistication of the western part of the Territories. Their strident urgings that it receive more self-government by being separated from the less modern eastern and high Arctic made division an important question for the Carrothers Commission. Its 1966 Report rejected the concept of division primarily because it could jeopardize the political position of the native people when at some time in the future they would become politically active.

This recommendation did much to discourage the proponents of separating a more advanced western part of the N.W.T. from the rest, although the suggestion recurred from time to time. Division again became a pressing issue when it took on its second and present form, that of a component of the native claims. Both the Métis in 1977 and the Dene Nation in 1979 proposed that the N.W.T. be divided so that structures of government could be created in the west to clearly protect native interests. However, these proposals have taken a back seat to the 1979 position of the Inuit Tapirisat of Canada, stated in a document entitled ('Political Development in Nunavut.')[17]

The ITC proposes that the Northwest Territories be divided so that the portion of it north of the treeline, including the Mackenzie Delta, will come to be ruled by its own government and to gain provincial status within fifteen years of when it becomes separate. The bases for this argument are the distances from Nunavut of the present seat of government in Yellowknife,[18] the uniqueness of the eastern and high Arctic, and the perceived unresponsiveness of the present government to the needs of the residents of what will become Nunavut. The determination of the ITC in promoting its proposals, and the ethnic homogeneity of the proposed Nunavut area, which precludes any significant opposition from other groups of residents in the area affected, have given the proposal a great deal of credibility. Indeed, it was the major question discussed by the Territorial Assembly at its session held in Frobisher Bay in October 1980. During this session the leader of the Assembly's Committee on Unity reported that the committee "has not been able to find a consensus, or even, at the moment, to see the opportunity for consensus, favouring the continuing existence of this territory as a single jurisdiction."[19]

Following the recommendations of the Committee, the Assembly endorsed the idea of division. It recognized that little information was available on the practical consequences of division and accordingly called for a referendum on the question to be held two years later to allow enough time for study and debate.[20]

Is division a wise response to the problems of distance and social diversity in the Northwest Territories? The problem with this question is that it is too abstractly stated. In reality the question of division has to turn on its practical consequences. If the goal of political development demands standards of responsiveness, efficiency, and legitimacy, then the proponents of division must provide specific arguments to address these criteria.

It is likely that the legislators of the proposed Nunavut will be able to be more responsive to their people than were the members of the Assembly of the N.W.T. simply because the Nunavut Assembly will be closer to the people and will have to bridge much narrower social gaps. In other words, they will likely be working on the basis of a much stronger consensus than exists within the N.W.T. as a whole. However, what is not so certain is the extent to which the Nunavut legislators will hold the powers they need in order to act responsively. It may well be that the population of Nunavut is so small that Ottawa will not consider it justified to transfer to Nunavut the substantial powers the ITC currently claims for it. Thus, division may freeze Nunavut into a junior position in Confederation. In contrast, a united territorial government might be able to press more effectively for fuller provincial powers. Whatever the extent of the powers it enjoys, the proposed Nunavut would swing virtually no weight in federal-provincial negotiations or negotiations between itself and Ottawa, again because it contains so few people. It is true that the N.W.T. as a whole exercises little power in such negotiations, but how responsive can Nunavut be to its people if it exercises even less clout in Ottawa?

Another problem affecting responsiveness is the technical issues that all contemporary governments must address. For example, in the case of Nunavut, protection of the environment requires an understanding of the intricacies of drilling for oil and gas and of pipeline design, construction, and operation. Dealing with private enterprise and with other governments requires the services of highly skilled lawyers, accountants, taxation experts, and resource economists. The present territorial government finds that it cannot afford to employ the depth of expertise to put it on a par with the federal government's army of experts or, in some cases, with the energy companies placing applications before the federal government. It is likely that the government of some fraction of the territories would be forced to maintain an even smaller technical establishment and be even more limited in its ability to retain expert consultants. This could force it to defer to Ottawa or corporate interests not simply because it was wrong on a question but because it lacked the resources to prove itself right.

In terms of the second criterion, cost efficiency, it will obviously cost more to operate several governments, although the exact extent of the cost difference would depend on how the costs of duplication would compare to the savings of the enormous sums of money presently devoted to travel by territorial officials around the N.W.T. and to other costs associated with the enormity of the present boundaries.

The third criterion, legitimacy, involves two questions. The first is the political balance in the respective portions of a divided Northwest Territories. In this regard, the likeliest candidate for division, Nunavut, raises the critical question of the ethnic composition of the electorate that would remain in the rest of the N.W.T. At present, the Dene Nation can derive some comfort in knowing that the total electorate of the N.W.T. is likely to contain a majority of native people for the foreseeable future. However, if the predominantly native Nunavut were to be removed from the N.W.T., the electorate would be more evenly balanced between native and non-native and the new-found native control of the Territorial Assembly could well be lost.

This prospect could lead to enough Dene and Métis opposition to Nunavut to cause Ottawa to reject division, or at least to give it a pretext for a policy of rejecting division that Ottawa had reached for other reasons. Already, concern about the Nunavut proposal has begun to be expressed by native spokesmen from the western portion of the N.W.T. For example, the Dene members of the Territorial Assembly argued for delay and very careful study rather than endorsement of the Nunavut proposal when it was discussed by the Assembly at its Autumn 1980 session.

However, the Assembly took a leaf from René Lévesque's book; it endorsed division in principle and a referendum to actually decide the question. The two-year delay before the holding of the referendum is prudent, because the Nunavut proposal pits the principle of native solidarity against that of native self-determination. This clash of principles will take time to resolve. It deserves the most careful treatment because of its implications for the future level of political development in the N.W.T. On the one hand, the rejection of Nunavut will produce great alienation above the treeline. On the other hand, if the Dene become a minority of the electorate—that is, if Nunavut is created, but the Dene metro model is not implemented—they are likely to view the Assembly again as illegitimate. This would prove fatal to the progress recently made in interethnic relations in the Mackenzie.

Another concern some people in the western portion of the N.W.T. feel about Nunavut is its economic impact. They fear that the dividing line proposed by the ITC will give Nunavut the bulk of the mineral and hydrocarbon wealth of the North while leaving the western portion with, in the words of one resident, "one large river and a lot of spruce trees." Also to be sorted out are the economic effects of division on Yellowknife, which owes much of its economic life to the territorial and federal government offices located there. The removal of even a substantial fraction of these offices could undermine the town's fragile economy.

The residents of Nunavut or of the Dene area envisioned by the metro proposal presumably will view their new government as legitimate because it will embody the wishes of the majority; the government ought to be staffed by officials responsive to the feelings of the people. However, legitimacy can still pose a problem in two senses. The first is that the new structures of government may put members of the minority in the new territory at a disadvantage and come to be viewed as highly illegitimate by this group. The proposals of the Dene and ITC are explicit in rejecting any form of ethnic government or infringement on the equal rights of all residents of the proposed new territories. However, the possibility for difficulties remains until the exact nature of the governments to be created is worked out. The second possible source of illegitimacy in the new territories may be the frustration of excessive expectations. It may well be that the proponents of division may give their people the impression that it will bring fuller and quicker solutions to their problems than the limited resources and the teething problems of the new government will permit. Widespread disenchantment could result and reinforce popular hostility to government and politicians.

The likelihood of any of these developments coming about is at present uncertain because the details of the division proposals have not yet been worked out and because division has not yet been approved. Before the issue can be properly considered, both in the North and by Ottawa, it will be necessary to specify at the very least the boundaries of the new territory or territories so that questions of electoral composition and resource distribution can be clarified; the form of government the new territory will have, including residence requirements for the electorate; the powers the new government will exercise; and the extent to which it will retain certain links—for example, shared authority over certain questions—with the rest of the Northwest Territories.

Division has been discussed for a long time and appears to be gaining credibility. Indeed, at the time of writing, it appears that further constitutional evolution may well be suspended until the question of division is settled. However, before it is settled, a great deal of work remains to be done to define the shape that division might take. Only when that shape becomes clearer will it be possible to judge its likely consequences for the political development of the North. Even more important, it is only in the process of defining that shape that the territorial and federal governments will decide their positions on the question.

8. The Role of Local Government

Local government can be an important vehicle for political education. It can teach the members of a community how to deal with conflict and reach satisfactory decisions on issues. It can persuade them of their personal political competence, encourage them to be active in politics, sensitize them to the limitations of their political positions and the need to react responsibly and realistically to these limits. Generally, it can give them the basis of a political analysis that will assist them to promote their own interests locally and at higher levels. To the extent that it meets the needs of the people, local government can be important in legitimizing politics as just and worthwhile.

The pursuit of this goal has produced a set of aggressive and often controversial approaches to the development of local government in the Northwest Territories. The first forms of local government were simply administrative arrangements in which local people played no formal role. The Hudson's Bay Company factors, the missionaries, and the RCMP performed the limited administrative tasks Ottawa wished undertaken in the North. In 1954 Ottawa sent Northern Service Officers to train the Indians and Inuit to take part in the Canadian political system.[21] This program encountered substantial difficulty. Because its purpose was basically assimilationist, it had to confront the difficult task of persuading native people that white political ways were better than the native ones that the native people had until then considered quite satisfactory. However, the NSOs often approached the people of their settlements in an insensitive and judgmental fashion, which produced alienation rather than education.[22] In addition after 1959, the position of Northern Service Officer was changed to that of "area administrator" with, as the name suggests, substantial administrative duties. These duties had two implications. First, they greatly reduced the amount of time the area administrator could devote to the political-education function. Second, they conflicted with the political education role, in that they gave the educator powers over such important matters as the granting of social assistance. Hard feelings from the administrator's exercise of these powers could make native people far less receptive to his efforts at political education. In addition, the exercise of these powers tended to be handled basically as an administrative matter; it was not usually thought appropriate to seek the advice of local people or a local council on such questions. Thus while the area administrator was attempting to socialize the native people in his community in the norms of democracy, their experience with government was autocratic. The predictable result was that northern natives felt confused, powerless, and alienated by their first contact with white political institutions.[23]

The Carrothers Commission recognized that even in the mid-1960s the residents of the N.W.T. wanted government brought closer to home. For many of the native residents, particularly in the east, it was difficult to feel much of a link with governments headquartered in distant centres. In response, the Commission recommended that a Department of Local Government be established as part of the government of the N.W.T.[24] This Department was created in Yellowknife in 1967. It established a development program to bring the people of the smaller communities in the North through a succession of stages of increasing understanding of political forms and of increasing responsibility until they attained the status of "hamlets" with elected councils exercising authority over a limited area of jurisdiction. This jurisdiction primarily involves the provision of what may be called "hard services," such as garbage pickup, water hauling, road maintenance and zoning.

Over the years, the program came to be strongly criticized. The structure of the local councils was an imposed southern structure that was alien to the existing political practices in the communities. It was inevitable that any local-government structure established would be alien to the Inuit, because their traditional social organization did not include specifically political institutions. Still, the structures imposed were too rigid to accommodate Inuit approaches to politics and often produced confusion and alienation among the native residents of the smaller communities.[25] Frequently, decisions made in council meetings merely reflected the consensus reached earlier by means of more traditional approaches to decision making. In communities with mixed populations, the native people tended not to take part in the councils because they were conducted in a language and using procedures they did not understand. In some instances, they were offended by white councillors whose approach was perfectly normal in white politics but an aggressive departure from native political practices. In none of these situations was the existence of "modern" governmental forms a reliable indicator of the degree of political development in the community.

Equally important was the relative powerlessness of the local councils. At the end of 1978, 26 of the 51 communities in the N.W.T. still held the status of settlements, which only permitted them to have local, primarily advisory committees—in other words, hardly any self-government. Even among the hamlets, C.M. Drury reported that "local councils and committees are perceived by the communities as possessing no real authority over those issues that are of vital importance to the lives of the residents of the communities."[26] Thus, the local council had no control over "soft services," such as education and social programs, nor over the land-use decisions that affected the traditional activities of the native residents of the communities. While the goal of the local-government program may have been to train people in the communities in politics, it actually schooled them in frustration.

Changing this situation did not seem to be a major priority of the Assemblies preceding the Ninth, nor of the Commissioner at the time, Stuart Hodgson, probably because they felt that the native people of the smaller communities needed to learn southern political forms in order to take part in the larger institutions of government affecting them. In one sense they have been vindicated; native people have become conversant with local council procedures and southern political concepts. However, they have used their growing political sophistication to push for solutions to the problems of local government. The voices of dissent became more strident and were reinforced by the election of the Ninth Assembly, a majority of whose members rejected the idea that local government in the smaller communities should be merely an extension of the territorial government, with primarily administrative responsibilities. Instead, they want the local councils to be acknowledged as a separate level of government for Yellowknife to consult rather than to command.

To achieve this goal, it has been proposed that a new Community Government Ordinance replace the present Hamlet Ordinance. This new Ordinance should be an improvement over the old system, for several reasons. First, it permits each community, within relatively broad limits, to decide the structure of its council and the rules of election to it. This should dispel some of the feeling among native people that the councils are foreign structures.

Second, the proposed Ordinance allows a community to decide that it wishes to take over responsibility for one or more programs such as social services, housing, health, economic development, renewable-resource management, and education. Thus, communities are freed from the restrictive principle that increased local self-government depends on the development of a larger tax base. This principle virtually guaranteed powerlessness to many communities in the eastern Arctic, which have no hope of attracting the economic activity needed to produce significant property taxes. Now it is proposed that, once a community decides to seek a new responsibility, it will negotiate with the responsible minister of the territorial government to demonstrate its understanding of the obligations involved in assuming the responsibility and its commitment to the task. This procedure ensures that local government evolves out of each community and has its support. Thus, it will not be an imposed and alien structure; nor will it be prematurely foisted on the community to suit the needs of the territorial government. Assuming that care will be taken to ensure that only appropriate transfers of responsibility occur, it should be unlikely that local councils will handle them in a manner that would lead to conflict in the community and disaffection with local government.

The third advantage to the proposed Ordinance is that it would end the competition in the Mackenzie Valley communities between band councils established under the federal Indian Act and the community councils established under the Ordinances of the territorial government. Currently, sixteen Mackenzie Valley communities have this often-troublesome dual system.[27] By permitting an amalgamation of the two bodies where the community requests it, the new Ordinance would provide a means by which the communities could simplify their politics.

All told, local government in the Northwest Territories appears on the verge of becoming better rooted in the communities and more relevant to their needs. Its legitimacy should grow as it comes to be seen as more responsive to community needs. The encouragement this growth gives to political participation should begin to realize the potential that local government possesses for contributing to the political development of the Northwest Territories.

The Yukon has tended to ignore local government as a vehicle for political development. The only incorporated local councils are in the predominantly non-native centres of Dawson, Faro, and Whitehorse. Local Improvement Districts existed in some other communities but handled only a narrow range of questions, usually involving hard services. They were merely advisory and tended not to involve native people. Beyond this, the territorial government has not attempted to use local governments as a device for providing political education, particularly to native Yukoners. Instead, it defines its role more conservatively as the provision of planning assistance and other advisory services to existing municipal bodies.

In the Fall of 1980, the Yukon Legislative Assembly passed a Municipal Ordinance ending the five local improvement districts and permitting smaller communities to become either hamlets or unincorporated settlements. This Ordinance resembles the system used in the N.W.T. during the 1970s, in that the unincorporated settlements have councils with only advisory status and the powers of the hamlets are largely restricted to the provision of hard services. It is not clear whether the new forms of local government will be accompanied by some effort by the territorial government at explicit political education.[28]

4. Political Parties

Political parties have come to be a universal feature of liberal democratic states in large part because they perform many services for the political system. While party politics does have its uglier moments, it is essential to the organization of the political system.[29] It recruits candidates for elections, organizes them into relatively few groups (thus making the voters' decision somewhat less complex), and encourages the electorate to vote, thereby adding to the legitimacy of the political order. Both during and between elections, parties provide organized means for people to communicate their wants and needs to those who may come to power or who are in power. To varying degrees, parties formally and informally contribute to the policy process by aggregating these needs—that is, trying to find reasonably satisfactory accommodations among them. Parties provide the stabilizing mechanism for parliamentary government because they organize a majority of support for the cabinet or clearly define the situation when the government holds only a minority. Finally, parties provide for continuity beyond the political lifespans of individuals and they enable the public to impose some small degree of accountability on elected politicians. While it is true that the party system in Canada is coming under increasing attack for the lack of choice, policy relevance, and accountability it provides,[30] its contributions remain substantial. Canadian politics could not function without it.

If the political systems of the North are to mature, they will have to take advantage of the benefits of party politics. In the Yukon, the process is already well under way in that the 1978 election was fought on party lines: fourteen of the sixteen elected candidates ran as Progressive Conservatives, Liberals, or New Democrats. Subsequently, a PC Executive Committee was established and operates on the principles of party government found in southern Canada.

The Northwest Territories have not evolved nearly as far. In part this may reflect the fact that party organization is foreign to native political culture. Party discipline, for example, may impose obligations on a native MLA that conflict with the expectations he and, more importantly, his constituents hold about his behaviour as an MLA. The evolution of parties in the N.W.T. will have to accommodate native political traditions, but it is unlikely to be prevented by them. Indeed, the stage has already been set. While the 1979 territorial election was not run on party lines, as of 1981 it is possible to see the beginnings of party development. Because the Executive Committee is now nominated by the Assembly rather than selected by the Commissioner, individual ministers or the whole Executive might be voted out of office by the Assembly unless a firm basis of support is organized in the Assembly. As was noted above, the usual means of guaranteeing this support has been the evolution of parties and the development of party discipline.

Several possible lines of party development are now visible. It is possible, if the N.W.T. is not divided geographically, that they may reflect the regional voting blocs—the western part against the eastern part—which appeared in some of the votes of the Ninth Assembly. This type of party system would discourage east-west integration and could focus on this axis of conflict many issues that are not really regional in nature. A second possibility is that the traditional southern parties (which are active federally in both territories) may establish at the territorial level the three-party system of federal politics.

As of early 1981, the federal parties were considering contesting the 1983 territorial election.[31] One problem they would encounter is that the distinctions between the Liberals and Conservatives in southern Canada have little relevance in the N.W.T. However, this consideration has not prevented the establishment of a southern-Canadian pattern of party competition in the Yukon and the already existing party structures in the N.W.T. may provide enough of a political focus to establish the same pattern despite its absence in the past.

A third possible route for the evolution of parties in the Northwest Territories is suggested by the fact that personality has been more important than party in determining the N.W.T.'s choice of MPs. If allegiance to southern parties is weak in the N.W.T., the parties may not take hold in the Territorial Assembly. Instead, the N.W.T. may follow the British historical experience of loose coalitions of individuals organizing to govern and to promote their own reelection. In other words, the N.W.T. might back into a party system if the members of the present Executive Committee decide to run on their record as a group. Already, the members of the Executive Committee are tending to refer to themselves as "the government" and principles of cabinet solidarity and secrecy are taking hold. These developments will make the Executive Committee a more closely knit group, as will the need for them to work together to meet the scrutiny of the Assembly. The likelihood that this process will stay on the rails is enhanced by the philosophical consensus among the members of the Executive Committee at the time this was written. While their positions diverge to some extent, they generally support the native claims and are concerned about ensuring that the North will receive a reasonable share of the benefit if megadevelopment is to occur. This shared perspective would provide an ample base for party organization, particularly if it is led by a single individual around whom the others can rally. This person must be credible in both the non-native and native communities, must be able to command the territorial public services, and must act as a buffer between the expectations of the people of the N.W.T. and the goals and activities of DIAND—not to mention the other federal agencies working in the North—and the federal cabinet itself.

The leader of the elected members of the Executive Committee, George Braden, could be such a figure. If he can successfully perform the complex balancing act and if he contests the 1983 territorial election and wins, then the N.W.T. will have evolved greatly in the direction of party politics and will begin to gain the benefits that party politics can provide in the form of increased political development. If, however, the Executive of the Territorial Assembly evolves differently, the question of the evolution of parties will remain unanswered and the legislative process will be limited by the lack of an organizational focus that a party system provides.

The Shape of Political Development

The political futures of the two territories can be anticipated to lie somewhere along a continuum whose ends represent the two contending visions this chapter has discussed. They are native claims on the one end and southern-style evolution towards provincial government on the other. The two are not mutually exclusive and that is why they occupy the same continuum. It is Ottawa's position that the attainment of the two visions can most usefully be understood as "separate but parallel" processes, a view that it may find comforting but that has in the past distressed the advocates of both visions, each of whom understandably wanted the pursuit of his vision to proceed first. As we have seen, this competition continues in the Yukon, but has subsided in the Northwest Territories.

1. Native Claims

As noted, the Dene, Inuit Tapirisat, and Yukon Indian claims all call for substantial changes to the political organization of the North. Whether they are ever accepted by Ottawa and regardless of the form that acceptance takes, the aspirations of the Dene and the ITC claims have been brought closer to realization by the emphasis on unity in the Ninth Assembly. These groups are developing cooperative relations with the Territorial Assembly and can expect a sympathetic hearing from it. Whatever the ultimate shape of the claims settlements, the native groups and the Assembly should be able to work out their implications in a mutually supportive fashion.

However, this situation is not replicated in the Yukon.[32] Not only do the Yukon government's processes not reflect native approaches to politics, but also its leadership has historically been unsympathetic to the Indians' goals. These leaders see little need to share power with the Indian leaders of the Yukon, in that the Indians at present have no power to share with them or, in their view, any ethical or legal claim to political authority. For their part, Yukon natives feel little incentive to participate in a government they believe they cannot deflect from its unresponsive and assimilationist policies, particularly since they form a minority of the Yukon electorate. As a result, neither side sees it as being in its interest to explore the possibility of compromise with the other; hence, relations between the Indians and the territorial government have remained tense.

This situation is the antithesis of political development because a political system can only be considered developed if the various groupings within it are reasonably well integrated. In response to this situation, the Council for Yukon Indians has proposed what is in effect a model of integration through the settlement of its aboriginal claim. It proposes that the native people receive authority over culturally relevant programs, such as education and social assistance, and over economic matters of particular importance to native people, such as wildlife management. Separate native institutions of government are likely to evolve to exercise these powers and the CYI is beginning to develop a structure and gather together the expertise that would be appropriate were it to take on some governmental powers.

How can such a proposal promote social integration? Even if the crude references to segregation are set aside, the CYI proposal does seem to point in the direction of separate native and non-native institutions, a situation likely to institutionalize racial separation in the Yukon. Several replies can be addressed to this concern. First, it must be recognized that the CYI claim will not create social separation in the Yukon. A very real social segregation already exists there: it is a hierarchical one with the native people on the bottom. This unhappy fact leads logically to the second and more positive reply that vertical segregation will only end when Yukon natives as a group achieve a position of equal status with non-natives. This status is in one sense psychological. At present, Yukon natives are victim to the debilitating legacy of decades of being an "internal colony."[33] While there are prominent exceptions, many Yukon Indians translate their feelings of powerlessness and frustration into apathy and personal failure. A claims settlement with a political element would stand as a dramatic symbol of new hope. In validating the Indian view of themselves as a people, it could instil confidence in native people and give them the courage to face the arduous process of rehabilitating themselves. They may then be able to survive existing intercultural tensions intact.

However, the claim settlement must match recognition with power, for two reasons. First, if native people have a degree of self-determination, they will be able to govern themselves in matters important to them. Second, real native power will inject into Yukon politics a completely new element; it will give the leadership of the Yukon territorial government an incentive to treat the native people seriously. The point is that, while the settlement of the claim may give the native people the authority to administer programs for its people, it will not compel the creation of separate programs. Native leaders can be expected to appreciate that the settlement will not provide them with unlimited funding. A decision to strike out on their own with the provision of certain services will be costly, particularly since the number of Indians is small compared to the cost of establishing governmental services. They will want to explore the possibility of some joint programing with the territorial governments. It in turn should prefer that prospect in order to avoid the dismantling of part of its public service. It will also want to avoid the loss of legitimacy that would be confirmed by a native decision to go it alone. Thus, both sides would feel strong incentives to cooperate. This cooperation would likely be promoted by the general economic strengthening of the Yukon anticipated to follow the claim settlement and could stand a reasonable chance of success because it proceeded on the basis of equality, not imposition by the strong on the weak.

The prospects for this sort of development cannot be estimated as very promising. To the extent that it does come to pass, it would have a difficult time coming to be accepted as legitimate in the Yukon because those who might see themselves as the victims of the situation—the long-term, non-native residents of the Yukon—are not now being prepared to understand how such a settlement could promote the political integration of the Yukon. They are also not being told that a settlement could overcome the Yukon natives' opposition to provincehood, which stands as a major obstacle to its attainment. Native and some non-native leaders have emphasized the economic benefits to all Yukoners flowing from a claims settlement, but they have not argued the long-term political benefits of enhanced social and political integration. Moreover, hardly any non-natives—who would be more credible to a non-native audience—have suggested this line of reasoning. As a result, the ground has not been prepared for accepting native political power. In any case, both Ottawa and the territorial government resist such a development: they can be counted on to ally at the claims-negotiating table and to emphasis the economic and land aspects of the claim at the expense of the political aspect. To the extent that they are successful, the future political development of the Yukon will remain highly prob-lematic, regardless of the legal form its institutions may take.

2. Provincial Status

In the legal sense, the North is a colony because its legal form is territorial, not provincial. The territories lack the sovereignty of provinces within their areas of jurisdiction. They cannot alter their own constitutions, in most cases do not control the uses to which their land is put, are limited in their financial powers, do not have direct jurisdiction over their native populations, and face the possibility that Ottawa might veto any legislation their assemblies pass. The legalistic response to this situation is obvious; the territories should be made into provinces.[34]

This solution has not been actively promoted in the Northwest Territories, which has come to political maturity much more recently than has the Yukon and whose agenda is complicated by the native majority and the unanswered question of division of the N.W.T. However, provincial status has long been a clarion call in the Yukon, particularly among the businessmen and professionals who have tended to dominate the Territorial Assembly. These people argue that Yukoners, as Canadians, deserve the same political rights and privileges as other Canadians. They assert that it is intolerable that democracy for them boils down to rule by a government thousands of miles away, in which their MP is merely one of 282. They also point out that provincial status should greatly improve the responsiveness of government. Finally, they argue that provincehood will make Yukoners less scornful of government. Ottawa will seem less grasping and arbitrary and the Yukon territorial government will enjoy more legitimacy because of its autonomy. In December 1977, the Yukon Legislative Assembly's Standing Committee on Constitutional Development presented its Second Report[35] to the Assembly. The keystone of this Report was a draft of a new Yukon Act "to establish and provide for the Government of the Province of the Yukon" with the full powers of a province, including control over resources and all lands other than national parks and land put aside in anticipation of the native-claims settlements. Since then, the territorial government has continued to push this position, achieving its greatest success with the promise by then–Prime Minister Joe Clark that before the end of his first term of office he would give Yukoners an opportunity to express their wishes in a referendum on provincial status for the Yukon. However, when he made that promise, he undoubtedly anticipated a longer tenure of office than he in fact achieved. He did not call a referendum and the Liberals show no interest in adopting his commitment.

While provincial status enjoys great support in the Territorial Legislative Assembly, a referendum would have been appropriate not only for its democratic symbolism, but much more importantly because it would give some clear evidence of public feelings on what is in reality a divisive issue in the Yukon. Indeed, it is quite likely that the provincial side would have lost in the referendum, for two reasons. The first reason, though most Yukoners would not phrase it this way, is simply that the Yukon has not attained a level of political development necessary for self-government to work. The gap between the native and non-native population of the Yukon and particularly between the native leadership and the territorial government would lead to great antagonism if the latter were permitted to be the final authorities over certain matters of great concern to the native people that the federal government now controls. At present the leadership of the Council for Yukon Indians sees its claim as a far more promising route for gaining political structures sympathetic to native needs than is provincial status. For this reason it resists any federal grants of power to the territorial government before the settlement of the claim. Native people are not yet a part of the territorial government's decision-making processes. There are notable exceptions, such as the establishment with the cooperation of the territorial government of a native-controlled school at Burwash Landing, but generally natives tend not to involve themselves politically with the territorial government. When they do, their activity tends to take the form of protesting some governmental action rather than working together with the government in the early planning stages of the policy process. In this way, they tend not to be involved in the crucially important formative stages of policy making. The result, not surprisingly, often is alienation.

The territorial leadership has tried to make provincial status more palatable for Yukon natives. It has suggested that the boundaries of territorial electoral districts be gerrymandered to ensure at least several constituencies, such as Old Crow, with clear and in all likelihood permanent native majorities. It also suggested the possibility of superimposing over the whole of the Yukon some electoral districts in which the electorate would be all native. Thus, the non-native population would vote in one set of ridings and the natives in another.[36] The suggestions have aroused very little native enthusiasm because they guarantee at best only minority native participation in the territorial government and the natives recognize that minority status guarantees them nothing.

They would feel more confident about their future if a second house, composed entirely of native people, were added to the Yukon legislature and given power to reject legislation from the other house that it felt to be hostile to the interest of the native people. However, if the members of this house could argue successfully that virtually all legislation affected native people, as native people, they then would be in a position to bring the business of the Yukon government to a halt. One safeguard against this development would be to give the second house only the power to delay legislation, but this might be too little power to provide a sufficient guarantee for the natives.

A second institutional device might be to set a longer residence requirement for voters than is usually applied in Canada. If, for example, only those people who had been in the Yukon for five years before election day were permitted to vote, native people might not form a majority of these "committed Yukoners," but they would certainly be close enough to it to command the respect of territorial legislators. While possibilities such as these might make Yukon provincehood more attractive to Yukon natives, there is no evidence that the elected leadership of the Yukon is willing to consider them seriously. Accordingly, it seems accurate to assume that the native people of the Yukon will continue to oppose provincial status for the Yukon at least until their claim is settled and they are in a position to assess the implications of the political structures they have been able to gain as part of their settlement.

For non-native Yukoners (who may be concerned to varying degrees about the role of the native people in the political future of the Yukon) the provincehood question turns on an assessment of the financial strength of the territory. Can the Yukon afford to be a province? This question assumes that, before provincehood is attained, the Yukon ought to have a sufficient tax base to pay for the standard of government services Canadians have come to expect, and to achieve it without either taxing Yukoners excessively or depending too much on handouts from Ottawa. In the fiscal year 1979-80, the federal grant to the Yukon amounted to $38 million. During this fiscal year, the Yukon's total budget amounted to $122 million.[37] DIAND calculated that if the Yukon were a province at the time with the added spending obligations of that status, its deficit would have been increased by $24 million.[38] Proponents of provincehood are not daunted by such figures, however. They predict that the economic growth resulting from provincehood will provide revenues to cover the deficit. They argue further that, if the Yukon received the resource revenues the provinces enjoy, the day of fiscal self-sufficiency is not far in the future. However, their crystal balls tend to give off something of a rosy glow; probably more accurate is the view of Mel Foster in a study prepared for the Yukon government in 1979:

> . . . the immediate economic prospects for Yukon give no indication of any significant realignment of Government of Yukon revenues; only in the longer term could a major impact such as large-scale Beaufort Sea petroleum production radically alter the level of Government of Yukon revenues and markedly improve its overall financial status.[39]

The proponents of provincehood respond to this type of judgment by insisting that, if the Yukon received resource revenues as the provinces do, it would soon be able to pay its own way. However, for its part, Ottawa is most reluctant to permit fewer than 25 000 Yukoners to monopolize the benefits of the mineral and hydrocarbon wealth that might be exploited in the future. Accordingly, the most that Yukoners can hope for is some kind of revenue-sharing agreement such as the Drury Report suggested for the Northwest Territories.[40]

In any case, the terms of this whole debate are misplaced because the basic assumption—that fiscal strength is necessary for provincehood—is incorrect. For example, the Atlantic provinces regularly receive large proportions of their total revenue from federal-government grants. In 1976-77, fully 71 per cent of the revenues of the government of Prince Edward Island came from this source.[41] Thus, there is no necessary reason why finances should stand in the way of the granting of provincial status.

Far more relevant are the practical consequences of provincial status. In the absence of a claim settlement reasonably satisfactory to all, provincehood would likely intensify the hostility between the non-native and native populations of the Yukon. It is true that the legal colonialism of the Yukon Act and the heavy hand of Ottawa would be things of the past. However, the economic dependence on Ottawa of the Yukon government and, with it, the frustrations of dependence would persist. More importantly, the economic life of the Yukon would still depend heavily on decisions taken outside the Yukon, in corporate boardrooms in the power centres of the continent. In this respect, while provincehood would be psychologically gratifying to many and grant the Yukon a degree of additional authority to deal with its problems, it would not undo the longstanding links of colonialism that have been the fate of the North since the first coming of the white men.

Ottawa's Position

This chapter has presented an optimistic picture of the North's political prospects—at least those of the Northwest Territories. While promising signs can be seen, the northern situation is tentative. Cooperative relationships are still in their infancy among the political groupings in the territories and they will only mature if they enjoy a supportive environment. If, however, the aspirations on which these relationships are based come to be frustrated, if northerners feel that vital decisions are continuing to be made in their absence or that they can best pursue their own interests through competition rather than through cooperation with their neighbours, then northern politics will return to the incoherence and conflict of the 1970s. There could not be a better recipe for stagnation.

Will the North stagnate or will it grow politically? The answer to this question will depend on many factors, but chief among them will be the policies of the federal government. As in all colonial situations, the colonial power, Ottawa, has the ability to define the terms of political debate. It alone has the power to respond to claims for greater self-determination. Only it can approve the massive development projects that may lead the native groups to view their situation as increasingly desperate—indeed, too critical to permit the luxury of a political evolution based on the slow gains made through cooperation with sympathetic elements of the nonnative population.

Ottawa most recently signalled its intentions in the cabinet document entitled "Political Development in the Northwest Territories,"[42] which it released in 1977 in conjunction with the appointment of C.M. Drury as Special Representative for Constitutional Development in the Northwest Territories. As has been noted, the paper rejected the basic political assumptions of the native claims and went so far as to incorrectly label some of them as racially separatist.

It also asserted that constitutional changes were a matter separate from settlement of the native claims and to be decided by different processes. While this position was stated with regard to the N.W.T., the principle behind it raises particular difficulties for the Council for Yukon Indians because the natives' minority position offers them little hope of controlling the territorial government. However, if cooperation continues between the native groups and the Legislative Assembly and Executive Committee of the N.W.T., the native peoples may be able to achieve their goals through the territorial government, or through the public governments that may be created to govern the regions of a divided Northwest Territories.

The 1977 paper indicated that Ottawa was willing to consider division of the Northwest Territories, though not on explicitly racial lines. It also favoured two forms of devolution. The first was to gradually restructure the governmental institutions of the N.W.T. in a fashion more consistent with responsible government. This would mean withdrawing from the decision-making processes of the territorial government. In the intervening years, this policy has been put into practice, particularly by reducing the role of the Commissioner as a legislator. The second form of devolution was actually to transfer more powers to the territorial government. However, it was not anticipated that control over non-renewable resources would be transferred. In this sense, Ottawa served notice that it did not intend to provide the North with direct access to the revenues that might make its governments financially self-sufficient. Finally, it warned against the simple assumption that the Northwest Territories would follow the well-travelled path from being a territory to provincehood. Instead, the paper suggested that many questions remained to be resolved and that the process of evolution was going to be a lengthy one.

The most publicized, though not necessarily the most significant, constitutional event since the release of the political-development paper was the Report of the Special Representative on Constitutional Development in the Northwest Territories, in January 1980. The Report is not government policy in that it is only advisory. However, the thinking of the Special Representative must be considered to be very close to that of Prime Minister Trudeau, for at least three reasons. First, they both attended the same meetings of cabinet at which the Liberals' northern policies were defined over the years. Second, Trudeau would have been unlikely to appoint an individual whose views greatly diverged from his own. Third, Drury is unlikely to have accepted the task unless he felt that his ideas were going to prove influential.[43] Not surprisingly, the Drury Report continued most of the thinking of the 1977 paper on political development. It rejected the idea that the N.W.T.'s political institutions be reshaped through the settlements of the native claims. Instead, it emphasized the devolution of powers from Ottawa to the territorial government and from Yellowknife to the communities, adding that, if the communities wished, they might band together to form regional governments to provide common services and a collective voice in dealing with the territorial government in Yellowknife.

In terms of devolution, Drury argued that it would be desirable for the territorial government to come to resemble the provincial governments in a variety of ways. First, the Commissioner should gradually withdraw from his role in the policy processes of the territorial government. Second, the financial relationships between Ottawa and Yellowknife should be transacted through the same mechanisms Ottawa and the provinces use. This would replace the present situation in which the territorial government has to negotiate its finances with DIAND, which in turn presents the N.W.T.'s financial needs to the Treasury Board in Ottawa. It appears that Ottawa has decided to implement this change and by doing this has given additional authority to elected northern politicians, although on terms that are not very generous financially.[44] Third, he suggested that Ottawa should deal with Yellowknife through the federal minister responsible for federal-provincial relations, rather than through DIAND. Fourth, Drury urged that the territorial government be assisted in beginning immediately to strengthen its civil service in order to develop the expertise to handle the increased powers of devolution. Fifth, Drury proposed that ownership of onshore non-renewable resources and responsibility for land-use planning be transferred to the government of the Northwest Territories. However, Ottawa would have overriding jurisdiction over these matters and receive any "extra-ordinary" revenues from resource development. In his words:

> ... Territorial revenues from royalties and other resource revenues should be subject to a "cap" beyond which they would be shared with the federal government. The sharing formula should be designed so as to be neither a disincentive to responsible resource development by the GNWT, nor a deterrent to the imposition by the GNWT of royalties, fees and other levies on resource use.[45]

While these exceptions are potentially significant, the impact of this proposal would be that the policy process—the public servants and the ministerial responsibility—for these important subjects would come to reside in Yellowknife and could serve as the basis for many initiatives in the area of economic development by the territorial government. Ottawa might intervene occasionally, but Yellowknife would generally control two very important devices for shaping its economic future. In any case, in view of its problems over jurisdiction and revenues with the resource-producing provinces, Ottawa is certainly not going to give the N.W.T. more than the Special Representative proposed.

In general, Ottawa is likely to come to treat the government of the Northwest Territories more as another government and less as an administrative arm. In promoting this development, Drury was attempting to put into practice the assumption that politics is about power; only by being given meaningful power will the members of a government—particularly the elected Assembly and Executive Committee—come to develop a sense of responsibility. Only if the government has power will the people of the territories respect it and come to it, rather than ignoring it in favour of taking their case directly to Ottawa.

It is easy to read the Drury Report as simply another report and to ponder the extent to which it will be implemented. In a sense, however, this speculation misses the point because, as in the case of Justice Berger, Mr Drury did more than merely issue a report; he conducted an inquiry Although less publicized than the Berger Inquiry, Drury's travels through the North brought him into contact with large numbers of northerners and permitted him not merely to question them, but to attempt to persuade them He did not achieve any consensus and his Report is more an agenda for future deliberation than a blueprint for the future. However, the process of his inquiry undoubtedly influenced the thinking of many northerners who will be politically active in the coming decade.

In addition, the day-to-day policy process is evolving the institutions of the territorial government in the directions Drury proposed. Devolution from Ottawa to Yellowknife has occurred and is likely to continue. For example, it is probable that Ottawa will soon transfer control over economic development programs and somewhat thereafter will transfer control over land-use planning, except for megaprojects.

One problem with this process and particularly with Mr. Drury's recommendations regarding it is that the decision as to how quickly devolution will occur usually is seen as a technical question in which the advice of the public service weighs particularly heavily and elected politicians tend to be passive. This is a problem if the public servants who are judging the ability of the government of the Northwest Territories to take on new powers belong to the organization, DIAND, from which the powers would be transferred. The Drury Report is a blueprint for dismembering DIAND's northern establishment. It proposes that DIAND lose its power over financial and other contacts between Ottawa and Yellowknife. In addition, DIAND's various activities would be transferred to those federal departments that conduct them in the South. Thus, for example, it would not be responsible for economic development, agriculture, energy, or environmental protection in the Northwest Territories. It would also lose its role as coordinator of the federal government's various northern activities. Will the members of DIAND resist this prospect? Many northerners see the DIAND establishment as eager to hold onto power, particularly because the adjustment demanded when the territorial administration moved North starting in 1977 disrupted many public servants' careers. The survivors of that experience are unlikely to relish the thought of an encore. Indeed, this may be why the 1977 paper was produced in the Privy Council Office rather than by DIAND. A similar rationale may have led to Mr. Drury's being appointed to advise the PM rather than the Minister of Indian Affairs and Northern Development, and may have contributed to Drury's recommendations to limit the role of DIAND in the North. This line of conjecture gains some credibility from the fact that Mr. Drury felt compelled to complain to the Minister of Indian Affairs and Northern Development that his Report was being misrepresented by DIAND. In his words, a summary of his Report contained in a draft Cabinet

Memorandum prepared by DIAND "reflects the spirit of an entirely opposing premise [to that underlying his Report], namely, the desirability of continuing colonial-type, interventionist control by the federal government over the NWT."[46]

Thus, while the fate of northern political development will be decided in Ottawa, it must be remembered that there are several Ottawas. The elected participants in the policy process will accede to institutional change if it:

1. Does not fundamentally obstruct their economic goals for the North;
2. Follows their belief that the basic unit of Canadian politics is the individual rather than the racial collectivity; and
3. Holds out a reasonable promise of responsive, efficient, financially responsible government.

The first two conditions may delay the institutional development of the North—particularly the Northwest Territories—and provoke native groups there to resume a hostile stance toward the territorial government. This could lead to the kind of confrontation that would make the third condition much harder to achieve. Official Ottawa will not actively promote this scenario, but it wishes to retain power. Its interpretations of the North to politicians may be coloured by this wish and could contribute to the evolution of this scenario.

Thus, at the start of the 1980s, it is possible to say that northern politics have evolved dramatically in the past decade. Institutional forms have developed tremendously and the dimensions of political conflict have come to be clearly articulated—a first step in the political process. What is not yet clear in either of the two territories is whether in the 1980s they will evolve processes to resolve these conflicts. These processes will have to be originated in the North and they will have to be social and not just political processes. They must evolve out of an understanding by northerners of their problems and of the need to cooperate to resolve them. Yukoners will have to learn to work together and the people of the N.W.T. will have to pursue their cooperative beginnings. They must not only satisfy Ottawa's minimum requirements, but also overcome the drag of bureaucratic inertia and, possibly, the concerns of non-renewable-resource developers who may be anxious about the uses to which northern governments might put their new-found powers. Provincehood is unlikely to come to the North in the 1980s. However, the pressure for change will be irresistible. Whether the changes are for better or for worse will depend on the complex meshing of the social processes of the North and the governmental processes of the South.

Notes

[1]The Eighth Assembly of the Northwest Territories, which sat from 1975 to 1978, contained a majority of native members, many of whom favoured development of the wage economy in general and northern megaprojects in particular, without making their approval contingent on settlement of the native claims. However, these members tended not to figure prominently

in the business of the Council. For this reason, it is accurate to characterize the Assembly as having been dominated by non-natives, as was the case in the Yukon where no native people sat on the Territorial Assembly.

[2]See p. 147. This is the thesis of Edgar J. Dosman, *The National Interest* (Toronto: McClelland and Stewart, 1975). The obvious exception to this judgment—the rejection of the application by the Canadian Arctic Gas pipeline consortium to build a natural-gas pipeline up the Mackenzie Valley—is in fact consistent with Ottawa's goals, as will be explained in Chapter 4.

[3]These attributes of political performance are discussed more fully in Harry Eckstein, "The Evaluation of Political Performance: Problems and Dimensions," *Sage Professional Papers in Comparative Politics*, Vol. II, no. 01-017 (1971).

[4]The most comprehensive and contemporary statement of the constitutional position of the Yukon is contained in David W. Elliott, *Some Constitutional Aspects of the Government of the Yukon Territory* (Whitehorse: Government of Yukon, 1978).

[5]In many respects, this evolution reflects the process by which Alberta and Saskatchewan gained provincehood. This evolution is discussed in L.H. Thomas, *The Struggle for Responsible Government in the North-West Territories, 1870-97*, 2nd ed. (Toronto: University of Toronto Press, 1978).

[6]See, for example, the First and Second Reports of the Standing Committee on Constitutional Development for Yukon, reprinted in R.F. Keith and J.B. Wright (eds.), *Northern Transitions*, 2 vols. (Ottawa: Canadian Arctic Resources Committee, 1978), Vol. II.

[7]Letter of January 25, 1979.

[8]The new position of the Commissioner was set out in a letter to the then-Commissioner, Ione Christensen, which is reproduced in *Musk-Ox*, Vol. 25, pp. 101-03.

[9]The present governmental structures in the Northwest Territories and the division of authority between the territorial and federal governments are set out in detail in C.M. Drury, *Constitutional Development in the Northwest Territories: Report of the Special Representative* (Ottawa: Supply and Services Canada, 1979), Chs. 4-6. These subjects are also discussed in detail and with interesting commentary in Louis-Edmond Hamelin, *Canadian Nordicity*, William Barr (trans.) (Montreal: Harvest House, 1978), Chs. 4 and 5.

[10]Advisory Commission on the Development of Government in the Northwest Territories, A.W.R. Carrothers (Chairman), *Report to the Minister of Northern Affairs and National Resources* (Ottawa: 1966). This document is summarized and assessed in Hamelin, *op. cit.*, pp. 114-19.

[11]This view received a great deal of exposure during the Berger Inquiry. Mel Watkins (ed.), *Dene Nation: The Colony Within* (Toronto: University of Toronto Press, 1979), documents statements to the inquiry primarily by Dene leaders and consultants. Martin O'Malley, *The Past and Future Land* (Toronto: Peter Martin Associates, 1976), records these presentations but also includes many statements by individual native people.

[12]Hamelin, *op. cit.*, p. 236.

[13]"Aboriginal Rights and Constitutional Development in the Northwest Territories," a Sessional Paper presented to the Second Session of the Ninth Legislative Assembly of the Northwest Territories by the Executive Committee of the Government of the Northwest Territories (February 15, 1980).

[14]Legislative Assembly of the Northwest Territories, *Debates*, Ninth Assembly, Second Session (February 22, 1980), p. 727.

[15]Government of the Northwest Territories, *Towards Decentralized Government* (Yellowknife: Government of the Northwest Territories, 1977).

[16]Drury, *op. cit.*, pp. 52-56.

[17]Report prepared for the Board of Directors of Inuit Tapirisat of Canada, to be discussed at the Annual General Meeting (Igloolik, September 3-7, 1979).

[18]Distance poses a particular problem for Inuit members of the Legislative Assembly who dislike being separated from their families during the sessions of the Assembly. Much longer periods of separation would be necessary to carry out the responsibilities of a member of the

Executive Committee. It has been suggested that the reluctance to accept this separation is a major reason behind the refusal of Inuit legislators to take up positions on the Executive Committee.

⁹Report of the Special Committee on Unity to the third session of the Ninth Assembly (October 22, 1980), p. 3, reported in the *Edmonton Journal* (October 23, 1980), p. B2.

⁰*Globe and Mail* (November 6, 1980), p. 10.

ᵃAlfred R. Zariwny, "Politics, Administration and Problems of Community Development in the Northwest Territories," in Nils Orvik (ed.), *Policies of Northern Development* (Kingston: Group for International Politics, Department of Political Studies, Queen's University, 1973), pp. 86-87.

²Hugh Brody, *The People's Land* (Harmondsworth: Penguin, 1975), Ch. 6.

³*Ibid.*, pp. 120-21.

⁴Carrothers Report, *op. cit.*, p. 188.

⁵A particularly strong statement of this assessment can be found in Wilf Bean, "Colonialism, in the Communities," in Watkins, *op. cit.*, pp. 130-41.

⁶Drury, *op. cit.*, p. 34.

⁷*Ibid.*, p. 37.

⁸*News/North* (October 17, 1980), p. A7.

⁹The functions of political parties are discussed in F.C. Engelmann and M.A. Schwartz, *Canadian Political Parties: Origin, Character, Impact* (Scarborough: Prentice-Hall, 1975), pp. 13-17.

⁰For example, John Meisel, "The Decline of Party in Canada," in Hugh G. Thorburn (ed.), *Party Politics in Canada*, 4th ed. (Scarborough: Prentice-Hall, 1979).

ᵃ*News/North* (January 30, 1981), p. A3.

²The politics of the Yukon are explored in Glen Toner, "Political Development in Yukon" (M.A. thesis, University of Alberta, 1978).

³This concept is examined in detail in G.V. Flores, "Race and Culture in the Internal Colony," in F. Bonilla and R. Girling (eds.), *Structures of Dependency* (Stanford: Stanford University Press, 1973).

ᵃThis proposal is being considered afresh by policy makers and academics in the light of Denmark's granting of home rule to Greenland in 1979. The analogies between this experiment in self-government and the wishes of Canadian northerners are many and could point the way to a future accommodation between North and South in Canada. At the very least, they may add credibility to northern claims by demonstrating that the road they wish to take has already been travelled. The Greenland experience is summarized in Peter Jull, "Greenland: Lessons of Self-Government and Development," *Northern Perspectives*, Vol. VII, no. 8 (1979). A fuller discussion can be found in Ole Oleson, *Home Rule for Greenland* (Ottawa: DIAND draft, 1979).

Reprinted in Keith and Wright, *op. cit.*, p. 269.

These suggestions are contained in "Meaningful Government for All Yukoners" (Whitehorse: Office of the Commissioner, 1975).

Presentation by Chris Pearson, Government Leader, Yukon Territory to the Eighth National Northern Development Conference (Edmonton, 1979), *Proceedings*, p. 30. The Northwest Territories are even more dependent: in the fiscal year 1979-80, the federal operating and capital grant to the Territories totalled $202.7 million out of a projected total territorial budget of $291 million. Drury, *op. cit.*, p. 110.

Mel Foster, *The Development of Greater Self-Government in the Yukon Territory: Finance and Economics* (study prepared for the Government of the Yukon, 1979), p. 141.

ᵃ*Ibid.*, p. 117.

See p. 119, below.

ᵃ*Ibid.*, p. 113.

Reprinted in Keith and Wright, *op. cit.*, p. 277.

He received no payment for undertaking the task.

[44]*News/North* (February 30, 1981), p. A13. In effect, the new arrangements limit increases in the amount of money Ottawa will transfer annually to the N.W.T. to the rate of growth of spending at the provincial and municipal level in Canada. However, it is likely that the N.W.T. will face additional expenses in the foreseeable future to deal with the particular stresses its people will encounter as development proceeds. The formula, being based on an externally derived growth formula, is not designed to take these special needs into account.
[45]Drury, *op . cit.*, p. 96.
[46]*News/North* (October 24, 1980), p. A5.

4/The Economic Future: Non-renewable Resources

The mineral wealth of the North has long been a mainstay of Canadian mythology. In this instance, myth and reality converge: the North does contain vast quantities of minerals, oil, and gas. However, the richness of these resources does not guarantee their production because it only represents one of five factors in the development equation. The second factor is cost: for a resource to be commercially viable, the price which it can command on world markets must be high enough to promise prospective developers an attractive return on investment. In the North this means that the resources to be tapped must be very rich, rich enough to offset extremely high costs of exploration, extraction, and transportation. Third, the special elements of uncertainty surrounding northern resource projects require a rate of return even higher than that normally required by resource developers. For example, untried technology and a less than predictable regulatory process tend to make the necessary return on investment less assured than it is in the South. The element of risk should not be exaggerated, since government taxation, subsidy, and regulatory policies tend to favour industry. Still, risk is an inevitable part of operating in the North. It always enters into corporate decisions on necessary rates of return and along with high costs makes uneconomic many resource deposits that would be quite attractive if located in the South.

The fourth factor is the relationship between price and supply. The simple rise in world prices of a resource found in the North may not necessarily lead to its exploitation. The reason is that as prices rise, formerly marginal southern resources will be developed in competition with what may be even more marginal northern resources. For example, world events such as the 1973 Yom Kippur War and the disorder in Iran at the start of the 1980s have turned Canadians' eyes toward frontier oil and gas resources. However, the price increases they produce—from $3 to $38 for a barrel of imported oil over the decade of the 1970s[1]—also make it economic to exploit deposits of oil and gas in southern Canada that were formerly uneconomic, and act as a spur to the oil and gas exploration industry. As a result, Canada at the start of the 1980s is experiencing a substantial surplus of natural gas, a surplus that moves farther and farther into the future the day when northern gas will be needed for Canadian consumption. This example demonstrates that it is incorrect to assume that substantial increases in price will automatically lead to northern resource development.

The fifth factor in the equation is politics. The definition of "the public interest" in government policy can breathe life into projects that would otherwise be stillborn. For example, a perceived need to reduce oil imports in order to lower the cost to Ottawa of subsidizing energy prices could lead it to favour otherwise unjustified northern energy projects. Ottawa's political needs can also abort economically viable projects.

The following discussion will examine the interplay of these five factors regarding the two most prominent non-renewable-resource sectors in the North, mining and oil and gas development.

Mining in the North

Oil and gas exploration has drawn the lion's share of southern attention because of the magnitude of the projects anticipated and the controversial public hearings on the proposed developments. However, mining remains a mainstay of the northern economy. It accounts for between 40 and 45 per cent of all goods and services produced in the North and directly employs between 20 and 25 per cent of the total northern labour force.[2] Indirectly, demand created by the mining sector provides for many additional jobs in the transportation, retail, and service sections of the northern economy. In the national context, the North contributes substantially to Canada's mineral production. In 1977, mines north of the sixtieth parallel produced all of Canada's tungsten, 44 per cent of its lead, 26 per cent of its zinc, 20 per cent of its silver, and 13 per cent of its gold.[3]

Despite these impressive figures, northern mining is an economically tenuous proposition. In some instances, huge deposits have been found, but are simply uneconomic to mine at present. For example, if the 111 million proven tonnes of coal in the Bonnet Plume Basin lay closer to potential users, they would make a tremendous contribution to the Yukon economy. However, their location in the north-central Yukon makes their development in the foreseeable future unlikely. Often, ore bodies only become economic if their developers receive substantial government support, particularly for the provision of infrastructure. For example, the Cyprus Anvil mine at Faro in the Yukon benefited from a more than $25 million federal-government investment in infrastructure[4] and the Nanisivik lead-zinc mine on Baffin Island received an estimated $16.7 million in the form of direct grants and infrastructure.[5] Once in operation, northern mines are frequently shortlived. For example, the Rankin Inlet mine produced for only five years,[6] the Cassiar Asbestos Mine at Clinton Creek in the Yukon operated for only eleven years,[7] and the Nanisivik mine was opened with enough ore on hand to operate for twelve years.[8] The economics of mining result in the short life span of mines, leading mine owners to seek to recoup their investment as quickly as possible. However, it can make for fluctuations in the territories' mineral production d, much more important, social disruption caused by the development of e mine, particularly if northern natives come to depend on it for wage ployment.

It is difficult to predict how successfully the northern mining industry ll handle these problems in the 1980s because the answer to the question ll depend on world prices for the metals the North can produce. In the kon, despite some optimistic predictions, mining will probably just keep ce with the 1970s.[9] The United Keno Hill Mine, which produces silver, d, zinc, and cadmium near Elsa, may well close because it appears likely to n out of economically viable ore. The same fate may befall the Whitehorse pper Mine. Rounding out the debit side of the picture, the Clinton Creek eration of Cassiar Asbestos closed in 1978. The asbestos fibre produced at s mine was shipped out of the territory on the historic narrow-gauge hite Pass and Yukon Railway. The loss of this important freight proved a ious blow to the already financially troubled railroad.[10]

In view of these problems, how is it possible to be at all optimistic about kon mining in the 1980s? First, the largest mine in the territory, Cyprus vil, extended its expected life span in 1978 when it acquired three nearby d-zinc deposits and subsequently proceeded to develop the nearest of these, Grum deposit. The development of this ore body gives a new lease on life the Tantalus Butte coal mine, a small operation that supplies fuel to prus Anvil. Second, spectacular gold prices have attracted large numbers placer miners to the old goldfields.[11] Third, of the several promising ospects—such as the Howard's Pass lead-zinc deposit and the MacMillan ngsten orebody on the Yukon–Northwest Territories border—at least one ght to open and add its production to the Yukon total.[12]

The 1980s are likely to see a stronger performance by mining in the rthwest Territories than in the Yukon. In 1979, seven mines employed 0 people and produced $437 million worth of zinc, lead, gold, tungsten, ver, copper, and cadmium in the N.W.T.[13] The largest of these mines is the ne Point lead-zinc mine on the south shore of Great Slave Lake, which ployed 570 workers. The economy of Yellowknife benefited from the erations of the Giant Yellowknife gold and silver mine and Cominco's n-Rycon-Vol gold and silver mine. Together, the two mines employed 610 rkers in 1979.[14] The Nanisivik lead-zinc mine on Strathcona Sound on ffin Island shipped its first ore in 1977 amid controversy over environ- ntal questions and the balance between the assistance given the mine by tawa and the mine's likely benefits to Canada.[15]

Looking to the future, Cominco is scheduled to open the Polaris Mine Little Cornwallis Island early in 1982. When it comes into production, s lead-zinc mine will be the northernmost metal mine in the world. Other ines scheduled for development are the Cadillac property west of Fort npson and the Lupin gold mine at Contwoyto Lake. While other operties offer possibilities of development in the 1980s, the health of

mining in the N.W.T. will be greatly affected by the growth of uraniu
mining. Substantial bodies of uranium-bearing ore have been discovered i
the Keewatin region. The Baker Lake decision,[16] while incomplete an
ambiguous, appears to have removed most of the obstacles the claim (
aboriginal title formerly presented to uranium exploration-and-develo;
ment firms. However, the price of uranium was depressed late in the 1970
even if it recovers, more profitable deposits of uranium in Saskatchewan m;
be developed instead of Keewatin deposits.

In the 1980s, northern mining seems likely to maintain or better i
contribution to the territorial economies in both output and employmer
However, the new northern political climate will increasingly come to jud;
it by other standards, such as the employment and business opportunities
offers to northerners—and particularly native northerners—and its soci
and environment impacts.[17] The mining industry has resisted these sta
dards,[18] but has begun to improve its performance. In the N.W.T., tl
industry faces a territorial government that recognizes the contribution
mining to the territorial economy but that refuses to subordinate its oth
goals to the interests of mining companies. It remains to be seen whether t
Yukon territorial government will find the will to require mines, or at lea
new mines, to meet more vigorous social-impact standards.

Oil and Gas

While the North will probably experience moderate growth in the minir
sector of its economy in the 1980s, it is likely to see energy megaprojects who
size, technological sophistication, and risks are spectacular.

The presence of oil north of the sixtieth parallel was one of the fir
discoveries made by white explorers. In 1789, Alexander Mackenzie e
countered it seeping out of the ground near Fort Norman.[19] This deposit w.
first tapped by a successful well in 1920 and the field has been supplyir
communities along the Mackenzie and in the western Arctic since 193
During the Second World War, it supplied oil for the Canol pipeline
Whitehorse. This project exemplifies the dependence of northern econom
development on events elsewhere. It was conceived in 1942 when the threat
Japanese military action against Alaska was thought to be imminent and w.
intended to supply fuel to support the Northwest Staging Route for fighte
flying to Alaska as well as bombers being delivered to the U.S.S.R. In 194
when the Japanese threat passed, the pipeline stopped operating, havir
carried oil for only about a year.[20] The pipeline was not economical
rational and could only be justified by considerations outside the realm
ordinary business calculations. This may well hold true for a lar;
proportion of the energy transportation proposals of the 1980s.

Interest in northern oil and gas lagged in the decade following the end
the Second World War. However, by the mid-1950s industry was becomir
aware of studies of the North done by the Geological Survey of Canad

hich showed substantial formations of the types of sedimentary rock in
hich oil and gas can be found.[21] The most promising were the Mackenzie
elta and Beaufort Sea areas and the Sverdrup Basin, an oval-shaped area
ncompassing roughly the Parry and Sverdrup Islands. Lancaster Sound and
avis Strait also contained interesting formations but were thought to be
naccessible because of the extreme technological problems involved. (See
igure 4-1.)

Although the potential had been revealed, exploration for hydrocarbons
n the North did not follow automatically. Areas in western Canada south of
ne sixtieth parallel were more attractive because they were closer to markets
nd less expensive to explore. It took two events to stimulate interest in the
orthern frontier. The first of these events was the 1961 promulgation of the
anada Oil and Gas Land Regulations that set out the conditions under
hich the industry would operate in the North.[22] They specified, among
ther items, the amount of land to be granted under permits and leases, the
umber of years a permit could be held, royalty rates on production, liability
or oil spills, and work requirements—how much money had to be invested
n exploring an area in order to maintain a permit for it. In this way, these
gulations divided between government and industry the benefits to be
ained from northern hydrocarbons and the risks to be borne in developing
nem. The division was intended to be highly attractive to the oil and gas
ndustry in order to overcome the problems of operating in the frontier area.

Figure 4-1
Oil and Gas Exploration North
of the Sixtieth Parallel

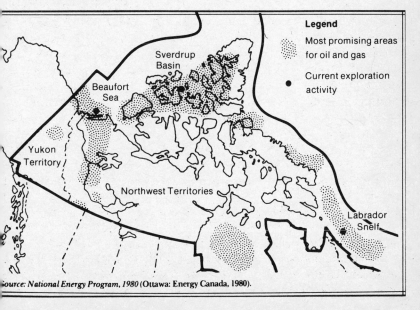

Source: National Energy Program, 1980 (Ottawa: Energy Canada, 1980).

However, it was strongly criticized as excessively generous to the industry an certainly far more generous than the comparable regulations in Alaska. Whether the regulations constituted a giveaway or not, they did lead t seismic activity and a small amount of drilling in the North, particularly i the lower Mackenzie Valley and, late in the decade, by Panarctic Oils in th Sverdrup Basin.

However, the role of the regulations was more to set the stage for th upsurge in exploration provided by the 1968 discovery of an enormou oilfield at Prudhoe Bay on the North shore of Alaska about 300 km west of th Alaska-Yukon border. This discovery is credited for increasing northern o and gas exploration spending from $30 million in 1968 to $200 million i 1972.[24]

It also led Humble Oil, a United States based firm, to try to send specially refitted tanker, the *Manhattan*, through the Northwest Passage determine the feasibility of using the Passage as a regular oil-shipping rout The 1969 and 1970 voyages of the *Manhattan* demonstrated that such a rou could be feasible with larger, more powerful, and more sophisticated ship but that it would be prohibitively expensive. Despite this conclusion, th damage inflicted on the *Manhattan* by ice, and its failure to navigate i chosen course, the mere fact that the voyages were attempted shocked Ottaw because it challenged the Canadian view that it held authority over i northern waters, at least concerning measures to prevent pollution. T emphasize its claim over northern waters, Ottawa passed the Arctic Wate Pollution Prevention Act in 1970, creating a 160 km Arctic Pollution Zon The firm rejection of this legislation by the American government led Ottaw to seek to reinforce its sovereignty in the North. During the 1960s, Panarcti Oils' small exploration program in the Arctic Islands had shown the flag i this part of the North. The federal government had gained a 45 per cer interest in Panarctic in 1966. In 1970, when the *Manhattan* episode showe the need for a more visible Canadian presence in the North, the cabine helped finance an expanded exploration program by Panarctic.[25] Ottawa participation in Panarctic was transferred to the crown corporation, Petrc Canada, in 1976. This transfer and Petro-Canada's acquisition of control c Pacific Petroleum in 1978 have made the federal government an activ participant in northern hydrocarbon exploration. This development seem likely to promote northern oil and gas activity, but also raises very troublin questions of conflict of interest, since Ottawa will increasingly have to mak hard decisions between its roles of developer and regulator of development.

Exploration continued actively during the first half of the 1970s an increased with the 1976 cabinet approval of Dome Petroleum's application t drill in the Beaufort Sea despite the anxiety of the public and the civil servic about the environmental risks involved.[26] Arctic drilling received a furthe stimulus with the introduction of the Frontier Exploration Allowance in th 1977 budget. This allowance—often referred to as the "super-depletion llowance—particularly benefited operators in the Beaufort Sea, most notably Dome Petroleum, because it provided extremely generous tax advantages to operators drilling extra-expensive wells, the type required in the Beaufort. It did less to aid Panarctic Oil's drilling because its wells were not sufficiently expensive to benefit very much from the most generous provisions of the allowance.

While the allowance helped a few companies, it did not prevent exploration from declining toward the end of the decade. There are several reasons for the decline. The first is the 1977 federal-government decision not to permit the construction of a pipeline to tap the reserves of gas found in the Mackenzie Delta. Because of this decision, the companies that had discovered the gas could not expect to receive any cash flow from it in the immediate future. This situation obviously dampened the industry's enthusiasm for undertaking further exploration. The downturn in exploration was intensified toward the end of the decade by the increased attractiveness of the western provinces, which were being examined again more carefully in the light of higher oil and gas prices. As a result, at the end of the decade, the National Energy Board had determined that Canada had a large surplus of natural gas in hand. This surplus meant that frontier gas—which would be expensive because of the costs of exploration, development, and particularly transportation—would be unable to find Canadian markets until the 1990s at the earliest. In addition, drilling off the coast of Labrador and around Sable Island produced discoveries likely to compete with northern oil and gas when the time comes for government and industry to decide which frontier reserves should be developed first.

A final factor contributing to the uncertainties surrounding northern oil and gas exploration at the end of 1980 was the National Energy Program presented to Parliament in October of that year. The National Energy Program appalled the oil and gas industry, which warned that what oilmen saw as crippling taxes could make operating in Canada significantly less attractive than in the United States. If the government persisted, the warnings went, the companies would take the traditional path of the multinationals and concentrate their activities in the more hospitable jurisdiction. This threat, self-serving though it was, gained extra credibility when, in one of the first acts of his presidency, Ronald Reagan "deregulated"; that is, he ended government price control on oil and gasoline in the United States, permitting prices to rise. The higher prices made operating in the United States even more financially attractive to firms whose Canadian operations, in their opinion, had been plundered by the new Canadian budget. The contrast could well draw exploration funds away from Canada and from its northern frontier.

However, a major goal of the National Energy Program is to promote development of oil and gas on Canada Lands.[27] To accomplish this goal, the government introduced Bill C-48, The Canada Oil and Gas Act, into

Parliament. This legislation amended the Canada Oil and Gas La~
Regulations to:

1. Require that firms holding permits on Canada Lands—that is, crow
   lands held by Ottawa—explore more aggressively on Canada Lands tha
   some firms had in the past.
2. Give Ottawa a 25 per cent interest in any holding on Canada Lan
   without Ottawa's having to pay anything for it.
3. Require that any operation be at least 50 per cent Canadian owned befo
   going into production.
4. Require a substantial level of Canadian content in exploration ar
   production activities.
5. Establish a new royalty scheme involving a 10 per cent basic rate and
   Progressive Incremental Royalty[28] to capture extra revenues from e
   tremely profitable wells or fields.

These changes make Canada Lands less attractive to the oil and gas indust
than they were under the former regulations. However, times have chang
since 1961, when Canada Lands did not appear to be very promisin
accordingly, favourable regulations were seen to be necessary to attract tl
industry's interest. Since 1961, what was then viewed as "moose pasture,"
quote one oilman, has become paydirt; hence, Ottawa can impose mo
stringent regulations on the industry in order to meet the governmen
northern-development and Canadianization objectives.

Nonetheless, the bill does have some appeal for the industry. First, tl
act would give the Minister of Energy the discretion to lessen the burden
requirements in particular cases. Second, the Petroleum Incentives Progra
(PIP) will compensate the industry for the act's more rigorous requirements.
PIP will also replace the super-depletion allowance on Canada Lands and tl
existing regular depletion allowance scheme,[30] with as many as three pa
ments:

1. "For exploration on the Canada Lands . . . all enterprises will qualify fe
   an incentive payment of 25 per cent of approved costs incurred in 1981 ar
   thereafter."
2. "Enterprises that are at least 50 per cent owned by Canadians and a
   Canadian controlled will qualify for a further additional incentiv
   payment equal to 10 per cent of approved costs incurred in 1981 ar
   thereafter.
   "For enterprises that are at least 75 per cent Canadian owned ar
   Canadian controlled, the additional incentive payment will be equal to §
   per cent of approved costs incurred in 1981 and thereafter."
3. "For oil and gas exploration anywhere in Canada, enterprises that are a
   least 50 per cent owned by Canadians and are Canadian controlled wi
   qualify for an incentive payment equal to 10 per cent of approved cos
   incurred in 1982 and 1983 and 15 per cent thereafter.

"Enterprises that are at least 65 per cent increasing to 75 per cent by 1986 Canadian owned and Canadian controlled will qualify for a 35 per cent incentive payment incurred in 1981 and thereafter." The government subsequently provided for a short-term incentive payment for 60 per cent Canadian-owned firms in order to support them while they attempted to increase their Canadian ownership.

In the most favoured case, then, 80 per cent of exploration costs will be borne by Canadian taxpayers. PIP generally will put more firms into a better position to explore Canada Lands than before because few firms were able to qualify for super-depletion allowances, whereas now any size of firm can qualify for PIP. The National Energy Program also provides these payments to defray costs of development: 10 per cent for firms 50 per cent Canadian owned, 15 per cent for firms 60 per cent Canadian owned, and 20 per cent for firms 75 per cent Canadian owned. All told, these exploration and production incentive payments make Canada Lands much more attractive to investors than formerly compared to the western sedimentary basin.

On the eve of the implementation of this policy, the northern oil and gas industry had modest production, growing reserves, and vast potential. At the end of 1980, three fields were producing gas. In the N.W.T., the Pointed Mountain field, located at the southwest corner, and the Norman Wells field had been producing for years. In the Yukon, the Kotaneelee gas field in the farthest eastern section of the territory went into production on a modest scale in 1979.[31] The only oil production came from the Norman Wells field.

Substantial discoveries of gas had been made in the Beaufort–Mackenzie Delta area. Panarctic Oils had located 453 million cubic metres of natural gas in the Arctic Islands by 1979 and expected to have located a total of 840 million cubic metres by 1981.[32] Both Dome Petroleum and Esso Resources had drilled exploratory wells in the Beaufort Sea that struck oil, but were only beginning to delineate the quantities they had found. The Geological Survey of Canada estimates that the Beaufort Sea and Mackenzie Delta contain between 9.4 and 12.3 billion barrels of oil and between 3.1 and 4.1 trillion cubic metres of natural gas, not all of which, of course, is necessarily accessible or marketable.[33] However, the majority of the estimated Beaufort-Mackenzie oil and gas deposits remains to be discovered and the rate of its discovery will depend on the sums invested.

The exploring companies actively drilling in the North were Esso Resources, drilling in the shallow waters of the Beaufort from man-made islands; Dome, operating in the deeper waters of the Beaufort using sophisticated shipborne drilling rigs; and Panarctic, drilling in the Sverdrup Basin both on land and through the ice, a technique which requires flooding the existing ice cover with water until it freezes to a thickness great enough to support the weight of the drilling rig and the entire drilling camp. In addition, Imperial and Aquitaine Canada had drilling programs in the South Davis Strait. Lancaster Sound had attracted interest, although Ottawa had deferred the first exploratory well proposed for the Sound because (concerns identified during the federal Environmental Assessment an Review Process into the proposed drilling program.

While fewer operators will be active in seeking northern oil and gas i the early 1980s than formerly, they are exploring promising geologica formations. It is safe to predict that sizable quantities of oil and gas will b proven by the middle of the decade. However, it is not at all safe to venture prediction on when these reserves will actually find their way to market. An decision to transport northern natural gas and oil to market involves complex of factors to challenge any decision-making process. The factors ai numerous, in many cases are only partially understood, and frequentl cannot be compared with one another to strike some kind of cost-benefi balance. Even if it were possible to obtain a degree of rational analysis of th questions involved, political issues only indirectly—but nonetheless ver importantly—connected to northern energy debates are likely to play a majo role in determining their outcome. Largely for these reasons, the polic process governing northern oil and gas development has in the past lacked clear sense of direction and has been so fragmented that its performance ca: only be termed erratic. While it has generally promoted development, it response to specific proposals—and thus the shape of northern energ development—are unpredictable.

The Northern Pipeline Decision

These themes are apparent from even a sketch of the major northern pipelin decision made to date, the 1977 decision to approve the construction of th Alaska Highway gas pipeline.[34] The northern pipeline story begins i earnest with the announcement by Imperial Oil in January 1970 of a majo oil discovery at Atkinson Point on the Tuktoyaktuk Peninsula. Althougl this find ultimately proved to be too small to be commercially viable, it immediate impact was to encourage policy makers in Ottawa who wer promoting an oil pipeline carrying Alaska oil across the Yukon and up th Mackenzie Valley. It also led to exploration programs by several companie: which began to find significant quantities of gas. When the United State decided to transport its Prudhoe Bay oil by means of the Alyeska pipeline t(Valdez on the south coast of Alaska and then by tanker to the mainlanc United States and when exploration in the Mackenzie Delta region continuec to produce relatively little sign of oil, attention turned to the possibility o constructing a natural-gas pipeline along the Mackenzie Valley. (See Figur(4-2.)

The cost of building such a pipeline carrying only Mackenzie Delta ga was felt to be too enormous to make the project economic. Only if additiona gas could be put through the line might the per-unit cost of gas delivery b(brought down enough to enable the line to be built. On the basis of thi: calculation, in March 1974 Canadian Arctic Gas Pipelines (CAGPL), a

Figure 4-2
Proposed Natural-Gas
Transportation Systems, 1977

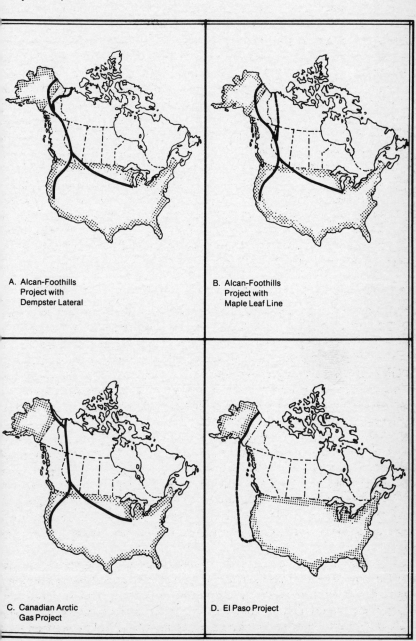

A. Alcan-Foothills
   Project with
   Dempster Lateral

B. Alcan-Foothills
   Project with
   Maple Leaf Line

C. Canadian Arctic
   Gas Project

D. El Paso Project

consortium of some of the largest multinational oil companies in the world, applied to the government of Canada for permission to build a pipeline across the northern portion of the Yukon and up the Mackenzie. At the same time, CAGPL's sister company, Alaskan Arctic Gas Study Limited, which was responsible for the American section of the line, submitted its application to the American government. Together the total of 4295 km of high pressure, 1220 mm diameter pipeline[35] they proposed would connect the gas reserves at Prudhoe Bay with markets in the United States. The pipeline was also originally intended to carry the Mackenzie Delta gas to market in the United States, because it was thought early in the decade that Canada had a great surplus of gas and oil, so it would benefit by selling the surplus abroad. In the fall of 1974 CAGPL proposed that its pipeline deliver the Canadian gas to Canadian rather than American markets.[36] This change of plan was necessitated by the growing belief that, rather than facing an energy glut, Canada was entering a period of drastic energy shortages. In such a situation it was very unlikely that the National Energy Board would authorize the export of Mackenzie Delta gas.

The CAGPL application pleased Ottawa, which favoured and indeed had actively promoted the construction of a Mackenzie Valley pipeline.[37] However, for public-relations reasons and to mollify the New Democratic Party, which at that time held the balance of power in the House of Commons,[38] the cabinet decided that a public inquiry should be held to study the questions surrounding the pipeline. In March of 1974, Mr. Justice Thomas Berger of the British Columbia Supreme Court was appointed to head the inquiry. Although Justice Berger was known to be sympathetic to native people, Ottawa did not anticipate how effectively he would orchestrate his inquiry to promote the native and environmental cause in the Mackenzie. To limit his impact, Berger was instructed to "inquire into and report upon the terms and conditions that should be imposed in respect of any right of way that might be granted across Crown lands for the purposes of the proposed Mackenzie Valley Pipeline. . . ."[39] These instructions did not ask him to advise whether the pipeline ought to be built. They only told him to study how best to undertake the project already implicitly approved.

However, even those in power may be frustrated by their failure to anticipate the consequences of their actions. Far from undertaking a perfunctory inquiry,[40] Berger proceeded to redefine his mandate and to build the political momentum that would make it very difficult for Ottawa to take his recommendations lightly.[41] He announced that he would consider the impact, not simply of a single gas pipeline, but also of a transportation corridor and of a gas-gathering system in the Mackenzie Delta as it might relate to the pipeline. This decision flew in the face of the cabinet's wish to minimize the anticipated impacts of the proposed development. Berger also decided to fund groups that wished to testify before him but that lacked the funds to make a detailed technical presentation. Ultimately, these groups received about $1.5 million.[42] He also ordered that all technical studies of the project, whether by government or corporations, be made public to ensure that all parties had the information they needed to prepare their testimony. Most important, in addition to holding technical hearings, Berger arranged for a series of community hearings in the Mackenzie Valley and for public hearings in major centres in southern Canada. The first set of hearings enabled him to defend his findings by saying that he had gone directly to the occupants of the land to be traversed by the pipeline and by quoting their testimony. The publicity given the community hearings captured the sympathy of many Canadians for the native people whose testimony was extensively reported by the press.[43] Berger could not possibly have provided the native people and particularly the Dene with a better platform for publicizing their position that there should be no pipeline until their claims had been justly settled and implemented. Public sympathy was reinforced by the southern hearings that featured churchmen[44] and others condemning the pipeline in widely reported statements that kept the pipeline question in the news much longer than would normally have been the case.

In this way, Berger's early decisions not only shaped and prodded public opinion but, more importantly, also ensured that the information his inquiry produced maximized rather than minimized the apparent costs of a Mackenzie Valley pipeline.

While Berger was shaping his inquiry, other forces were also at work. In September of 1974, Robert Blair, president of Alberta Gas Trunk Line[45] withdrew from the Arctic Gas consortium. He and Kelly Gibson of Westcoast Transmission committed their firms to pursuing their own northern gas pipeline through their joint subsidiary, Foothills Pipe Lines. In March 1975, Foothills filed an application with the National Energy Board to build what was called the Maple Leaf Line, a 1067 mm diameter line solely to carry Mackenzie Delta gas to Canadian markets. In August 1976, it applied to build the Alcan pipeline,[46] a separate 1067 mm[47] line running from Prudhoe Bay along the route of the Alyeska oil pipeline to Fairbanks and then along the Alaska Highway, through British Columbia and Alberta, ultimately delivering its gas to American consumers. (See Figure 4-2.)

In addition to the Berger inquiry, two other inquiries were also underway. The National Energy Board began its consideration of the three pipeline proposals in 1976. In its 214 days of public hearings involving over 37 000 pages of transcript,[48] it examined natural-gas supply and demand projections, engineering design, and technical feasibility as well as contractual, financial and economic questions. In addition, it departed from its traditional focus on these questions to study the socioeconomic impact of the pipelines on the regions through which they would pass. In doing this, it revealed its sensitivity to the political climate in which it operated and the criticism it was receiving for the narrow standards on which it had formerly judged proposals. During 1975 and 1976, the American Federal Power

Commission examined the applications of Arctic Gas, Alcan Pipeline Company (the American sister of Foothills), and El Paso Alaska, which sought to build a gas pipeline across Alaska, to liquefy the Prudhoe Bay natural gas and then deliver it by tanker to the mainland United States.

All of these processes converged in the hectic spring and summer of 1977. On May 2, the Federal Power Commission issued its report stating that either of the two proposals that traversed Canada was acceptable, and that the El Paso project was a less desirable alternative. This decision had two consequences. First, it put the ball squarely in Canada's court. Second, it cast doubt on what was thought to be the frontrunning corporate contender, Arctic Gas, by suggesting that the United States was willing to accept its competitor. On May 9, Justice Berger released his report recommending that no pipeline be built in the Mackenzie for a period of ten years in order to allow time for the settlement and implementation of the native claims in the Valley and that no pipeline ever be built across the environmentally sensitive north coast of the Yukon.

While a few scenes remained to be played in the drama, these recommendations doomed Arctic Gas. However, it was the July 4 report of the National Energy Board, which held the regulatory authority over the project, that actually sounded the death knell for Arctic Gas. The NEB endorsed the Alcan Pipeline over the Arctic Gas proposal, but directed that it be routed through Dawson and then south along the Klondike Highway to the Alaska Highway. This stipulation was intended to bring the pipeline closer to the Mackenzie Delta and in this way reduce the cost of a pipeline that might be built along the Dempster Highway to carry Mackenzie Delta gas. The possibility of a Dempster pipeline enabled Ottawa to meet its anticipated critics. It could argue that it was providing means by which Mackenzie Delta gas could come to market and, thus, that it had considered the needs of the interests—the oil companies and local business—that had been depending on the production of Mackenzie gas. The Board also recommended that Foothills be required to pay up to $200 million to cover "the socio-economic indirect costs of the pipeline project in the area north of the 60th parallel."[49]

While the National Energy Board decision was bringing down the curtain on the Mackenzie Valley pipeline, the scene was being set for Ottawa's ultimate approval of the Alaska Highway route. In March, Ottawa launched two inquiries into the route. The first was a study by the Department of Fisheries and the Environment's Environmental Assessment and Review Office. The second was an inquiry chaired by University of British Columbia Dean of Law, Kenneth Lysyk, into the social and economic impacts of the proposed pipeline on the Yukon. Ottawa was forced to establish these inquiries in view of the precedent set in the Mackenzie, but was reluctant because of the problems it was encountering with the Berger Inquiry. However, it was able to minimize the likelihood of these inquiries turning into showcases for pipeline opponents. First, the Environmental

Assessment Review Process (EARP) panel was composed solely of public servants, who would be unlikely to diverge too greatly from government policy.[50] Second, the inquiries had only a very limited period of time to gather evidence and prepare their reports. In the end, the July 28 report of the EARP panel[51] played a relatively minor role in the decision-making process because it followed the Berger and National Energy Board reports. Also, it was weakened because it had to qualify its conclusions because it simply had not been able to gather the information needed to make its recommendations definitive. It reported that it could not evaluate the Dempster route at all for lack of information and that further study was required to produce plans that would minimize impact on the Alaska Highway route itself. It did, however, report that the Alaska Highway route was acceptable environmentally.

On August 2, the Alaska Highway Pipeline Inquiry reported that "we think that the social and economic effects can be kept within acceptable limits" if Ottawa required "an advance payment toward the settlement of the Yukon Indian Land Claim, compensation [for social and economic costs] from the pipeline company ... and deferral of the commencement of construction of the pipeline [to August 1, 1981]."[52]

This final report acquiescing to the Alaska Highway route, the support of the three opposition parties for the route and the report of a public-opinion poll showing Canadians to favour the route[53] smoothed the way for the cabinet's August 8 selection of the Alaska Highway route. Negotiations with the American government began on August 17 and were concluded on September 20. These negotiations rerouted the pipeline along the entire length of the Alaska Highway rather than through Dawson. This reduced the cost of delivering American gas but added to the cost of the Dempster pipeline by increasing its length. To compensate Canada for the benefit it would receive, the American government worked out a formula for offsetting extra Canadian costs. However, the benefit that Canada might actually realize from this formula is debatable.[54] A second concession by Ottawa was that the $200 million socioeconomic payment to be made by the company would take the form of a Yukon Property Tax to be paid to the territorial government. This is a far different obligation on the pipeline company from the requirement that it pay its property tax plus the special compensation payment.

Bill C-25, the Northern Pipeline Act, was passed by Parliament in April 1978, despite the strong objection of Yukon natives, to whose unsettled claim the act pays only the most trivial lip service.[55] The act put into effect Ottawa's agreement with Washington and established the Northern Pipeline Agency to oversee the construction of the pipeline. The act requires the Agency to establish terms and conditions to govern the socioeconomic and environmental impacts of the pipeline. However, it denies virtually all appeal to the judicial system by those who feel they have been damaged or will suffer damages as a result of pipeline-related activities and cannot persuade the

Northern Pipeline Agency of their case. In this sense, and in pushing aside the native claim, the impact of the act is to expedite the pipeline. This bias will avoid costly delays in pipeline construction but denies those harmed by the pipeline the protection customarily provided by the Canadian legal system.

Explanations of the Northern Pipeline Decision

The northern pipeline decision was much more than a single decision: it was a sequence of a great many decisions. While all are interesting and contributed to the final outcome, they really reduce to two critical decisions. The first was the decision to build a pipeline at all; the second was the actual choice of which pipeline to build. These decisions can be explained in terms of two different approaches. The first is to consider in the abstract the "public interest" as it would be affected by the construction of a pipeline. The second is to examine the politics of the question, which reflects the merits of the proposals in the light of the public interest but which ultimately rests on a much broader calculation of factors.

The Northern Pipeline and the Public Interest

The following aspects of the northern pipeline applications involved the most significant implications for the "public interest" in Canada. The political significance of each of the factors will be considered later, but a reliable rule of thumb is the standard of colonialism: impacts on the North tended to play a smaller part than did the impacts on Canada altogether. The factors are presented here in a highly abbreviated fashion because to explore them fully would require volumes. Despite this summary treatment, they are most important because future megaproject decisions in the North will raise the same kinds of questions. In other words, this catalogue of factors represents a checklist for understanding the implications and the politics of future projects.

The pipeline applications raised two types of environmental problems. The most obvious was the damage a pipeline might inflict on the environment, particularly on the fish, bird, and wildlife populations along its route. The coastal route across the northern Yukon proposed by Arctic Gas seemed to pose a particularly great threat to the huge Porcupine caribou herd. It was partly his concern for this herd that led Justice Berger to recommend against any pipeline route across the northern Yukon and in favour of designating this region a national wilderness park. Another critical area identified was the Mackenzie Delta, because a pipeline route across it was thought to threaten important fish, bird, and whale populations. In other areas, threats to these populations were anticipated to take a variety of forms, but it was felt that environmental damage could be held within acceptable limits if the pipeline construction and operation followed adequate and effectively enforced environmental protection guidelines. For example, uffer zones could be created around sensitive areas such as waterfowl nesting tes. Also, construction could be limited to times of the year when animal opulations had migrated away or were not going through delicate stages in eir life cycles, such as the caribou calving season.[56]

Government can set standards for industry, but these guidelines alone re no guarantee of responsible behaviour, particularly if following them ould cost millions of dollars. For example, Justice Berger anticipated that eather conditions or reduced productivity by the pipeline crews might row the pipeline construction off schedule and create strong pressure on e contractor to continue construction past the time of year when it was nvironmentally desirable to do so.[57] To prevent such actions, native and nvironmental groups argued that Ottawa establish penalties large enough o have a deterrent force. However, the Northern Pipeline Act only provides or a maximum fine of $10 000 a day. When viewed in the context of the huge ums of money involved, this represents "a paltry sum . . . no more than a cense to breach a condition"[58] and suggests that Ottawa's commitment to nvironmental protection is modest at best.

A second category of environmental problem was the damage the nvironment could inflict on the pipeline. While land slides and erosion were en to create some difficulty, particularly at stream and river crossings, the reatest damage was anticipated to be frost heave. Frost heave could exert a trong enough upward pressure on a buried pipeline to cause it to rupture, articularly if varying soil conditions produce strong heave on one section of e line and much less pressure on an adjacent section. While a rupture ould not cause great environmental damage, it would force the pipeline to hut down. Gas deliveries would cease while the line was being repaired and is disruption of service would be most expensive. Arctic Gas undertook xtensive research to develop an elaborate strategy for dealing with the roblem. However, its credibility suffered when it was discovered during the ourse of the inquiry that its calculations were based on readings from a alfunctioning piece of laboratory apparatus. By the close of the inquiry, rctic Gas had not been able to demonstrate that it had mastered the problem f frost heave.

In general, environmental factors, while far from the primary considera- on, seemed to favour the Foothills (Yukon) application. First, the Alaska Iighway route avoided the areas of greatest sensitivity. While it did cross ome areas with permafrost, they were less extensive than in the Arctic Gas roposal. Also, the Alaska Highway route travelled along an already existing orridor and accordingly was thought to involve less environmental disrup- on than a pipeline across the virgin north Yukon. Finally, the Foothills roposal was a political masterpiece of timing and information manipula- on. It was introduced so late in the decision-making process and with so uch less research behind it than was the case with Arctic Gas, that it was a ery difficult application to scrutinize effectively. Potential critics lacked the time and the detailed information that had enabled them to review the Arctic Gas application so rigorously. In this way, while the rejection of Arctic Gas was the rejection of a project that had not demonstrated its environmental adequacy, the acceptance of the Foothills pipeline was in no way the selection of a project proven ecologically sound. However, in its eagerness to approve one of the applications, Ottawa chose to take Foothills' assurances on faith hardly evidence of a strong commitment to environmental protection.

Economics

The economic issues surrounding the northern pipeline decision were exceedingly complex. Not only were they numerous and intricately inter related, they were also volatile; the assumptions on which some of them were based changed drastically over the lengthy decision-making process. The major issues during this process were the macroeconomic effects of the pipelines, the pipelines' contribution to Canada's energy supply, and the financing of the pipelines. A fourth issue, less significant in the ultimate decision, was the impact of the proposed pipelines on the northern economy

Macroeconomic Effects

By 1981, the estimated price tag for the Alaska Highway gas pipeline was in the neighbourhood of $30 billion.[59] Had it been built in the period anticipated for the construction of the Alaska Highway pipeline, the Arctic Gas line would have been even more expensive. Projects such as these are so enormous that they could well affect the total operation of the Canadian economy. For example, they might command such large amounts of goods and services as to raise Canada's rate of inflation. Similarly, they might demand so much financing as to increase rates of interest charged by Canadian banking institutions. In addition, other Canadian enterprises might find machinery, labour, materials, and credit in short supply. If these enterprises were in the manufacturing sector of the economy, many jobs might be delayed and long-term growth sacrificed to the relatively short-term boom of pipeline construction.

In other words, while a megaproject brings some obvious benefits, it also imposes opportunity costs, the lost benefits of opportunities foregone as a result of the decision to build the project. The opportunity cost in building a northern pipeline might have been to reinforce Canada's historic tendency to concentrate on the extraction of primary resources and to suffer an underdeveloped manufacturing sector. This "deindustrialization" could well obstruct the industrial strategy Ottawa is attempting so desperately to develop.

Other macroeconomic effects were the impact of the proposed pipelines on the international value of the Canadian dollar and on Canada's international balance of payments. After much analysis using computer models of the Canadian economy, the NEB concluded that the economy could absorb the macroeconomic effects of any of the pipeline proposals.[60] However, this was not an endorsement of the predictions of the pipelines' proponents that their projects would produce vast macroeconomic benefits for Canada.

Energy Supply and Demand

One of the strongest arguments of the pipeline promoters in the mid-1970s was that Canada urgently needed additional supplies of natural gas to overcome the imminent shortage. Only an estimated 200 million cubic metres of gas had been discovered in the Mackenzie at the time. However, the pipeline groups maintained that drilling results indicated that the Delta contained at least the threshold volume of 450 to 510 million cubic metres needed to make a Mackenzie Valley pipeline financially feasible. Indeed, contracts were being signed or discussed that would have committed 650 million cubic metres for export alone.[61] As it turned out, additional gas was not found: in 1977, the estimate of the volume of gas which had already been located was reduced to 150 million cubic metres.[62] This development virtually doomed the Maple Leaf line.[63] It also hurt the Arctic Gas proposal, although not as seriously because it could rely on the Prudhoe Bay gas it carried to finance it.

If the contribution the Mackenzie Delta could make to Canada's gas supply seemed to diminish at a critical time in the northern pipeline decision-making process, the apparent need for the gas also diminished. By 1977, it was becoming clear that new discoveries of gas in western Canada were creating an actual surplus over and above anticipated Canadian needs for a good many years. Canada no longer needed frontier gas as urgently as both government and industry had previously thought.

As a result of these changes in the apparent supply of and demand for frontier gas, the public interest in the construction of the northern pipelines came to be redefined. Formerly it had been to supply Canada. If American gas was to be carried or Canadian frontier gas sold to the United States, the justification was to finance the basic goal of the pipeline—meeting Canadian energy needs. In the middle of the 1970s, this basic goal seemed less compelling and the economic benefits of providing a transportation corridor for American gas came to the fore. The development of the Mackenzie Delta reserves was therefore no longer vital for Ottawa. In this revised context, the Foothills project could compete with Arctic Gas.

Financing

Finding the capital to construct the proposed pipelines would be one of the major challenges facing the proponents because the sums needed were so huge and because the projects involved complex and in some cases unique engineering techniques that had yet to be proven in actual operational situations. These factors were largely responsible for the price tag on the Alyeska oil pipeline's rising from an initially estimated $900 million to over $9 billion, a cost overrun large enough to strike terror into the heart of any banker.[64] To ease the fears of the financial community, the pipeline proponents sought a variety of concessions from Ottawa. Among these were methods of calculating their taxes to put their projects on a stronger financial footing.[65] In addition, they sought a "full cost of service, all-events tariff." In the words of the National Energy Board, a full cost of service tariff was one "equal to the serving Company's (the pipeline owner's) costs of providing service, rather than a fixed rate or amount . . ."[66] An all-events tariff would be paid—even if delays in completion of the pipeline or events such as pipeline rupture disrupted the deliveries of gas. In other words, cost overruns and project failures would be paid for by the shipper of the gas, by the companies receiving the gas, or by the customers to whom they distributed it, but not by the pipeline companies.

Possibly the most contentious financing question involved the possibility that government might be called on to provide guarantees to the financial backers of the pipeline that it would assume the financial obligation should the pipeline company prove unable to bear the burden. In other words, might Ottawa ultimately have to shoulder the financial risk of building this monumental project? The question was so contentious because the provision of a guarantee might:

1. Reduce the company's incentive to build and operate the project efficiently;
2. Give Ottawa a special interest in seeing the project built quickly and at the lowest cost, an interest in conflict with its responsibility to regulate the project's environmental and social impacts; and
3. Place a great burden on Canadian taxpayers without their receiving any compensating benefit.[67]

Arctic Gas forthrightly admitted that it would require a degree of government guarantee of its financing. Despite objections that its plans were not financially superior to those of Arctic Gas and that the members of its consortium were smaller and financially weaker than the members of the Arctic Gas consortium, Foothills maintained that it would require no guarantees of its financing from the Canadian government. While the sceptics persisted, Foothills' insistence put Arctic Gas in a bad light. As a following discussion will note, while Foothills has not yet sought government guarantees, it has encountered great difficulty in organizing its financing. These difficulties emphasize the point made in Chapter 1 that the non-renewable resources of the North will have to be particularly rich to compensate for the economic costs and substantial uncertainty surrounding their development.

Social Issues

The social impact, including economic effects, of pipeline construction and operation on the areas through which it would pass constituted a third set of issues. As was the case with environmental and economic impacts, the construction phase was thought to involve the greatest threat, for it would bring large numbers of workers into sparsely populated areas. The problems common to boom towns were anticipated to result. To minimize such difficulties, Justice Berger recommended that the camps housing the pipeline labour force be located away from the smaller native communities, that workers be discouraged from visiting these communities, and that the camps themselves provide superior food and accommodation to reduce the need workers might feel to leave them and the frustration they might want to vent when they did enter northern communities.[68] While the terms and conditions governing the Alaska Highway pipeline require Foothills to provide a high standard of camp facilities, the fact that the pipeline will parallel the Highway through the Yukon means workers will have easy access to the communities, which cannot be completely sheltered by means of Berger's expedient of limiting access to them.

A second and much broader social issue was how the proposed pipelines would affect the natives' severe community, family, and personal problems. Spokesmen for the Dene Nation and those sympathetic to it anticipated that the construction period would draw native workers away from the traditional sector of the economy—which they saw as both viable economically and important culturally. They expressed the fear that such industrial activity would not provide a long-term substitute for traditional economic activities because pipeline operation would involve few jobs, which, in any case, would require education or experience that few native workers possessed. To answer this concern, Arctic Gas attempted to minimize the importance of hunting, fishing, and trapping for native people and to argue that wage employment was the only viable alternative to what was in effect a moribund way of life. In one of the most controversial findings of his inquiry,[69] Justice Berger disagreed with this viewpoint and recommended that active steps be taken to protect the native economy, of which traditional activities are such an important part.[70]

Over and above the threat to the traditional economy was the more general concern that industrial development in the North would further degrade native life.[71] It was anticipated that native people would experience the pipeline as yet another—but more massive—instance of uncontrollably powerful outside forces swamping them and submerging their efforts to find their way in an alien culture. Their alienation was anticipated to show itself in increased violence, alcoholism, suicide, mental distress, and family breakdown. The pipeline proponents and the Berger and Lysyk inquiries proposed a variety of measures to mitigate these problems. While these would have proven helpful, in Justice Berger's words:

There can be no control over how many families will break up, how many children will become delinquent and have criminal records, how many communities will see their young people drifting towards the larger urban centres, and how many people may be driven from a way of life they know to one they do not understand and in which they have no real place. Such problems are beyond anyone's power to control, but they will generate enormous social costs. Because these costs are, by and large, neither measurable nor assignable, we tend to forget them or to pretend they do not exist. But with construction of a pipeline, they would occur, and the native people of the North would then have to pay the price.[72]

The psychological impact of the pipeline was anticipated to hit native people particularly hard because of their anxieties over the absence of any guarantees about their future. In other words, they needed the confidence in their tenure on their lands and their authority to administer their own programs to cushion the social impact of the pipeline. Only a claims settlement would provide these guarantees. This point was repeated time and again by Dene and Yukon Indian spokesmen who emphasized their position that there be no pipeline before their claims were settled and implemented. The pipeline's proponents agreed and repeatedly urged an early settlement of the claims, but were helpless to achieve this goal because they were not a party to the negotiations. In the end, Berger recommended a ten-year moratorium on pipeline construction in the Mackenzie. He felt that this would allow the settlement not only to be negotiated but also to take effect and to give Dene society the resilience it would need to survive pipeline construction culturally intact. The Lysyk inquiry proposed an eighteen-month delay (to August 1 1981) in the proposed commencement of construction of the Alaska Highway pipeline.[73] It was hoped that this would provide time for the settlement of the Yukon Indian claim, but it would not allow any breathing space for its implementation. Ottawa demonstrated its limited sympathies to the native position by setting a January 1, 1981, date for the beginning of construction In the end, however, the financial difficulties faced by the pipeline have pushed the commencement of the main construction activities in the Yukon well past Lysyk's proposed date.

As has already been noted, it was suggested that the pipeline company bear the cost of the programs needed to remedy the social problems accompanying the pipeline. However, as this idea evolved during 1977, it became quite diluted from its earliest conception. Here again, northern considerations were subordinated to Ottawa's imperative of pipeline promotion.

The Politics of the Northern Pipeline Decision

The environmental, technological, economic, and social factors discussed above all played their parts in the northern pipeline decision, but political factors determined the significance of these parts—particularly the decision whether to build a northern gas pipeline at all. In truth, it was less likely a decision than an assumption, which early in the 1970s became part of the conventional wisdom in Ottawa.[74] Its status as an article of faith owes something to the pipeline appearing as the "new improved" model of the northern vision that had periodically stirred the Canadian imagination. More importantly, industry vigorously promoted an oil pipeline from 1968 to 1970.[75] Ottawa mandarins allowed themselves to become committed in principle to it prematurely, when its benefits were obvious but its costs had not received careful examination. This commitment was transferred to the concept of a gas pipeline after the approval of the Alyeska project ended the possibility of a Canadian oil pipeline. A gas pipeline was rendered all the more credible by the development of an apparent gas shortage, particularly after it was officially recognized by the NEB in 1975.[76] The Arctic Gas proposal was also supported by the most intense lobbying effort ever undertaken by any corporation in Canadian history, reinforced by over $150 million of research and development. In addition, once the Federal Power Commission had ruled the El Paso route, which would have avoided Canada completely, to be inferior, Ottawa felt it important not to deny Washington a land bridge across which to transport its gas. This very aspect of the project attracted criticism in Canada because it was thought to jeopardize Canadian sovereignty and to move Canada and the United States closer to a continental energy policy, which would benefit the latter at the expense of the former.[77]

In the final analysis, it was recognized that the construction of any of the proposed northern pipelines would not significantly improve Canada's short-term energy situation, although it would likely be beneficial in creating a cash flow for companies that had found gas in the Mackenzie Delta and in this way encourage them and others to continue to search for additional gas and oil. However, this prospect alone would not justify the expenditures and risks involved in approving a pipeline.

Three factors confirmed the decade-long drift toward pipeline approval. The first was the anticipated boost to the lagging Canadian economy from pipeline construction. The second was the wish to defer to the wishes of the United States. The third was simply the existence of an option for cabinet to sidestep the accumulating opposition to the Mackenzie Valley pipeline. It was the Foothills option that created the second crucial question facing Ottawa in 1977—which of the pipeline applications to select. In the absence of an alternative, Justice Berger might well have felt compelled to moderate his firm recommendations in order to bring them into the realm of the politically acceptable. In the process, he might have destroyed the impact of his report and given the cabinet a freer hand. Without an alternative, the cabinet would probably have approved the Arctic Gas proposal. However, Canadian public opinion had been aroused by the strength of native opposition to a Mackenzie Valley pipeline and by the release of the first

volume of the Berger Report. The years of careful examination of the Arcti
Gas proposal had also identified a variety of environmental and technologi
cal deficiencies in it. In contrast, the Alaska Highway proposal had receive
only very cursory scrutiny because Ottawa did not want to appear to b
dictated to by Washington and, accordingly, felt compelled to decide befor
September 1977, when the President of the United States was required by law
to make his choice public. This time limit hindered opposition from
mobilizing against the Foothills project and prevented inquiries from
investigating it as thoroughly as the Arctic Gas project had been studied.

In addition, as has already been noted, the Yukon had had more contac
with white society than had the Mackenzie Valley. This fact made it seen
better equipped to deal with the social problems likely to accompan
pipeline construction, a view that Justice Berger supported.[78] The nativ
people of the Yukon were not nearly as militant or vocal as the Dene.[7]
Canadian public opinion had taken less notice of them and would be les
aroused by a project that undermined their claim rather than the Dene claim
The provision for the Dempster Highway pipeline gave the appearance o
providing for the development of Mackenzie Delta gas and, of course, th
main pipeline itself would satisfy American needs. Finally, selecting th
Alaska Highway route would enable cabinet to avoid rejecting the advice o
the variety of inquiries it had initiated into the question. When all was saic
and done, the Alaska Highway route enabled cabinet to achieve its basic goal
and minimize its political losses. It was a marginal project, but the bes
available. Given that the rejection of all the applications was not seen as ar
option, it received the official nod.

The Northern Pipeline Decision-Making Process

The fashion in which the northern pipeline decision was reached demon
strates several of the themes of the Appendix. The first is simply the colonia
emphasis apparent in the process. Northerners were completely excludec
from the process during the early years when Ottawa was developing it.
commitment to a northern pipeline.[80] Their interests could not have beer
taken very seriously in 1977 in view of Ottawa's haste to reach a decision tc
conform to an American timetable, even though much was not known abou
the northern impact of the Foothills project.

That this was the case merely reflects another of the themes of th
Appendix—the primacy of power. At every stage in the northern-pipelin
policy process—the bias in favour of constructing a pipeline, the decision tc
appoint Justice Berger, the support for Arctic Gas, and ultimately the choic
of the Foothills project—the Liberals in power in Ottawa were swayed by th
pressures brought to bear on them by those who had the political resources tc
press their case. The distribution of resources among the participants in th
process was predictable, but the impact of these resources turned out to be fai

less straightforward than might have been imagined. While size and wealth favoured Arctic Gas, they could not match the public sympathy mobilized by the Dene and the flexibility, bordering on opportunism, of Foothills. The lesson here is that the Dene and Foothills used their limited resources far more effectively than did Arctic Gas. Strategy and commitment can go a long way towards compensating for deficient political resources if the circumstances are favourable.

In the case of the northern pipeline decision, these circumstances owed a great deal to the fact that the decision did not simply occur, but rather evolved as a protracted interplay between process, power, and influence. The long evolution made positional politics particularly important. For example, the energy industry was able to involve itself intimately in the early stages at a time when all other interests were excluded. This early industry-government relationship was more than simply a case of industry's successfully seeking favourable government policies, such as support for an oil pipeline or early approval in principle for Beaufort Sea drilling. It also involved Ottawa's pressing the industry to organize itself into the most effective consortium for promoting the northern developments, which Ottawa had already presumed to be desirable. The Arctic Gas consortium that evolved out of this process could not fail to enjoy the sympathy of Ottawa, which had acted—if not as its parent—at least as its godparent. The result of the early stages of the process was that basic understandings were established solely between government and industry. These understandings were so entrenched by the time other interests entered the fray that these less-well-placed groups found them to be unassailable. Although their public positions may have been unequivocally stated, these groups were forced to confine their strategies to second-order questions such as routes, timing, and conditions.

Throughout the process, the industry's power guaranteed its initial privileged position, although the fortunes of individual consortia rose and fell. Government bias in favour of industry meant that it was more receptive to information and pleading from industry and that its discourse with industry tended to proceed under a presumption of shared interest. The lack of this presumption in dealing with native and environmental groups led Ottawa to discourage communication from them. For example, Ottawa refused to fund groups wishing to put their cases before the National Energy Board. Without this funding, very few groups could take this important but very expensive step: the industry side of the pipeline debate therefore predominated at the NEB hearings. Also, Ottawa refused to devote nearly enough funding to environmental studies on the North for fear that they would produce findings that would assist critics of northern energy projects.[81] As a result of these and other restrictions on the free flow of information, environmental and particularly native groups' relations with Ottawa tended to assume an oppositional tone that further turned Ottawa against them. In this way, information flows through the policy process came to reflect the initial biases of the policy makers and the distribution of power among the participants.

The many years over which the pipeline decision evolved made it inevitable that its context would change and with it would change the standards by which the various proposals were judged. This feature of the process placed a premium on flexibility. As has already been noted, Foothills showed itself to be a political chameleon, changing its plans to match changes in supply estimates, demand forecasts, and financing considerations. In contrast, Arctic Gas apparently assumed that its plan was so superior and its position with Ottawa so favoured that it did not need to change in any fundamental way. In the end, time passed it by. This fate could befall proposed northern megaprojects in the future because government approval of them is likely to rest on a shifting rather than a fixed set of considerations. Change is particularly likely because proposed northern megaprojects will continue to involve staples whose value is determined globally. The economics of such projects depend on factors beyond the control of the Canadian government or of any single corporation or handful of corporations. Not only are these not controllable, they may not even be predictable at the time an application for a megaproject is filed. In addition, new information about resource supplies or unforeseen obstacles to their development in the North may also dictate changes, as may shifts in the Canadian political climate. Because of all of these possibilities, the rationale on which an application is originally based may not be adequate to see it through the regulatory process; hence, firms applying for project approval will need to be as flexible as possible.

Changes in the context of the policy-making process necessarily built a degree of non-rationality into it. Some assumptions formed in the late 1960s still held sway in 1977 when the formative circumstances had passed. Policy makers were aware of the changed circumstances, but insulated themselves from full exposure to the evidence of how great the changes had been. Also, being human, they tended not to adjust their "operational codes" even to the changes they recognized. The result was that the pipeline decision owed something to historical factors, not just to what would have been the rational basis for it—the situation in 1977.

The rationality of the decision also suffered because Ottawa prematurely decided on the Mackenzie Valley route, concentrated its efforts on it, and subsequently found itself without adequate information to properly assess the Alaska Highway route. Decision makers often try to simplify their task or save scarce funds by focusing on a narrower range of policy options than they might. If their selection is correct, they have operated in a highly efficient fashion. However, if circumstances lead policy elsewhere, they have gambled and lost. This problem is compounded when government discourages supporters of other options from developing their proposals. The efforts of such groups could lead to the early identifications of problems in the favoured proposal and to the development of bodies of information on alternatives that may turn out to be very valuable. Ottawa spurned these benefits in preparing for the 1977 pipeline decision. As a result, it decided on the basis of insufficient information—that is, on a less rational basis than could have been possible.

Some observers have suggested that the rationality of the northern-pipeline policy process was limited by its "drift," the lack of a policy on northern development that was clearly understood by all those involved in the making of the decision.[82] However, an examination of the record reveals that government officials by and large shared the basic goal of northern development based on megaprojects in general and a pipeline in particular. Drift did occur, but at a more specific level than is sometimes suggested; in the absence of a national energy policy and an industrial-development strategy, Ottawa experienced great difficulty with the second-order question, the choice between the alternatives facing it. Aside from its role in the creation of the Arctic Gas consortium, it proved unwilling to take the initiative in structuring the terms of this choice. Instead, it reacted to initiatives taken in the private sector or by the United States. Ottawa therefore left to others much of the agenda setting for the pipeline decision—and the power that flows from this function. A free-enterprise approach to industrial development would laud this kind of exercise of the authority of the marketplace. However, the sheer magnitude of the pipelines' impacts on Canada suggests an opposite conclusion. Because Ottawa brought into play a variety of regulatory devices, it recognized that it had a legitimate interest in such a project and an obligation to control it. However, it did not define its role any more broadly than this. Whether out of respect for the marketplace, deference to political pressure, an inadequate information base, lack of purpose, or inexperience in what was a new form of policy challenge, it handled the evolving pipeline issue much more passively than it might have.

These, then, were some of the most significant aspects of the pipeline decision. Considerations of power not only determined the outcome of the process, but also shaped its structure to reinforce the position of the favoured interests. In this context, the wellbeing of the colonial North and other questions of the national interest became merely abstract and academic in view of the lack of political resources to back them. The duration of the pipeline policy process, its complexity, and the number of individuals, inquiries, and institutions contributing to it all added elements of non-rationality to the process. This non-rationality was compounded by Ottawa's inability to define in any detail the national interest in the issue and to commit itself to an aggressive pursuit of this interest. As a result, *ad hoc* considerations and the political resources to press a particular interpretation of these considerations on Ottawa acquired particular prominence. While this is not a surprising result, it is an important one in that it limited Ottawa's ability to perform its function. The question to be answered is whether

Ottawa will have learned from the experience and begun to put into place a more rigorous and open policy process based on a clearer statement of goals and a fuller commitment to pursue them. The answer to this question lies in Ottawa's handling of the second generation of northern energy-megaproject applications.

The Fate of the Alaska Highway Pipeline

At the time of writing, Foothills' political magic had not been translated into a viable pipeline. Despite the support of both the Canadian and American governments, Foothills had been unable to assemble the massive financing required to underwrite its project. Its problems had been several. First, regulatory agencies delayed handing down rulings on the rate of return the pipeline companies could receive and on the price to be paid for Alaskan natural gas. This footdragging prevented customers from signing contracts for the gas, which prevented Foothills from using firm orders as the basis for seeking credit, the usual approach used by the industry to finance its projects. Second, the financial community was anxious about the possibility of cost overruns and about the financial strength of the pipeline companies. In the words of one investment analyst, "... four of the world's largest oil companies, with total assets of $32 billion, had problems financing the $8 billion Alaska oil pipeline while the total American natural gas industry, which ultimately must support the $14 billion [sic] Alaska Highway pipeline, has total assets of only $19 billion."[83] Third, a variety of reasons led the producers of the gas at Prudhoe Bay to balk at the prospect of helping to finance the pipeline. Fourth, Foothills did not seek the government-financed participation or even guarantees of its debts, which would have done much to bolster the confidence of the financial community in the project. Fifth, drastically increased energy prices made Alaskan gas profitable to deliver, but they also brought into production in the rest of North America large quantities of gas that can be delivered more cheaply and with less danger of cost overruns than can Alaskan gas.

All of these factors make the construction of the Alaska Highway gas pipeline far from assured. However, it can be argued that the prospects for the pipeline are improving. In the summer of 1980, the Prudhoe Bay producers did agree in principle to help finance the project. In July 1980, the Canadian cabinet approved a controversial plan to "prebuild" sections of the pipeline in southern Alberta and British Columbia. This $680 million project will deliver to the United States southern Canadian gas considered to be surplus to Canada's needs. This gas will inject some revenue into the pipeline project and reduce its overall cost by permitting early—hence less expensive building—of part of it. However, it means the export of an anticipated 65 million cubic metres of gas over seven years without any American agreement to replace that gas with equivalent amounts when Alaskan gas actually begins to be delivered.[84] As a result, the outcome of the northern-pipeline decision at the end of 1980 was not a project to bring Canadian gas to

Canadian markets, nor even to deliver American gas to American markets. Instead, it was to export Canadian natural gas.

Whatever may be thought of this outcome, it did promise an improvement in the economics of the pipeline, and Foothills was confidently predicting that "phase two" of the project—the main line from Prudhoe Bay to connect with the prebuilt section, now called "phase one"—will be ready to operate in 1985. Changes in the political climate in the United States also appear to favour the pipeline. Events in Iran since the overthrow of the Shah may persuade American politicians that energy self-sufficiency is an urgent goal, requiring the swift completion of the Alaska Highway pipeline. The election of Ronald Reagan as President may well reinforce this sentiment. If it does, this development will demonstrate once again the unpredictable nature of the policy process governing northern megaprojects. This volatility should be kept in mind when weighing the prospects for the northern megaprojects of the future. If political and economic forces combine to doom the pipeline, the consequences for Foothills are unlikely to be as drastic as the rejection of the Arctic Gas application was for that consortium. The prebuilt section will be in place and Foothills will still have a number of irons in the energy fire, thus demonstrating that the winning strategy for northern developers is to maximize one's range of options and one's flexibility in responding to the shifting demands of the political process.

The Next Generation of Northern Energy Projects

Although the Alaska Highway pipeline was hanging in the balance at the end of 1980, various other projects were being advanced to transport northern energy resources. It appears reasonable to anticipate that the decision-making process that will judge them will have improved from what governed the earlier northern-pipeline decision. Environmental study is continuing and may provide a sounder information base than was available for the first decision. Similarly, the Environmental Assessment and Review Process is now firmly established and mobilizing to carry out its mandate more effectively. For example, at the end of 1980, the Federal Environmental Assessment and Review Office established a Beaufort Sea Environmental Assessment body in anticipation of receiving applications from Dome and Esso Resources. This step should shorten the time needed for effective study of such applications.[85] The growth in the abilities of the territorial public services and in the determination of northern politicians will make it more difficult—but certainly not impossible—for Ottawa to exclude them from decision-making processes. Finally, native groups are much stronger than they were during the period in which Ottawa's pipeline prejudice took shape.

However, none of these factors may count for much in the face of Ottawa's determination to proceed with a project.[86] Ottawa is likely to continue to place great emphasis on the following southern factors. First, oil is in sufficiently short supply that large finds in the North could well make valuable additions to total Canadian reserves. Second, energy became a public policy issue of the first order in the 1970s and Ottawa lost credibility because of its poor grasp of Canada's hydrocarbon supply and demand. As a result, it now recognizes a great need to know about the extent of Canada's energy reserves, including the North's potential contribution to them.[87] This need will lead it to create incentives to encourage northern exploration. These incentives are likely to take the form of approving northern reserves' coming into production before Canada has an economic need for them. Canada has a substantial surplus of natural gas and no need to go to the lengths required to deliver northern gas to southern-Canadian customers. However, Ottawa is likely to approve the production of northern gas for export in order to provide cash and encouragement for continued exploration. A third consideration is that the western oil-and-gas-producing provinces can be expected to continue to oppose elements of federal energy plans that they feel infringe on their rights as owners of the oil and gas found within their borders. Oil and gas found on Canada Lands improve Ottawa's bargaining position with these provinces if they can be brought into production without excessive costs.

These considerations should be kept in mind when attempting to anticipate the fate of the proposed projects described in the following section. The history of the Foothills projects should also be kept in mind; the nature of what is proposed can change quite dramatically—as can cost estimates, particularly if projects are delayed. The following details were correct in early 1981, but may well become dated quickly. For this reason, they will only be briefly sketched. (See Figure 4-3 for a map of the proposed routes.)

The Norman Wells Pipeline

In 1980 the National Energy Board and an Environmental Assessment and Review Process panel studied a proposal by Interprovincial Pipe Line Limited to construct a $360 million, 305 mm pipeline from the Norman Wells oilfield to connect at Zama, Alberta, with the oil pipeline network serving southern Canada. This pipeline is projected to carry 25 000 barrels of oil a day, starting in 1983. The oil would be produced as a result of a $460 million expansion program to be carried out by Esso Resources Canada, the owner of the oilfield.[88]

The hearing process revealed a variety of problems with the application. Federal environmental-protection officials attacked its inadequate environmental-impact information and its allegedly simplistic plans for dealing with permafrost problems.[89] Its anticipated social impacts also caused substantial concern. As in the case of the Arctic Gas application, spokesmen for the Dene Nation condemned the concept of a pipeline before a settlement of the Mackenzie Valley claims.

Undoubtedly foreshadowing its position on other northern energy projects, the government of the Northwest Territories supported the Dene,

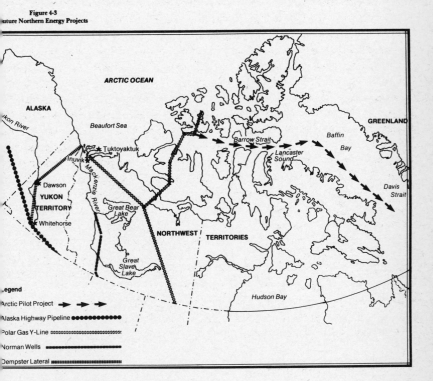

Figure 4-3
Future Northern Energy Projects

although it proposed only a two-year delay in approving the pipeline. It was suggested that this ought to provide enough time for a claims settlement to be reached but would not bind the pipeline to the claims-negotiation timetable, should the latter become delayed as had happened in the past. In addition to this position, the government of the Northwest Territories used the pipeline application as an opportunity to engage in positional politics by claiming a larger role in northern-megaproject assessment and the financial base it will need to underwrite the expanded powers and autonomy it seeks. Specifically it recommended:

1. A joint territorial/federal northern based mechanism be developed to manage the construction and operation of the project [this in contrast to the Northern Pipeline Agency, which is responsible solely to Ottawa].
2. Joint territorial/federal planning [of all nonrenewable resource development in the Mackenzie Valley and Delta and the Beaufort Sea].
3. Guaranteed supply of refined products [to northern communities

suffering from high fuel costs and potentially from problems of unavailability of fuel].

4. Resource revenue sharing to meet our needs and to build for the future.[90]

The National Energy Board approved the project in April 1981 despite these objections and without recommending that cabinet accept any of the conditions proposed during the hearings. Indeed, Bill C-48 emphatically rejects the first, second, and fourth of the territorial government's recommendations and is silent on the third. In all likelihood, Ottawa will find the pipeline to be in its interest because it will replace about 7 per cent of Canada's crude-oil imports at a saving of about $1 million a day at 1980 prices. Ottawa probably also recognizes that approval of the pipeline will put pressure on the leaders of the Dene Nation to moderate their claim in order to obtain an early settlement. It might also view a Norman Wells pipeline as the first stage of a pipeline to the Beaufort Sea to extract the deposits of oil that Dome and Imperial Oil recently announced. While all of these reasons seem likely to lead Ottawa to approve the project, the cabinet may be persuaded to qualify its approval by the EARP Report on the project released early in 1981, which recommended a year's delay in the commencement of construction to enable Esso Resources to satisfy a variety of environmental conditions and to give Mackenzie Valley residents more time to prepare for the project. The report also urged an intensification of efforts to negotiate the native claims still outstanding in the Mackenzie Valley and the creation of a trust fund out of a portion of the revenues that the pipeline will provide the federal government, including the use of the trust fund as one of the items to be negotiated.[91] As has been argued previously, Ottawa is very unlikely to look with favour on these latter recommendations.

The Dempster Lateral

As has been explained, the 1977 pipeline decision provided for a pipeline linking Mackenzie Valley gas reserves with the Alaska Highway pipeline at Whitehorse. In view of the difficulties in financing the main portion of the pipeline, this project has been given a low priority by both government and industry, a situation unlikely to change in the foreseeable future. In the words of François Bregha:

> It is ... difficult to judge today [1979] whether a Dempster pipeline will constitute the most attractive energy option available to Canada in the late 1980s or early 1990s. A significant discovery in the Arctic archipelago could, for instance, postpone the development of the Mackenzie Delta and perhaps even preclude it together. Conversely, a large strike in the Beaufort Sea could accelerate the development of this frontier region although not necessarily by a Dempster pipeline. If the reserves are large enough, a Mackenzie pipeline may be economically preferable to a Dempster pipeline. It is also conceivable that this gas would find its way to market by tanker.[92]

we will see, several of these possibilities are more likely than the prospect
t the Dempster pipeline will be approved soon.

e Arctic Pilot Project

consortium composed of Petro-Canada, Dome Petroleum, Melville
ipping, and Nova, An Alberta Corporation, is proposing this project to
the Drake Point gas field that Panarctic Oils has discovered near the
rthern end of Melville Island. Anticipated to begin operation in 1986 and
cost $2.25 billion, it will carry this gas—155 million cubic metres had been
oven as of June 1980—160 km to Bridport Inlet on the south shore of the
and. There it will be liquefied for shipping year-round by specially
signed icebreaking tankers which will pass through Parry Channel and
n south through Baffin Bay and Davis Straight to a location either on the
ait of Canso or near Gros Cacouna on the St. Lawrence.[93] At this location it
ll be regassified and enter the TransCanada Pipeline system to supply
nsumers in eastern Canada. However, the net effect of the Arctic Pilot
oject is not to supply Canadian markets, but to provide exports to the
ited States. A brochure describing the project explains:

> . . . 6.4 million daily cubic metres of Arctic Pilot Project gas will enter the
> Canadian pipeline system in Eastern Canada and equivalent volumes of
> "exchange" gas will be exported through existing pipeline facilities from
> Western Canada to the U.S.
> The agreement calls for an additional 6.4 million cubic metres a day of
> conventional gas to be exported from Western Canada.[94]

us, the net effect of the Arctic Pilot Project will be to export 6.4 million
bic metres of western-Canadian gas daily.

The project seems to offer a variety of advantages. As its proponents
phasize, it is a pilot project—in other words, in part a learning experience.
e comparatively small scale of the project should provide relatively
expensive experience in northern gas production, which should prove very
luable in preparing for future development. Similarly, while the icebreak-
g tankers will be built in foreign shipyards, provision has been made for the
hnology to be transferred to Canadian industry. If this transfer can be
ectively accomplished, Canada would be in the forefront of polar shipping
hnology because the tankers will represent the state of the art. Their
yages will help reinforce Canadian sovereignty in the North. They will
o provide income to Panarctic, which has been exploring in the North for
decade and a half without generating any revenue from sales, and will
courage exploration elsewhere in the Arctic. The economics of the project
e themselves attractive, for it will cost much less than a pipeline. The main
vantage will not be that its cost of delivering gas will be significantly lower
an a pipeline's, because it will deliver smaller volumes; instead, the
raction lies in the greater ease of raising the smaller sum of money involved

and the likelihood that cost overruns will also be smaller. A 10 per cent co
overrun on a $2 billion project is unpleasant enough, but a 10 per ce
overrun on a $10 billion project is an appalling prospect, particularly
backers who would have to seek the additional funding from the financi
community. Another advantage of a relatively low initial cost is that
requires a much lower threshold volume of gas to be economically feasib
than does a more expensive pipeline system. In other words, gas deposits t
small to justify a pipeline can be developed by using tanker-transportatic
systems.

Another advantage of the Arctic Pilot Project is its incremental nature.
pipeline only begins to deliver gas and earn income after the total sum
money budgeted to build it has been spent. In contrast, a tanker project can I
phased in and begin to earn money as soon as all of the land-based faciliti
are in place and the first tanker is ready to sail. The income earned by the fir
tankers will help pay for those that may follow. In addition, if circumstanc
change, it may be decided that only two tankers are justified and no more w
be built, or that their design should be altered. A pipeline is not nearly
flexible: its capacity must be decided in advance and it tends to becon
uneconomic if it is not operated at full capacity. In addition to the
advantages, the project's promoters argue that it will provide the Canadia
employment and balance-of-payment benefits usually associated with nort
ern energy projects, particularly those with an energy-export component.

The Arctic Pilot Project has not provoked the fierce opposition th
Arctic Gas pipeline proposal attracted. In part, this lack of opposition can I
attributed to the lack of detail of the company's plans to implement i
promises concerning northern social impact and preferences on hiring an
buying as well as to the lack of environmental information for the land an
sea areas to be affected. It is also partly due to the absence of a loc
population of indigenous people on Melville Island. In addition, th
combination of a federal election, the Quebec referendum and subseque
constitutional and energy conflict in southern Canada distracted many of th
southern groups that opposed Arctic Gas and drowned out those who di
raise their voices in objection to the Arctic Pilot Project.

The project is likely to be approved. Much more than the threshol
volume of gas has been proven by Panarctic and delivery contracts have bee
signed. The project cleared a major regulatory hurdle in November 198
when the Federal Environmental Assessment and Review Office found it
be environmentally acceptable, provided certain conditions are met.[95]

However, at the time of writing both the National Energy Board and th
cabinet must still approve the project. Whether they will may depend mo
on the cut and thrust of interdepartmental politics in Ottawa than on an
other factor. When the project was originally conceived, natural gas wa
thought to be in short supply in Canada and it was thought that the proje
would provide some relief for this situation. However, more recently gas ha

en found in abundance as its price has risen and Canada does not have an mmediate need for Arctic Islands gas. The practical impact of the Arctic ilot Project, then, is not to supply immediate Canadian energy needs, but in fect to export substantial quantities of southern-Canadian gas to the United ates.

Nonetheless, Canada's past experience with exporting apparent gas urpluses suggests that this may not be in the best interests of the country, espite the eagerness of the industry to see export permits approved and its ish flow thereby improved. Moreover, there is some reason to believe that is markets in both the United States and Europe will remain "soft" for a umber of years and unreceptive to the high price of Pilot Project gas. In this ay the Pilot Project is more of a transportation-technology and macro-onomic-benefits project than an energy project. This shift from the riginal rationale that prompted the project's conception should appeal to me federal departments, such as Finance, Industry, Trade and Commerce, nd Transport. However, Energy, Mines and Resources may look more and ore askance at a project that—at least in the short run—may be losing its itionale as an energy project and in fact trading precious energy resources or a variety of side benefits. To the extent that Energy, Mines and Resources oes come to view the project in this fashion and, given its strong position in ne Ottawa hierarchy and the personal strength of its Minister, it could make ne Arctic Pilot Project the centre of a political storm of the first order when it omes before cabinet.

Whatever the outcome, the evolution of the Pilot Project mirrors that of ne northern-pipeline policy process, in that in both cases projects were onceived on the basis of given sets of assumptions, which subsequently nanged in ways that reduced the need the projects were intended to satisfy. Iowever, the weakening of their rationales led not to their termination but to ne developing of a new rationale or the giving of an increased emphasis to hat had formerly been only subsidiary arguments supporting the project. his history demonstrates the momentum that megaprojects can develop: ne financial capital and personal commitment invested in them can make nem difficult to abandon. It also suggests that the slowness of the regulatory rocess—a frequent subject of complaints on the part of megaproject roponents—may be frustrating and financially costly, but may perform the aluable service of winnowing out projects lacking sufficient research and evelopment.

he Polar Gas Pipeline

he future seems less certain for the Polar Gas pipeline, the second project eing developed to transport Arctic Islands gas to market. The consortium eveloping this proposal—Petro-Canada, Panarctic Oil, TransCanada ipeLines, the Ontario Energy Corporation, and Tenneco Canada—is xpected to make application early in 1982 for a Y-pipeline to bring gas from the Arctic Islands and from the Mackenzie-Beaufort region. These two line would join together at a point as yet undecided but which would be rough! in the area of Great Bear Lake. The gas would then proceed to market alon one of four possible routes. This project is expected to cost about $7 billion i 1978 dollars and to deliver up to 93.5 million cubic metres of gas daily.[96]

Combining the reserves of the Arctic Islands and the Mackenzie-Beaufo would undoubtedly provide enough natural gas to fill this pipeline, but th fact alone far from guarantees the project's construction in the foreseeab! future. One problem the consortium must face is frost heave in discontinuot permafrost, the difficulty that made the engineering aspects of the Arctic G application appear suspect. Polar Gas has expressed confidence in its abilit to handle the problem, but its solutions have not yet been subjected to th scrutiny of any regulatory agency or hearing process. In addition, Polar G must develop the technology to enable it to construct underwater pipelin under exceedingly difficult circumstances. The greatest problems are antic pated to arise in M'Clure Strait. The pipeline crossing here will be 122 kr long, up to 503 m deep, and permanently covered in ice between 2 m and 13 r thick. Because ice islands can extend as much as 35 m below the surface of th water, it has been anticipated that the pipeline will have to come ashore into tunnel as much as 50 m below the surface.[97] Polar Gas has already spent ove $70 million on devising engineering solutions to this and other problems an obviously will not proceed unless it is confident in the technology it ha developed. However, technical failures during the construction or th operation of the pipeline are likely to be extremely expensive because of th difficulty of making repairs and the great costs of financing delays i building or interruption of gas delivery. This prospect requires that th pipeline's engineering be as foolproof as possible and be well supported witl backup systems; in other words, this pipeline will be very expensive. Thi cost and the possibility of breakdown—which can never be ruled ou completely—will make investors anxious about the project.

Any northern energy proposal raises questions of local social, economic and environmental impacts. While native groups have expressed oppositior to the approval of the project before the settlement of their claims, they hav had little more to say about these impacts because Polar Gas will explain i detail its plans for dealing with them only when it files its forma application.

Another uncertainty, which has already been discussed, is how soor southern Canada will need the gas that the Polar Gas project will deliver. I would appear that this need will not develop for a good many years. Ir addition, it is still uncertain how the Polar Gas and the Arctic Pilot project relate to each other. Both seem to be designed to carry much of the same Arctic Islands gas. The likely prior approval of the Pilot Project raises the question of the availability of this gas for the Polar project and the extending farther into the future of southern Canada's need for this gas. Promoters of the projects believe that they are complementary rather than competitive. They

rgue that the Pilot Project will be small scale, an interim measure primarily
) provide cash flow during the delay needed to implement the much larger
'olar Gas Project.[98] This is a plausible reading of the future, but so too is the
rediction that the Pilot Project will substantially weaken the case for the
onstruction of the Polar Gas project.

eaufort Sea Production

Iaving invested $850 million by the end of 1980 in its activities in the
eaufort Sea,[99] Dome Petroleum is applying its characteristic energy to
eveloping plans to bring into production some of the reserves it has
iscovered. Its approach involves the construction of artificial islands, 0.8 km
vide, called Arctic Production and Loading Atolls. Production wells will be
rilled on the perimeter of the atoll; the actual loading of special icebreaking
inkers will take place in the protected harbour within the atoll. The likeliest
ocation for the first of these islands would be Dome's Kopanoar well, about
20 km northwest of Tuktoyaktuk, which is estimated to tap between one and
wo billion barrels of recoverable oil. The cost of developing this geological
tructure is estimated to be $6 billion in 1980 dollars, about half the amount
eeded to supply an equivalent amount of oil from a tar sands plant,
ccording to Dome Petroleum's calculations.[100]

While a deposit the size of the Kopanoar find would be a large and
minently developable one in southern Canada, plans for production from
uch a site in the Beaufort Sea raise significant engineering and environ-
nental problems. While Esso Resources has constructed almost twenty
rtificial islands in water up to 20 m deep, these exploration islands are very
uuch smaller than a production island would be. It is not yet certain how
uuch additional stress a production island would have to face from the
normous pressure of the ice found in the Beaufort. Oil spills remain a
roblem for which an adequate technology has not yet been demonstrated to
xist. The Beaufort–Mackenzie Delta area is extremely important biolog-
cally: a spill could have serious consequences. In addition, it could create
nternational problems if it were carried by ocean currents to the shores of
ther northern countries. Local social and economic impacts are, as always, a
natter for concern. However, Dome has sponsored the Beaufort Sea
Community Advisory Committee as a communication line between itself
nd the local communities in the area and this device could help anticipate
nd relieve the pressures usually associated with non-renewable-resource
evelopment. In addition, Dome has actively promoted the employment of
ocal people on its projects. The experience gained on Dome-Canmar[101]
rillships and shore facilities should assist the local labour force to compete
ffectively for jobs at the production stage. However, while Dome thinks that
hat stage could come as early as 1985, it has not yet made a formal
pplication to government to proceed with it.

In addition to Dome, Esso Resources has been active in the Beaufort. In
980 it made what could well be a very large discovery at its Issungnak

artificial island. This find is sufficiently encouraging to lead Esso and i
partners in the project to invest another $30 to $35 million in addition to th
$70 million already spent to drill another well, which should give a cleare
picture of the extent of the deposit found.[102] However, until this informatio
is available, no decision on development planning will be made.

Northern Impacts

The preceding discussion has considered anticipated northern energ
projects primarily in the light of southern factors, because these factors wi
weigh most heavily in Ottawa's decision on the projects. At the same time
these projects represent one of two types of responses to the economic an
social problems of the North, or at least are argued by their proponents t
promise to alleviate these problems. In view of the debate about the economi
future of the North, the question is the extent to which these projects will i
fact help the North. This question cannot at present be answered because th
degree of industry and federal-government commitment to this goal has yet t
be determined. It is only possible to cite the historical record to date by way c
identifying the following key issues.

1. **Change** will undoubtedly accompany megaprojects and add to the socia
stress already so severe in the North. Government can choose among fou
responses to these stresses. The first is to refuse to permit a project to be buil
Ottawa did this in the case of the Mackenzie Valley gas pipeline, but onl
because of the availability of a politically easier alternative, which can b
argued to have threatened similar social problems in the area through whic
it is planned to pass.

The second approach is to make financial provision for the socia
disruption, in one of two ways. First, the project developer may be required t
set aside a sum of money to pay for the indirect—that is, social—costs of th
project. This approach was recommended for the Alaska Highway pipeline
but ultimately legislated in a fashion that makes it unclear whether the sun
involved is a payment over and above regular property taxes or simpl
replaces those taxes. The concept has not been suggested in the context of th
Norman Wells pipeline or any of the other projects being anticipated in th
North. The second financial response to social costs would be for Ottawa t
agree to share revenue gained from the project with the territory in which it i
located. The territory will have to pay the costs of servicing land; providin
clinics, schools, and other facilities; and generally extending its services
While the general funding it receives from Ottawa may expand to accommo
date these costs, adequate funding is not guaranteed. Ottawa's explicitl
funding of the costs of providing infrastructure for northern development
would ensure that northern governments do not suffer in order to provide fo
projects whose principal benefits are felt elsewhere. To date, Ottawa has no
adopted such a policy.

The third response to anticipated social problems is to require th proponent of the project to undertake measures to mitigate these difficulties. The terms and conditions of the Alaska Highway pipeline set by the Northern Pipeline Agency, to the extent to which they are respected, should ease much of the pressure. However, they unavoidably address only second-order questions. They cannot provide the guarantees that native people are seeking in the form of a fourth possible response by Ottawa to the increasing social pressure they will experience with development. This response, of course, is a prompt and just settlement of their aboriginal claims. The failure to reach claims settlements creates a dilemma for northern natives as they contemplate participating in or even merely supporting megaprojects. They may gain short-term material benefit, but at a long-term political and cultural cost. Until the settlement of the claims, this problem will be impossible to avoid.

2. **Resource revenues** could provide the financial base for more responsive and responsible government in the North. However, as has already been noted, Ottawa has not granted the territories significant revenues from this source.

3. **Employment** could be a major benefit of these projects in view of the growing unemployment problem anticipated as much more of the youthful northern population reaches working age. The record to date on northern employment has been mixed, but some encouraging signs can be noted. First, the government of the Northwest Territories has begun to assist corporations to prepare northerners for employment on their megaprojects and has achieved some success in this area. Second, rotation systems for northern workers are being handled with somewhat more flexibility, thus making them more attractive to native workers. These developments hold out some promise of increasing the proportion of northerners working on mega-projects, but there will undoubtedly remain room for improvement in individual projects. On a broader scale, means will have to be found for handling the social stresses created by employment itself—for example, the tensions of family separation when the father works at a distant site and the disruption of traditional collective social patterns by the individual pay-check.

4. **Increased northern business opportunities** ought to accompany mega-projects. In some instances they already have. For example, in 1979, Dome spent $16 million in the Northwest Territories.[103] However, to ensure such benefits from other megaprojects, they will have to be encouraged or required to depart from the common pattern of obtaining supplies directly from the South. In addition, business-development grants or loan guarantees may need to be given to northern firms to enable them to provide the services and goods required and the worker-training program must be expanded further.

5. **Environmental impacts** on the North could be severe. The performance of the government of Canada in protecting the northern environment leaves a great deal to be desired and it seems able to learn from its past mistakes only very gradually.

Conclusion

This catalogue shows that the northern benefits from northern megaprojects are at present more potential than real and that tangible social costs can be anticipated from them. This is not to say that the benefits will not be realized, but only that the question remains open. The uncertainty surrounding this aspect of these projects matches that surrounding the need to proceed on northern megaprojects at the pace urged by their promoters. From the North's perspective, this haste forecloses options deserving of consideration. Chapter 5 is devoted to the examination of these options.

Notes

[1]Energy, Mines and Resources Canada, *The National Energy Program, 1980* (Ottawa: Energy, Mines and Resources Canada, 1980), p. 3.

[2]Ewan Cotterill, "Resources and the Economy," *Proceedings of the Eighth National North Development Conference* (Edmonton, 1979), p. 15.

[3]*Musk-Ox*, No. 25 (1979), p. 104.

[4]*Canadian Annual Review, 1967*, pp. 195-96.

[5]Robert B. Gibson, *The Strathcona Sound Mining Project*, Background Study No. 4 (Ottawa: Science Council of Canada, 1978), p. 69.

[6]K.J. Rea, *The Political Economy of Northern Development*, Background Study No. 3 (Ottawa: Science Council of Canada, 1976), p. 69.

[7]Mel Foster, *The Development of Greater Self-Government in the Yukon Territory: Finance and Economics* (Whitehorse: Government of Yukon, 1979), p. 16.

[8]Gibson, *op. cit.*, p. 77.

[9]Foster, *op. cit.*, pp. 8-49.

[10]Foster, *op. cit.*, pp. 80-87, discusses the declining fortunes of this railroad. At the end of 1980 it was reported that the railroad was losing about $1 million a year and that its owners were considering closing it and concentrating on the firm's profitable trucking operations. *Edmonton Journal* (December 3, 1980), p. C20. If this were to happen, it would represent a final stage in the gradual triumph of truck transportation in the North over the earlier forms of water and railroad.

[11]Placer mining, as contrasted with other technologies, extracts gold from sand and gravel deposits by using large quantities of water to separate the heavier gold from the lighter sand and gravel.

[12]As Foster notes (*op. cit.*, p. 40) the MacTung mill site is actually located in the Northwest Territories and it remains to be seen which of the two territories will receive the royalties and the spinoff benefits the mine will provide.

[13]Government of the Northwest Territories, *Annual Report, 1979*, p. 27.

[14]*Ibid.*, p. 28.

[15]Gibson, *op. cit.*, presents a full and balanced review of the issues.

[16]See Chapter 2, pp. 72 and 73.

[17]The types of issues to be raised are examined for the Nanisivik case in Gibson, *op. cit.*, pp. 55-122, and for the Pine Point and Cyprus Anvil cases in E.B. Peterson and J.B. Wright, *Northern Transitions* 2 vols. (Ottawa: Canadian Arctic Resources Committee, 1978), pp. 65-150.

[18]Its position is set out in the *Report of Northern Mineral Advisory Committee* (Ottawa: DIAND, 1979).

[19]Rene Fumoleau, *As Long as This Land Shall Last* (Toronto: McClelland and Stewart, n.d.), p. 152.

[20]R.F. Keith *et al.*, *Northern Development and Technology Assessment Systems*, Background Study No. 34 (Ottawa: Science Council of Canada, 1976), p. 23. Additional sources of information on the Canol pipeline are P.S. Barry, "The Prolific Pipeline: Getting Canol Under Way," *Dalhousie Review*, Vol. 61, no. 2 (Summer 1976), and H.T. Udea *et al.*, *The Canol Pipeline Project: A Historical Review* (Cold Regions Research Engineering Laboratory Special Report 77-34, October 1977).

[21]Terence Armstrong, George Rogers, and Graham Rowley, *The Circumpolar North* (London: Methuen, 1978), p. 97.

[22]SCR 61-253.

[23]Douglas Pimlott, Kitson Vincent, and Christine McKnight (eds.), *Arctic Alternatives* (Ottawa: Canadian Arctic Resources Committee, 1973), pp. 337-39. It has been argued that Ottawa was so eager to encourage hydrocarbon development in the North that it allowed the oil industry to be the primary author of these regulations. See Andrew Thompson and Michael Crommelin, "Canada's Petroleum Leasing Policy—A Cornucopia for Whom?" (Ottawa: Canadian Arctic Resources Committee, March 1973), p. 1.

[24]H.W. Woodward, "Northern Canada: Resources and Resource Extraction—Policies of Development," in Nils Ørvik (ed.), *Policies of Northern Development* (Kingston: Group for International Politics, Department of Political Studies, Queen's University, 1973), p. 33.

[25]This episode is discussed in Edgar Dosman, "The Northern Sovereignty Crisis, 1968-70," in his edited volume, *The Arctic in Question* (Toronto: Oxford University Press, 1976). Dosman links the *Manhattan* incident to cabinet's decision in favour of continuing to support Panarctic in *The National Interest* (Toronto: McClelland and Stewart, 1975), p. 46.

[26]Douglas Pimlott, Douglas Brown, and Kenneth Sam, *Oil Under the Ice* (Ottawa: Canadian Arctic Resources Committee, 1976), pp. 12-15, chronicles the events leading to this approval.

[27]*The National Energy Program, 1980* (Ottawa: Energy Canada, 1980), pp. 42-45.

[28]The Progressive Incremental Royalty is explained in *The National Energy Program, 1980*, pp. 46 and 47. It should be noted that such a device may permit so many deductions in the calculation of the net profit subject to the royalty as to make it virtually impossible for Ottawa ever to realize any income from it. This point is explained in some detail in *Northern Perspectives*, Vol. 5, no. 4 (1977), pp. 3-4.

[29]*The National Energy Program, 1980*, pp. 39-41.

[30]The allowance on Canada Lands expired in April 1980; the rest of the allowance scheme will be phased out by 1985.

[31]Foster, *op. cit.*, p. 57.

[32]Charles R. Hetherington, "At the Turning Point—Toward a Viable Future," in *Proceedings of the Eighth National Northern Development Conference* (Edmonton, 1979), p. 130.

[33]*Edmonton Journal* (October 1, 1980), p. H1.

[34]Space considerations make it impossible for this book to describe this labyrinthine process in the detail it deserves. Fortunately, an excellent treatment of the subject is available in François Bregha, *Bob Blair's Pipeline* (Toronto: Lorimer, 1979). Useful additional detail can be obtained in Donald Peacock, *People, Peregrines and Arctic Pipelines* (Vancouver: J.J. Douglas, 1977) and Earle Gray, *Super Pipe* (Toronto: Griffin House, 1979). The former is sympathetic to Foothills Pipelines, while the latter favours Canadian Arctic Gas in its assessment of the northern-pipelines decision. Both condemn Justice Berger in no uncertain terms.

[35]"Some Questions about the Arctic Gas Pipeline" (Toronto: CAGPL, 1976).

[36]Keith, *op. cit.*, p. 25.

[37]Dosman's *The National Interest* is devoted to this theme.

[38]Bregha, *op. cit.*, p. 45.

[39]PC 1974-641 (March 21, 1974), reprinted in T.R. Berger, *Northern Frontier, Northern*

Homeland: The Report of the Mackenzie Valley Pipeline Inquiry 2 vols. (Ottawa: Supply and Services Canada, 1977), Vol. I, p. 205.

[40] Ottawa suggested to Justice Berger that he should submit his report no later than January 1975 (Bregha, p. 47).

[41] *Ibid*, pp. 47, 115-20.

[42] Peacock, *op. cit.*, p. 160.

[43] The flavour of this testimony is caught in Martin O'Malley, *The Past and Future Land* (Toronto: Peter Martin Associates, 1976), pp. 5-17, but the inquiry process also tended to polarize opinion and embitter relations between natives and non-natives in the Mackenzie Valley.

[44] The response of Canadian churches is sympathically described in Roger Hutchinson, "Native Peoples in a Technological Society: The Struggle for Self-Determination," a paper delivered to the XIVth Annual Congress of the International Association for the History of Religions (Winnipeg, 1980). It is less favourably described in Gray's *Super Pipe*.

[45] In 1980 renamed Nova, An Alberta Corporation.

[46] The project retained this name until 1977 when it was named the Alaska Highway Pipeline to avoid confusion about its relationship—there is none—with Alcan, the Aluminum Company of Canada.

[47] In 1977, the proposed diameter of the line was increased to 1220 mm.

[48] National Energy Board, *Reasons for Decision: Northern Pipelines*, 3 vols. (Ottawa: Supply and Services Canada, 1977), Vol. I, p. I-13.

[49] *Ibid*, p. I-176.

[50] Bregha, *op. cit.*, p. 110.

[51] Alaska Highway Pipeline Environmental Assessment Panel, *Interim Report to the Honourable Romeo Leblanc, Minister of Fisheries and the Environment* (Ottawa: Supply and Services Canada, 1977).

[52] Kenneth Lysyk, Edith Bohmer, and Willard Phelps, *Report of the Alaska Highway Pipeline Inquiry* (Ottawa: Supply and Services Canada, 1977), p. xvi.

[53] Bregha, *op. cit.*, pp. 129, 149.

[54] *Ibid*, pp. 157-59.

[55] Bill Webber *et al.*, "Presentation to the Commons Special Committee on Northern Pipeline Legislation on Behalf of All the Yukon Indian Associations." The draft bill is critiqued in more general terms in *Northern Perspectives*, Vol. 6, no. 2 (1978).

[56] Berger, *op. cit.*, Vol. II, pp. 97-98.

[57] *Ibid.*, Vol. I, pp. 22-27.

[58] "Presentation to the Commons Special Committee on Northern Pipeline Legislation on Behalf of All the Yukon Indian Associations" (Ottawa: 1978), p. 15.

[59] *Northern Perspectives*, Vol. VIII, nos. 7 and 8 (1980), p. 1. This sum includes a $3 billion cost-overrun fund and a $6 billion conditioning plant to prepare the gas for shipment.

[60] National Energy Board, *op. cit.*, Vol. II, p. 4-206.

[61] Bregha, *op. cit.*, p. 44.

[62] National Energy Board, *op. cit.*, Vol. I, p. 2-125.

[63] In May 1977, Foothills withdrew its application to build this line, largely because it had been superseded by the Alaska Highway–Dempster scheme, which was not weakened by the failure to expand the proven Mackenzie Delta gas reserves.

[64] They were not the only source of cost overruns. For example, litigation by environmental groups seeking to block the pipeline produced expensive delays.

[65] National Energy Board, *op. cit.*, Vol. II, p. 4-30.

[66] *Ibid.*, p. 4-30.

[67] Bregha, *op. cit.*, p. 186.

[68] Berger, *op. cit.*, Vol. II, p. 65.

[69] The Berger inquiries process and findings have been hailed by some observers and condemned by others. Favourable opinion can be found in Lewis Auerbach, "The Berger Report Sets an Important Precedent in Assessing Technology's Effects," in Keith and

Wright, *op. cit.*, and E.R. Weick, "The Assessment of Industrial Impact on the Northern Frontier," *Canadian Issues*, Vol. II, no. 2. The most common criticisms levelled are contained in L.C. Bliss, "The Report of the Mackenzie Valley Pipeline Inquiry, Volume One: An Environmental Critique," and "The Report of the Mackenzie Valley Pipeline Inquiry, Volume Two: An Environmental Critique," *Musk-Ox*, No. 21, and J.C. Stabler, "The Report of the Mackenzie Valley Pipeline Inquiry, Volume One: A Socio-Economic Critique," *Musk-Ox*, No. 20.

[70]Berger, *op. cit.*, Vol. I, p. 122.

[71]*Ibid.*, Ch. 10.

[72]*Ibid.*, p. 161.

[73]Lysyk, Bohmer, and Phelps, *op. cit.*, p. xiv.

[74]Dosman, *op. cit.*, develops this theme throughout its discussion of the 1968-75 period.

[75]*Ibid*, Ch. 5.

[76]*Ibid*, p. 201.

[77]Bregha, *op. cit.*, pp. 200-03.

[78]Berger, *op. cit.*, p. xiv.

[79]Gurston Dacks, "Lost in the Shuffle? Land Claims and the Alcan Pipeline," *Canadian Forum*, Vol. LVII, no. 673 (August 1977), p. 13.

[80]Dosman, *op. cit.*, pp. 25, 70, 75.

[81]Dosman, *op. cit.*, p. 157.

[82]Bregha, *op. cit.*, p. 190.

[83]*Edmonton Journal* (October 26, 1978), p. H7.

[84]*Ibid.* (July 18, 1980), pp. 1-2. The concluding chapter of Bregha, *op. cit.* (revd. 1981), details and analyzes the circumstances leading to the decision to permit construction of the prebuild, or phase one—as Foothills now refers to it.

[85]*Ibid.* (October 28, 1980), p. C11.

[86]*Northern Perspectives*, Vol. VIII, no. 2, offers a recent example.

[87]*The National Energy Program, 1980*, p. 44.

[88]*Edmonton Journal* (October 20, 1980), p. A12.

[89]*Edmonton Journal* (August 27, 1980), p. G3.

[90]*News/North* (October 31, 1980), p. M2.

[91]*Edmonton Journal*, (January 22, 1981), p. A3. See also *News/North* (January 23, 1981), pp. 1 and 2.

[92]Bregha, *op. cit.*, p. 159.

[93]*The Globe and Mail*, Toronto (October 16, 1980), p. B3.

[94]"Arctic Pilot Project Brochure" (Calgary: Petro-Canada, 1980), p. 16.

[95]These are summarized in *Arctic Seas Bulletin*, Vol. 2, no. 11 (November 1980).

[96]*News/North* (July 11, 1980), p. A8.

[97]*Oilweek* (March 31, 1980) report of speech by O.M. Kaustinen, Vice President, Engineering, Polar Gas.

[98]Gordon Jones, Executive Director, Canadian Arctic Petroleum Operators Association, presentation to "A Century of Canada's Arctic Islands 1880-1980," Symposium of the Royal Society of Canada (Yellowknife, August 1980).

[99]*Edmonton Journal* (October 30, 1980), p. F1. These activities are described in Dome Petroleum, *Five Years of Progress* (Calgary: 1980). Excerpts from this document discussing the use of tankers to ship Beaufort Sea oil are contained in *Arctic Seas Bulletin*, Vol. 2, no. 4 (April 1980). Environmental concerns raised by Dome's plans, particularly by the speed at which it wishes to implement them, are addressed in Vol. 2, no. 12, of the *Arctic Seas Bulletin*.

[100]*Alberta Report* (June 20, 1980), p. 17.

[101]Canmar is the abbreviation for Canadian Marine Drilling Ltd., Dome's wholly owned subsidiary that actually undertakes Dome's drilling program.

[102]*Edmonton Journal* (November 10, 1980), p. C17.

[103]Braden, *op. cit.*, p. 6.

5/The Economic Future: Renewable Resources

> Over the long term—that is, a period in excess of forty or fifty years—the value of food, fibre, power and other uses of renewable resources far exceeds that of mineral or non-renewable resource development.[1]

While this opinion may or may not accurately predict northern experience in the future, it at least casts doubt on the insistence of megadevelopers that the future of the northern economy is and ought to be dependent on the exploitation of non-renewable resources. In arguing the economic significance of renewable resources, it emphasizes such questions as the exact value of these resources, the nature of the competition for them, and how public policy protects them and regulates access to them.

The Value of Hunting, Fishing, and Trapping

While renewable resources are important, it is not at all clear how important. However else they may differ, authorities on the subject agree that there does not exist at present adequate information on the following basic features of the renewable-resource economy:[2]

1. The size of fish and animal populations.
2. The number of fish and animals currently harvested.
3. The actual weight of meat obtained from this harvest.
4. Reliable measures of the real economic benefits to native people of the harvest.[3]
5. The maximum sustainable yield of the harvest of the various types of fish, marine mammals, and animals harvested.
6. Techniques for increasing the sustainable harvest above current levels.

To these sources of uncertainty must be added conflicting interpretations of the health of the traditional economy—that is, the sum total of benefits that native people receive from it and the extent of their commitment to it. In the face of this uncertainty, two schools of interpretation have developed. They come into play whenever a megaproject is proposed for the North, with probably the most bitter and well-documented clash being the debate during and after the Berger Inquiry.

One school of thought argues that hunting, fishing, and trapping produce little economic benefit to native people. Members of this school argue that relatively few native people engage in either full-time or regular part-time trapping[4] and that the income they earn from both furs sold and all forms of meat obtained is relatively low. Those who hold this point of view assess the worth of food obtained on the basis of exchange value—that is, the price at which such food changes hands in northern communities. This is usually quite a low price because making food available to others in one's community frequently involves social as well as economic considerations, which lead the hunter to accept little more than token payment.[5] Second, standard accounting practice gauges the income from hunting, fishing, and trapping as net income rather than gross income—that is, deducting from the value of food and fur produced the cost of the weapons, shells, traps, gasoline, store-bought food, and other items needed to produce the food and furs. In the words of James Stabler, one exponent of this approach, "When *net* values are used—and this is the only methodologically acceptable procedure—the importance of fish and animal harvest [in the Mackenzie Valley] is greatly reduced."[6] Those who minimize the significance and potential of renewable-resource-based activities argue that the renewable-resource sector is too small to sustain the growing native population and that, in any case, young native people are uninterested in life on the land.[7]

The other school of thought—advocates of renewable resources as the basis of a viable northern economy—refute these assertions point by point. They include in their estimates of the number of trappers all those who consider themselves to be trappers, even though they may not be active in trapping in the year the count of trappers was taken. They also include those who earn only a small amount of money from part-time trapping because these sums of money may represent substantial additions to their total revenues and because even limited participation in trapping can fill an important cultural need. They argue that the basis for determining the worth of food harvested should not be exchange value, because it understates values for the reason suggested above. Instead, calculations should be based on replacement value, the cost of purchasing an equivalent amount of food in a local store. This calculation would produce a much greater value for the food harvest. This higher value, they argue, would remove much of the impact of the net-income argument, because it would produce a calculation of gross income substantially above costs of production.[8]

In reply to those who doubt the interest of native northerners and particularly young natives in the land, proponents of an enhanced renew-able-resource economy argue that the job preferences of young native people as expressed in surveys taken in the first half of the 1970s are not necessarily reliable indicators of sentiment in the 1980s. The "colonial mentality" of self-doubt and cultural denial among native people is giving way to an affirmation of cultural identity largely as a result of their increasing political organization, which is of quite recent origin. In addition, the promise of wage employment from megaprojects has not been realized for most northern native people.[9] Finally, the growth anticipated for the native population of the North promises that few native people will be able to rely on wage employment. Accordingly, most will continue to operate in a mixed economy in which they derive their income from seasonal employment, government transfer payments, and from hunting, fishing, and trapping.

In following this pattern they will continue to enjoy a particular benefit of native or "country" food, its high protein content as contrasted with meats available in North American supermarkets. For example, 100 g of uncooked ringed seal, walrus, and polar bear contain 32, 27, and 26 g of protein respectively. In contrast, chicken, the highest protein nonnative meat, contains 20 g, steak 16, and pork 12.[10] Thus, country food is not only inexpensive and preferred by native people, but also highly nutritious.

Possibly the greatest attraction for native people of even part-time hunting, fishing, and trapping lies in its cultural significance. The land and its wildlife occupy a central place in native religion. Hunting, fishing, and trapping put native people in that traditional context and reaffirm their place in the spiritual world. In this way, native subsistence hunting, fishing, and trapping differ from sport or commercial fishing and hunting, in that the latter have no religious significance.

Hunting, fishing, and trapping satisfy a number of additional psychological needs for native people. These activities link them with the succession of their ancestors who lived on the land and so build a sense of continuity with the past in which all human beings find psychological security. These activities also involve one of the few satisfying economic roles to which natives can plausibly aspire. Unemployment and welfare dependence are far from psychologically gratifying. However, the alternative of wage employment places the native worker in an environment that tends to be organized on the basis of alien assumptions in which he tends to occupy a subordinate position and in which he must cope with the expectation—either of his employer, foreman, non-native coworker, or himself—that he will fail, and in which, in any case, jobs are not readily available.

In contrast, hunting, fishing, and trapping, while hard and not particularly lucrative, are at least activities that native people control. The individual trapper decides when and how to trap. He can choose to trap with a partner, with members of his family, or alone. He can decide what equipment and supplies he needs to trap and how hard he ought to work on his trapline. In all of these decisions—while he must respect some governmental regulations, such as those pertaining to the registration and allocation of traplines, and economic realities—he need not submit himself to the authority of someone from another culture whose assumptions and values he only partially understands. In addition, the hunter or trapper approaches these activities free of the presumption that he may fail because he is ethnically unsuited for them. He may fail, but at least his failure is not racially preordained as it may appear to be in the case of wage employment.

Hunting, fishing, and trapping, then, are activities in which native people can take part free of the feeling of powerlessness and inefficacy that have made contact with white society so alienating for them. In this way, these activities are not only psychologically satisfying because they embody elements of tradition. More significantly, they are psychologically satisfying because they are controlled by the native person himself, and organized in a fashion that makes sense to him, not according to some alien logic.

Even if the native people do work for wages, part-time hunting, fishing, and trapping provide a balm for the alienation that employment often creates and in this way performs a function at least as important as its narrow economic function. Similarly, if they work in larger centres or megaproject sites, the opportunity to return to the land intermittently compensates for the strangeness of the surroundings in which they are employed. However native people spend the rest of their time, hunting, fishing, and trapping reinforce the sense of community among them because these occupations are central to their shared self-definition. Here culture reflects both economic and social structures. In the words of Peter Usher:

> If the land and its resources provide the economic basis of native society, the small communities and outpost camps provide the social basis of it, and indeed each is the precondition of the other. The small communities and camps are the hearth of native society; and economic development, if it is to benefit native people, must therefore be consistent with the viability and health of small community life.[11]

It may well be that forms of wage employment coupled with adequate job opportunities will outdate this assessment, but at the start of the 1980s, these seem distant prospects. Also, it must be recognized that Usher's description underplays the ill health of native society caused by the breakdown of small community and camp life. However, given that assimilation of native people into northern non-native society seems both unlikely and unattractive to most native people, regaining the values of native life seems to be the only approach to establishing a relationship between non-native and native that meets native needs. Only the kind of strengthened land-based economy Justice Berger so strongly endorsed is likely to secure these values by linking them in a living, functional way to native forms of income and economic activity. Other forms of income and work will be important, but because they do not hold out the same promise of sustaining native society and cultural values, because they are not native-controlled, and because their economic payoff is not at all certain, native people must rely on hunting, fishing, and trapping for cultural and social as well as some degree of economic sustenance.

While the native economy relies heavily on renewable resources for both subsistence and commercial uses, these resources are more and more attracting the attention of others, whose desires are increasingly coming into competition with those of the native people. Non-native sports hunters and fishermen resent their own access to game and fish being restricted while native people are exempt from limits because Ottawa grants them a virtually unlimited right to harvest wildlife for subsistence, although not commercial, purposes.[12] Northern sportsmen and the northern tourist industry, which would benefit from more generous game quotas to attract southerners, form a vocal lobby in the territorial capitals.

Commercial harvesting may reduce the stocks on which subsistence harvesting depends. Commercial fishing has not yet proven to be as serious a problem, as has been the case elsewhere in Canada. However, problems may well arise in the future: competition has in the past severely affected native trapping. Native trappers traditionally trapped only as many animals as was consistent with ensuring a continuing animal population and let areas "rest" by not trapping in them for a period of time, thus allowing the animal populations to increase. However, white trappers have tended to trap out areas completely, destroying the native economy dependent on them. It could be argued that instances of natives' overtrapping can be explained by the anticipation that whites will soon enter a trapping area and deplete it. In this way, both directly and indirectly, white commercial fur harvesting can destroy the native economy.

Environmentalists recognize that the Canadian North is one of the world's few remaining relatively unspoiled wilderness areas and are pressing for the creation of a system of parks and preserves to maintain the particular esthetic qualities of these rare environments. It is quite possible that native hunting, fishing, and trapping in any such preserves will be curtailed to some degree in order to reduce interference with the wildlife populations. Southern groups concerned about the cruelty of trapping practices may demand that native trapping methods be altered or may attempt to reduce the southern demand for the pelts the native economy produces. Finally, economic planners may wish to regulate the harvest of renewable resources to maximize their dollar value whether or not the means of attaining this goal are consistent with native practices.

To the competition from these groups, which value the renewable resources of the North, must be added the competition native people must face from a whole range of economic activities associated with the wage economy. Developers for whom the land represents not sustenance and identity but "overburden" cannot help but deplete stocks of fish and wildlife by their activities. Thus, their activities represent a claim on the renewable resources of the North, in that, to the extent that they reduce the quantity of these resources, there will be that much less for the native economy to harvest.

To the value of the wildlife harvest must also be added the income earned by the forestry industry in both territories.[13] While small in comparison to the mining and energy industries, forestry provides jobs to native workers in the Yukon and the Mackenzie Valley and offers some opportunity for seasonal

mployment to fill in the slack times in the annual cycle of wildlife
arvesting. Forestry, of course, can also jeopardize wildlife harvesting
ecause it degrades animal habitat, a possibility requiring that the needs of
1e forest industry be integrated into the total strategy for renewable-resource
1anagement.

Renewable Resources and Public Policy

The value of renewable resources to both native and non-native interests
oses a complex problem for the makers of public policy. First, they must
ecide what priority to attach to the values that the various groups with an
1terest in northern renewable resources press on them. In the case of native
unting, fishing, and trapping, policy makers must assess the potential
ontribution of these activities to the economic and social wellbeing of native
eople and must do so in the light of the options open to native people. In
ther words, they will have to choose between those who assert that native
eople have no option but to become increasingly dependent on wage
mployment and to subordinate their land-based activities, and those who
rgue that native people have no option but to base their future on an
nhanced renewable-resource harvest, supplemented but not superseded by
ther forms of income, including wage employment. To the extent that
olicy makers agree with the opinion of Justice Berger that renewable-
esource harvesting should form the basis of the native economy, they will
ave to determine how actively government policy should work to promote
1e development of this harvesting. At present there is great room for
1provement at the level of both the individual harvester and the land-based
onomy all told.

The Berger Report discusses this subject at substantial length[14] and it is
nly possible to briefly summarize Justice Berger's recommendations here. In
is view, the major problem facing the individual native hunter, trapper, or
sherman is a simple lack of cash. Land-based activities produce substantial
uantities of fur and food, but whatever is used for subsistence purposes
roduces no money, hence cannot contribute toward the payment of the costs
f equipping oneself to work on the land. To meet this problem—
articularly in the short run—may require that outside sources of cash be
1jected into the land-based economy. For example, floor prices for furs may
e set, grants and production subsidies given, and a form of unemployment
1surance be provided, all to stabilize and increase the cash income of native
ildlife harvesters. Possibly some of the cash payment of the native-claims
ettlements might be used to subsidize the activities of native hunters,
appers, and fishermen.

Berger emphasized that such sources of aid to individuals must be
1pplemented by measures to strengthen the land-based economy as a whole.
this economy could achieve a position of self-sufficiency, it would be better
1le to defend its worth from the arguments of megaproject developers that it

ought to be cast aside because it is moribund. Self-sufficiency would end dependence on external funding which inevitably brings external control with it. It would also reduce the feeling among natives that their economy and those who take part in it are judged as less than worthy by that part of society whose financial contribution now sustains them.

Self-sufficiency can be attained in several ways. The first is to increase production. For example, the Berger Report suggests that the Mackenzie Valley could sustain fur harvests twice those currently being taken and that there also exists substantial room for increased food production, particularly of fish.[15] The increased production of food could lead to an active commerce providing this food to settlements that at present cannot supply their needs for native food and accordingly have to rely on less satisfactory store-bought food. This is a possibility actively being studied for the eastern Arctic by the government of the Northwest Territories and the Inuit Development Corporation.[16] A second spur to self-sufficiency is to strengthen the whole range of secondary activities associated with fish and wildlife harvesting. Among the possibilities the Berger Report suggested are fur tanning, garment manufacturing, food processing, the processing of marine oils, handicrafts, tourism, and the management of renewable resources.[17] Not only would these activities add to the income derived from the renewable-resource side of the native economy, they would also meet the important criterion that they can generally be organized in small units and usually in community units. In this way they can be controlled locally by native people according to their practices for making decisions. This will reduce greatly the likelihood of their becoming alienated from these activities because they feel unable to control them.

Increases in harvesting and in processing the harvest will require active encouragement. One goal of native claims is to put into native hands the regulatory means and financial powers to provide this encouragement. However, whether it is native people themselves or government, some agency will have to address the problems that have plagued renewable-resource-based enterprises in the North. Berger summarizes these problems as including:

> . . . inexperienced or even incompetent management and personnel, failure to develop appropriate technology, poor quality machinery and facilities, inadequate maintenance, slow resupply, inadequate or insecure financing, lack of local involvement and control, improper understanding of the local situation, failure to take advantage of local expertise and skills, jurisdictional problems within governments, rapid turnover of administrative personnel in Ottawa or Yellowknife, bureaucratic red tape, and inability to make quick decisions and to take quick action.[18]

Clearly, what is involved here is a whole complex of problems that will require a variety of responses.

As Berger noted, policies of providing better and more stable incomes to individuals and strengthening local industries will only work if steps are aken to ensure the overall health of the renewable-resource-based economy. One such step is simply to develop the types of information needed to maximize the yield from this economy without harming it over the long run. A second such step would be for government to acknowledge—as the native claims seek—that the native peoples enjoy the right to fish and wildlife that akes priority over that of others who seek to press their claims for a share of hese resources. The native people need not monopolize them, but they must be assured sufficient supplies to sustain their economy. In Berger's words, his acknowledgement should extend to the recognition that:

> 22. Native people consider renewable resources, particularly fur, fish, game and timber, to be essential to their identity and their way of life. These resources must be the cornerstone of native economic development, and neither the initiatives nor the benefits can be appropriated by others. It follows that any attempt to develop these resources by means or programs that are non-native in design and execution are not only destined to fail in the long-run, but they will also generate resentment and hostility.
>
> 23. A proper role of government, whether federal or territorial, is to facilitate the availability of capital and of technical assistance to the people under its care. . . . If, however, funds continue to be made available, and programs continue to be developed and administered only under tight government control and regulation, then native people will be suspicious of both the motives and the benefits, and these programs will end in failure. The control and administration of such developments must lie in the hands of native people.[19]

natives must develop themselves not by ottawa

Finally, and possibly most important, government must decide whether the renewable-resource economy or the non-renewable-resource economy will receive top priority in the North. That such decisions are required is obvious when a megaproject is proposed. However, it is equally required when Ottawa comes to determine the regulatory regime that will govern exploration for and development of minerals and hydrocarbons. These regulations both determine the extent of non-renewable-resource-related activity on the land—as in the case of mineral exploration near Baker Lake—and influence the likelihood that megaprojects will be proposed. In addressing this question, Berger concluded that "the production and processing of renewable resources must be regarded positively as a desirable social and economic goal [and that] the critical thing is that priority be given to the strengthening of the renewable sector now."[20] Berger acknowledged that megadevelopment will take place, but urged that decisions on large-scale developments give full and fair consideration to the native economy and provide those active in it with effective means of influencing the decision-making process.

The Governmental Response

Berger's conclusion serves as a reminder of the variety of users who are competing with native people for access to renewable resources and thus of the complexity and political sensitivity of attempts to regulate activities affecting these resources and to divide the benefits to be derived from them. Not surprisingly, the range of governmental policies designed to respond to this situation is exceedingly broad. The policies themselves defy easy generalization because Ottawa is pursuing a variety of goals in the North and has created different types of policies with very different purposes in mind. In addition, jurisdiction over these policies is shared by three governments: wildlife management has become the responsibility of the territorial governments and responsibility for the management of land use through the administration of the Territorial Land Use Regulations is likely to be transferred to the territorial governments in the near future. Policies may not be clearly stated. They may fail to anticipate the special kinds of issues a particular megaproject application may raise. Finally, policy on many matters is currently in an evolutionary stage. For example, the powers of the Federal Environmental Assessment and Review Office may well increase as it comes to be more accepted—or less feared. Similarly, the settlement of native claims may establish new relationships and priorities affecting northern renewable resources. These conditions do not preclude the study of government policies on renewable resources; however, they do caution that these policies be recognized as both complex and changing.

1. Parks and Preserves

Because some areas of the North exemplify so magnificently the beauty and power of its landscape or contain rare land forms or important biological resources, they have been proposed or designated as parks or preserves. The most prominent of these sites are the four northern national parks administered by Parks Canada. The oldest of these parks—and largest at 45 000 km²—is Wood Buffalo National Park, established in 1922, which straddles the Alberta-N.W.T. border. Nahanni National Park, for which 4765 km² of land was set aside in 1971, became in 1978 one of the first two sites in Canada to be designated a World Heritage Site by the United Nations Educational, Scientific and Cultural Organization. This designation recognized the impressive Nahanni canyon, the 90 m high Virginia Falls and the wildlife abundance of the Park. The 21 470 km² Auyuittuq National Park on Baffin Island was created in 1972 because of its dramatic landforms showing the results of glacial action. Because of its remoteness it is not frequently visited, but its existence does guarantee the preservation in its natural state of a beautiful and rare form of Canadian landscape. Kluane National Park— which covers 22 015 km² of the mountains in the southwest corner of the Yukon—was proclaimed in 1976 and received World Heritage Site designation in 1979 because of its natural attractions, which include the largest non-polar glacial system in the world, its variety of vegetation communities, and its populations of rare animals.

In addition to these existing parks, six more sites are being considered as possible future National Parks.[21] (See Figure 5-1.) Of these, the Northern Yukon National Wilderness Park[22] is particularly interesting because it is seen as an important step in preserving the Porcupine caribou herd[23] and because it has aroused considerable controversy. In his Report, Justice Berger recommended the creation of such a park. Hugh Faulkner, then-Minister of Indian Affairs and Northern Development, followed up on this recommendation (which had also been made by others) in 1978 when he withdrew from further development all land in the Yukon north of the Porcupine and Bell Rivers. This decision, which prompted great unhappiness among mineral and oil exploration interests, paved the way for this 39 000 km² area's being declared a National Park or a national wilderness area, possibly in conjunction with an adjacent area in Alaska that the Porcupine herd occupies for part of its annual cycle. Together, the two areas would comprise the Arctic International Wildlife Range.

The International Biological Program,[24] which existed from 1964 to 1974, was created to identify areas of particular biological or physiographic importance in the hope of encouraging governments to set these areas aside

Figure 5-1
National Parks in the Yukon and Northwest Territories

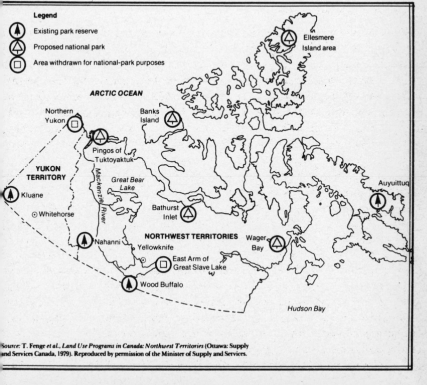

Legend

Existing park reserve

Proposed national park

Area withdrawn for national-park purposes

ARCTIC OCEAN

Ellesmere Island area

Northern Yukon

Banks Island

Pingos of Tuktoyaktuk

YUKON TERRITORY

Kluane

Great Bear Lake

Mackenzie River

Whitehorse

Auyuittuq

Bathurst Inlet

Nahanni

NORTHWEST TERRITORIES

Yellowknife

Wager Bay

East Arm of Great Slave Lake

Wood Buffalo

Hudson Bay

Source: T. Fenge *et al., Land Use Programs in Canada: Northwest Territories* (Ottawa: Supply and Services Canada, 1979). Reproduced by permission of the Minister of Supply and Services.

for conservation purposes. In 1975, the Minister of Indian Affairs and Northern Development gave approval in principle to the idea of ecological sites being designated in the North. Committees set up under the IBP have identified 152 such sites. While none of these sites has yet received formal ecological-site status, the Bracebridge-Goodsir site on Bathurst Island, also known as Polar Bear Pass, was approved in principle in 1978 and is likely to receive final approval in the near future.

The Northwest Territories contain three game preserves and four game sanctuaries;[25] the Yukon contains two preserves and two sanctuaries.[26] While there are no bird sanctuaries in the Yukon, sixteen migratory bird sanctuaries have been established in the Northwest Territories under the Migratory Birds Convention Act.[27]

2. The Regulatory Regime

While the granting of park or preserve status to areas of biological significance protects these sites, it can only be the beginning of a comprehensive approach to safeguarding the renewable resources of the North. More general protection is afforded through the acts of Parliament and the territorial ordinances that cover the entire area of the North, not merely the sites of greatest biological interest. The body of legislation that touches on environmental protection in the North is too substantial to describe in detail here, and accordingly only the most important acts will be described.[28]

Territorial Land Use Regulations

One of the legislative cornerstones of this protective structure is the Territorial Land Use Regulations first issued under the Territorial Lands Act in 1971 and amended in 1977.[29] These regulations are intended to limit the environmental damage caused by such land-use operations as driving large vehicles crosscountry, using explosives, drilling, earth moving, and establishing large camps or fuel-storage depots. Under the Regulations, anyone planning such operations must apply for a land-use permit. The DIAND Engineer designated under the Regulations can issue relatively promptly a Class B permit for smaller operations or a ("minor") Class A permit for larger but straightforward operations. Larger projects, if they are complex or raise important questions of policy, requiring a ("major") Class A permit, are referred to the Land Use Advisory Committee of the relevant territory. If a permit is granted, it is subject to a list of conditions relating to such aspects of the operation as:

> ... the location and area of lands that may be used; timing of operations; type and size of equipment that can be used in the land use operation; the type, location, capacity and operation of all facilities to be used; the methods to be followed for erosion and flood prevention; the handling of toxic material; the protection of wildlife and fisheries habitat; the protec-

tion of places of ecological, archeological, recreational or scenic value; methods for brush disposal . . .[30]

The permittee's compliance with these conditions is checked by means of regular visits by land-use inspectors.

The Territorial Land Use Regulations have proven a reasonably effective regime for managing many land-use operations, but they suffer from a variety of weaknesses. First, they do not cover some quite significant operations. While it is not reasonable that they should regulate each and every movement on the land, some sizable operations can be undertaken without having to come under the scrutiny of the Regulations. In addition, the Regulations do not cover operations in which the Minister has disposed of surface rights.[31] For this reason, mines and energy projects do not come under the Regulations. These activities are regulated by other pieces of legislation, but there is no guarantee that these acts enforce the same degree of environmental care required under the Regulations. In the Yukon, for example, the Yukon Quartz Mining Act provides for virtually no environmental protection.[32] The Yukon Placer Mining Act presents a more complicated case because the sections of it dealing with water management have been superseded by the Northern Inland Water Act. Still, in the judgment of the author of the Yukon *Land Uses Programs in Canada* study,[33] traditional and environmentally damaging approaches to water use commonly continue among Yukon placer-mining operations.

A second problem is the degree of rigour of the application-review process; applications are virtually never denied. Departmental officials justify this record by noting that the review process itself reduces the likelihood of unsatisfactory applications coming forward for final judgment. Applicants either amend their proposals to meet departmental standards or, if they are unwilling to do so, withdraw their applications if they are unlikely to be approved. Whatever the validity of this explanation, the staffing of the land-use permit system leaves room for doubt about its rigour. The Land Use Advisory Committees consist solely of public servants; hence, they deny active representation to private groups and individuals who may be particularly interested in environmental protection. This representation is also denied to mining, oil, and other development interests, but their views are amply represented by the large proportion of public servants on the Committees who come from departments of government committed to non-renewable-resource development. While the Committees should represent development concerns, they should also display a commitment to environmental protection. This commitment would be more certain if the Committees contained more representatives from the Department of Fisheries and Oceans and, indeed, if the whole process were administered by that department rather than by DIAND, which has a substantial interest in non-renewable-resource development.

Effective environmental protection is made all the more problematic because the Regulations give the Land Use Engineer a great deal of discretion in attaching conditions to permits and in deciding which applications to refer to the Land Use Advisory Committee. While such discretion builds flexibility into the process, it equally reduces the guarantees of environmental protection that the regulations should provide.

Arctic Waters Pollution Prevention Act

This act[34] was passed in 1970 primarily as a response to the attempted voyage through the Northwest Passage of the American tanker *Manhattan*. At the time, Ottawa felt itself under great pressure to affirm its sovereignty over these waters and the vehicle it chose for the task was both necessary and as inoffensive as possible: pollution-prevention legislation. The intent of the act is to regulate the design and operation of Arctic shipping and waste disposal in Arctic waters, which are defined to include the land areas that form the Arctic Ocean watershed. The act prohibits the deposit of waste except with special permission; makes polluters liable for the costs of cleanup operations and for losses caused by acts of pollution and requires that plans for operations that could lead to water pollution be reviewed in advance; has led to the establishment of Arctic Waters Pollution Prevention Regulations which, among other provisions, can be used to shut down offshore drilling operations if pollution emanates from them; and provides for inspection of potential pollution-producing activities by pollution-prevention officers.

Northern Inland Waters Act

This act,[35] which dates from 1972, and the regulations promulgated under its authority "provide for the conservation of inland water resources and the maintenance of water quality standards through control of the uses to which fresh water may be put in the North."[36] Anyone seeking to use water for other than domestic or emergency purposes must obtain a licence from the Yukon or Northwest Territories Water Board. In deciding on applications, the Boards can approve the deposit of waste in waterways, apply a range of conditions to proposed water uses, and demand a security deposit from water users. The act provides for inspection of water-use operations and for the shutting down of operations that violate the conditions of their permits. While this very rarely occurs, other legal options under the act can have the same effect,[37] and a variety of options are available for dealing with less serious problems. The Water Boards differ from the Land Use Advisory Committees, in that private individuals as well as governmental officials sit on them and in that they are required to hold public hearings on all applications. However, it has been argued that these hearings need to be improved by the provision of more information and earlier notification of applications to the public so that interested parties will be better able to prepare to take part in the hearings, which in turn will seem less like a closed operation.[38] It has also been argued, as with the Land Use Regulations, that

DIAND's primary responsibility for the administration of this act creates conflicts of interest with its development role and has led to situations in the past in which the public interest in environmental protection may not have been well served.[39]

The Fisheries Act

This act, as amended in 1977,[40] is designed to protect fish—taken to include crustaceans, shellfish, and marine mammals—fish habitat, and fishing grounds by imposing fines of up to $10 000 or jail sentences of up to two years if a deleterious substance is allowed to enter a body of water that supports marine life. The Fisheries Act has been an important piece of legislation because, of course, almost all bodies of water support some degree of marine life. This fact gives the Fisheries Act as broad a coverage as the Northern Inland Waters Act. However, in contrast to that act, the Fisheries Act has been tested in court on many occasions and accordingly prosecutors tend to bring charges under it rather than under the less-tested Northern Inland Waters Act.[41] This practice has made the act a significant deterrent to carelessness by such northern-development operations as pipeline construction, onshore and offshore oil drilling, and all types of mining.

The Canada Oil and Gas Drilling Regulations

These regulations[42] set standards for a variety of aspects of drilling operations, including environmental protection measures, require a review of proposed drilling programs, and impose a particularly stringent review for offshore drilling activities. These provisions are all to the good, but may not produce the desired effect if, as has appeared to be the case in the past, Ottawa cannot bring the manpower to bear to effectively oversee the drilling activities undertaken under the authority of these and other regulations.[43]

Other Legislation

In addition to the above pieces of legislation, environmental protection in the North is sought by means of a variety of federal acts that apply throughout Canada. This legislation includes the Clean Air Act, the Environmental Contaminants Act, the Canada Water Act, the Ocean Dumping Control Act, and the Migratory Birds Convention Act. In addition, several territorial ordinances covering matters such as wildlife management, public health, forest protection, and environmental quality offer degrees of protection for the natural environment.

All this legislation arms government with a full arsenal for the protection of the renewable resources of the North. However, this fact does not by itself guarantee that the northern environment will in fact be adequately protected. Indeed, there are too many examples in which federal government authorities have used the large discretionary powers they enjoy under the legislation to approve activities that jeopardized or actually damaged the natural environment.[44] While this history proves the academic point that legislation by itself is no safeguard without consistent and effective application, far more relevant is the fact that the northern environment remains in jeopardy not only from the megaprojects planned for it, but also from the day-to-day administration of environmental protection legislation in a myriad of cases—each of which is relatively small, but which taken together can result in substantial environmental damage.

3. The Environmental Assessment and Review Process

The legislation and regulations discussed above cover activities whose size and anticipated impacts are less than those associated with megaprojects. It has come to be recognized that megaprojects require a special process of review so that their implications can be considered publicly and in a single forum to avoid the duplication of effort and waste of time likely to occur if they were scrutinized by a more fragmented review process. It has also been recognized that ideally this consideration should occur as early as possible to avoid the making of premature commitments and to permit the results of the environmental review to be available at the early stages of planning, before crucial and irreversible decisions are taken.

In December 1973, the federal cabinet created the Environmental Assessment and Review Process[45] (EARP) to begin to deal with these problems. The process begins when a department or agency of the federal government—this includes the territorial governments, which come under DIAND—assesses the environmental consequences of projects for which it is responsible. These projects may be ones that it is itself undertaking, such as construction of a hydro project by the Northern Canada Power Commission, or they may be proposed by a private interest to a federal department. An example would be the Alaska Highway pipeline or the Arctic Pilot Project. The department may reach one of three conclusions:

1) There are (a) no anticipated adverse environmental effects associated with the project or (b) the anticipated environmental effects are known and are not considered significant.
2) The nature and scope of potential environmental effects cannot be readily determined during preliminary screening.
3) The anticipated adverse environmental effects are considered to be significant and the project requires a formal environmental review by the Department of Fisheries and the Environment.[46]

If Decision 1 is reached, the project will proceed subject to normal regulatory requirements but without any further reference to EARP. If Decision 2 is reached, an Initial Environmental Evaluation (IEE) of the impact of the project is prepared by or for the initiating agency to give it enough information to decide. If it subsequently decides that impacts are not significant, the project proceeds. If the impacts are anticipated to be major, the result is the same as if Decision 3 had been reached; an Environmental

Assessment Panel composed usually—but not always—of public servants is appointed to evaluate the environmental impacts of the project.

Its first act is to produce guidelines for an Environmental Impact Statement (EIS), "a detailed, documented assessment of the environmental consequences associated with the project . . . prepared in accordance with the guidelines issued by the Panel."[47] This statement is intended to be a more elaborate and rigorous document than the IEE. The EIS provides the focus for hearings at which public reaction to the proposed project is obtained. After this exercise, the panel prepares a report for the Minister of Environment Canada. The report may recommend approval for the project, approval conditional on its being modified or rejected. The Minister and the minister of the initiating department then make two decisions. The first is whether to accept the recommendations of the panel. The second is whether to make its report public. If they disagree, the dispute will have to be resolved in the cabinet itself.

The EARP process has attracted criticisms.[48] First, the process depends on the initiating department to determine whether a project is likely to involve significant environmental impacts. Such a judgment will be inescapable in some cases, but others may be less clearcut and the incentive to avoid the delay and possible frustration of one's wishes by submitting them to another department's scrutiny may persuade a department that the impact of a project is, after all, not sufficient to merit its submission to EARP. For example, the federal Department of Energy, Mines and Resources has not submitted the drilling activities in the waters off Labrador to an EARP study, although DIAND felt that the similar drilling program proposed for the South Davis Strait and Lancaster Sound required scrutiny by EARP.[49] It has been argued that the experience to date has been that federal departments have not shirked their responsibilities under EARP.[50] However, this diligence does not provide a guarantee for the future; should the Department of Fisheries and Oceans and a sponsoring department disagree over whether a proposed project should be subjected to an EARP review, the dispute would be settled at the level of cabinet, where the Minister of Fisheries and Oceans is invariably in a very weak position.[51]

Second, the IEE and the EIS are prepared by the initiator of the project and not by an agency that is both independent and committed to environmental protection. As a result, it is frequently the case that the proponent has more information about the ecological systems and their reaction to the proposed development than does the Department of Fisheries and Oceans, which accordingly is in a poor position to challenge unwarranted assertions in an Environmental Impact Statement. An EARP panel can challenge an EIS as insufficient, but it may find—as in the case of the Alaska Highway pipeline— that such an action simply limits its role in the ultimate decision. It can also challenge errors in an EIS, but may not catch all cases of exaggeration and understatement. In this way, the documentation aspect of EARP can limit its success as an instrument for environmental management.

Third, the members of EARP panels are in most cases civil servants who are seconded from their departments for the life span of the panel. While their primary responsibility during this time is to the panel, it is very difficult for them to act in a truly independent fashion. They have assimilated the general values of the public service from which they have been drawn, which may now lead them to interpret the public interest in the case under study in the way they might have, had they not come from this background. They also recognize that they will return to the public service on completion of their task and, while acting with integrity, may not wish to create problems for their colleagues and superiors on questions that involve subjective judgment calls. Even if they withstand the pressures on them to produce politically acceptable advice, the fact of their being public servants will make it appear that their work lacks the independence that should characterize a proper environmental review, thereby undermining its credibility.

Fourth, public participation in EARP is not as full or as guaranteed as it might be. The Federal Task Force on Environmental Impact Policy and Procedure, whose 1972 Report led to the creation of EARP,[52] emphasized the need for public participation by means of four arguments:

(1) Affected persons likely to be unrepresented in environmental assessment and decision processes are provided an opportunity to present their views.
(2) Members of the public may provide useful additional information to the decision-maker, especially when values are involved that cannot easily be quantified.
(3) Accountability of political and administrative decision-makers is likely to be reinforced if the process is open to public view. Openness puts pressure on administrators to follow the required procedure in all cases.
(4) Public confidence in the reviewers and decision-makers is enhanced since citizens can clearly see in every case that all issues have been fully and carefully considered.[53]

However, public hearings only appear in an EARP review if the ministers of Fisheries and Oceans and the initiating department permit them to. EARP does not encourage and assist residents of local communities—those most immediately affected—to comment on proposed projects. Public access to the information needed to prepare a submission to an EARP panel is limited; there is no requirement that the studies on which an EIS is based be made available for public scrutiny; nor is there a clear and compelling requirement regarding the amount of information about the project that must be made public. Moreover, subject to the discretion of the two ministers involved, even the guidelines to the preparation of the EIS and the EIS itself may be kept secret. As if those wishing to respond to proposals placed before EARP are not sufficiently hampered by the lack of information on which to base a response, they are further limited by the fact that EARP makes no provision for funding the preparation of briefs by groups wishing to appear before it. Justice Berger recognized that the cost of participating in a relevant fashion in a hearing would be prohibitive for many of the people and groups most directly affected by the proposed project. By ignoring this reality, the format of EARP discourages public participation and reinforces the image that it is a closed process.

A fifth problem with EARP is its lack of clout. EARP panels cannot subpoena witnesses or documents, cannot force applicants to prove statements contained in their application, and may not be able to obtain important governmental documents relating to the application they are considering.[54] These weaknesses greatly impair EARP's rigour as a review process. The report of an EARP panel is not policy, but rather only advice to the minister, who is free to ignore it if he or she wishes and who may be overruled if the initiating minister can make a convincing case to cabinet. The whole EARP mechanism is tenuous because it lacks a legislative basis. Because it was created by Order in Council rather than by Act of Parliament, it can be modified, suspended, or terminated without any public debate or advance warning.

Finally, EARP is a weak instrument of environmental protection, not only because of its lack of power, but also because of its narrow scope. Because it must examine projects submitted to it, it does not necessarily consider a full range of alternatives to such projects and in this way may not be able to propose the environmentally best project for the circumstances. In addition, there is no requirement that FEARO (the Federal Environmental Assessment and Review Office) prepares in advance for anticipated proposals in order to prevent situations arising in which it must defer to a sponsoring department because of a lack of information. Even more important, since it only considers projects one at a time, the combined impacts of several projects are not likely to command its attention. Particularly when one project itself involves tolerable environmental impact but is likely to lead to others—as in the case of the Arctic Pilot Project—the cumulative impacts of all of them should be weighed or the North could suffer what has been termed "destruction by insignificant increments."[55] EARP tends not to take the big picture into account.

An EARP Scorecard

EARP's structural flaws reflect the fact that Ottawa ranks environmental protection below a variety of other goals such as energy development and management of the economy. In the context of these priorities, FEARO has struggled to establish itself and has scored some successes. Its rejection of a 1977 proposal by Norland Petroleum to drill in the extremely sensitive Lancaster Sound region and the acceptance of its advice by the minister established some credibility for it in the North, as did its refusal to be completely stampeded by time constraints in its examination of the Alaska Highway pipeline proposal in the same year. In 1980, it established a

Beaufort Sea office in Vancouver to develop a basis of expertise in advance of anticipated proposals for oil and gas developments in that area. Its recommendations have also led to the initiation of a regional planning study of Lancaster Sound. Both of these steps should greatly improve its ability to handle development proposals and reduce criticism about its competence in dealing with specific applications. Finally, FEARO is actively promoting in Ottawa changes in its terms of reference that would close some of the loopholes identified above. The foremost of these loopholes would be to replace the principle of departmental self-assessment with a system by which FEARO itself decided whether the likely impacts of a proposed project were great enough to merit the project's being subjected to an EARP review.[56] Another is to provide funding to people wishing to participate in EARP hearings.[57]

While these developments demonstrate a great deal of commitment by FEARO's staff, they do not signal a significant change in FEARO's weak political position or a willingness to take a strong stance against a project that seems to enjoy the cabinet's favour. For example, the EARP report on the Arctic Pilot Project, released late in 1980, identifies a variety of unanswered questions about the environmental impact of the project. However, it gave its approval, asserting that "major impacts can be mitigated." Given the lack of information available at the time, this conclusion should at least have been presented as a hope rather than a prediction, particularly since it was based in part on the assumption that new scientific information will be developed before the project actually begins operations and will resolve some of the potential environmental problems. This type of congenial assumption would have more appropriately come from the proponent of the project rather than from the one body that should have been particularly cautious about assessing future impacts. The Report also examined the proposal as an isolated project rather than applying Justice Berger's approach of considering the cumulative impact of the range of future projects that the approval of the Pilot Project would encourage. In this sense, the EARP Panel committed the kind of error of narrowness for which the EARP process has consistently been criticized.[58]

Environmental-impact assessment in the North is a complex undertaking. Basic knowledge about ecological systems is usually lacking, as is an understanding of how the interrelationships that make up the systems will be affected by the intrusion of a new force or set of forces associated with a megaproject. Even if this information were available, it would not automatically lead to an acceptable evaluation of proposals because the tradeoffs between costs and benefits are questions of value, not of fact. There is no single answer to the question of how much environmental degradation should be tolerated in order to gain a certain additional supply of energy. In its report on the Arctic Pilot Project, the EARP panel seems to have made this judgment call—as it would have to in order to fulfill its mandate. However, the answer it provides seems to lie closer to the interests that cabinet has indicated it has in such projects and farther from the special commitment to environmental protection that should be what EARP is all about. Possibly EARP has little room to manoeuvre when considering energy megaprojects in the scarcity-conscious 1980s. However, if that is the judgment of its officials, then it can be effective in the less politically sensitive cases but cannot hope to be more than a marginal force for environmental protection.

4. Comprehensive Land-Use Planning

In creating EARP and an array of specific pieces of legislation, Ottawa has committed itself to a regulatory approach to protecting the northern environment. While this approach does set standards and discourage more extreme abuses, it is a weak and partial response to the challenge of protecting the natural resources of the North and allocating them among competing uses in the most desirable manner. A regulatory regime is almost by definition reactive, in that it usually does not come into action until private developers present proposals. This gives them and not the government the initiative in land-use planning. The decisions that result from these applications when taken together comprise a hodgepodge of *ad hoc* judgments. The total result may be unsatisfactory because each decision was taken without much consideration of its impact on the overall pattern of northern land use.

In addition, decisions may come to be applied far afield from the area where they were intended to be applied. For example, Dome-Canmar was first given permission to drill in the Beaufort Sea on the basis of likely environmental impacts in the areas in which they were proposing to drill. Their more recent holes have been located quite a distance from their first drill sites, but have been authorized on the basis of the earlier environmental work rather than on evidence about the present working locations.[59]

Further severe problems arise because government frequently lacks the scientific information to judge the impacts of proposed developments and because the regulatory processes as they are currently structured do not encourage interested individuals and groups to come forward with their points of view, which could play an important role in placing proposed developments in a clearer context. This criticism is particularly important in terms of socioeconomic factors because the regulatory process does not guarantee that the human values involved here will be fully considered. For their part, prospective developers criticize the regulatory process because it involves a substantial degree of uncertainty about the fate of their proposals. They feel that a system with clearer ground rules would reduce the risk involved in spending large sums of money on development applications and would encourage more developers to bring them forward. They also argue that the current system involves an excessive "regulatory lag," which adds greatly to the cost of making development proposals.[60]

An answer to many of these concerns is to adopt a policy of comprehensive land-use planning, which would set about to recognize that, in the words of John Naysmith, there is "an increasing awareness of the composite value of northern lands, including associated renewable as well as non-renewable resources, and a growing demand for rights to use the land for a variety of purposes. . . ."[61] Naysmith argues that this development will become more intensive with the passage of time and that it requires a comprehensive land-use planning process that "takes into account the composite value of northern land and incorporates a course of action for guiding and determining decisions respecting the allocation of land for various uses . . . based first on a consideration of the natural capability and limitations of the land."[62]

While many approaches can be adopted in designing such a process, the approaches to process usually involve certain common elements. The first is an extensive inventory of the biological and physical natures of the area under consideration, including existing uses, ownership, permit, and tenancy rights. The second is to identify the uses likely to follow from the nature of the area and the values that all of the parties interested in the land attach to it. A third is to allocate the land into a variety of categories of use appropriate to its nature and to the values attached to it. For example, Naysmith suggests four categories.[63] Occupancy-use areas would include farms, residences, settled areas, and business sites in and near settled areas. Integrated-use areas would include forests, recreational wilderness, territorial parks (which are chosen more for their recreational than for their ecological significance), and lands particularly suited for hunting and trapping. Natural and scientific areas would include the parks under the Parks Canada program, such as natural parks, natural landmarks, wild rivers, and marine parks; historic, archeological, and ecological sites; and key wildlife areas. Finally, extensive-management areas would be the likely locations of megaprojects related to subsurface resources. The fourth element in the process, which presumably would be found at all stages of it, is a citizen-involvement component. It should not only obtain the best possible factual information and find the balance that best accommodates the divergent wishes of those involved, but also—and more importantly—should enhance their understanding of the logic and fairness of the process and their commitment to the resulting plan. For this reason, any plan should be flexible enough to accommodate changes in values or available information. The plan should confirm rights on the land and direct prospective developers of the land by identifying those areas in which developments are more likely to be approved, thereby reducing the uncertainty that developers now feel as they try to anticipate the response of the regulatory process to their proposals.

The federal government has moved tentatively in the direction of comprehensive land-use planning. However, its efforts have yet to bear fruit and the record to date makes it less than certain that they will ultimately yield bountiful harvest. Between 1975 and 1977 an unsuccessful attempt was made to develop a Mackenzie Delta Regional Plan.[64] Since then, planning exercises, which are still going on, have been mounted for the Tuktoyaktuk Peninsula and the Baker Lake area. In addition, the Lancaster Sound Regional Study was initiated in 1979. A draft Green Paper on Lancaster Sound, released early in 1981, contains much excellent information on the environment of the Sound and on potential conflicts between competing uses of the Sound and poses questions that must be considered if the competition between various uses is to be regulated in a coherent fashion. However, the Green Paper is disappointing because it goes no farther than this, its authors referring to use it as a springboard for public discussion. This book has argued that public participation is highly desirable, but not at any price. The lack of conclusiveness of the Green Paper suggests that the process leading to the production of a firm policy on Lancaster Sound will take so long that Ottawa will have made several crucial decisions before the policy intended to guide these decisions is in place.

The early exercises in comprehensive land-use planning represent first steps; as a result, they show particularly clearly the problems of land-use planning as an approach to environmental protection. The basic reality is simply that the North is too huge an area to study in the depth required for a proper planning exercise. Such an effort would be prohibitively expensive and would exhaust the human resources of government, industry, northern peoples, and environmental-protection interest groups. Even studies for relatively limited purposes may not be adequately supported or comprehensive enough. For example, the Eastern Arctic Marine Environmental Study (EAMES), initiated by Ottawa in 1977 to obtain enough environmental information to judge drilling applications on a regional basis, has been criticized officially as inadequate.[65] If comprehensive planning is going to occur, it will have to evolve over a period of many years. In the meantime, unavoidably, planning exercises are done only for areas of immediate development potential. Therefore, again, the industry's priorities take the lead: studies come to be defined in terms of industrial interest rather than the public interest. However, even putting these serious problems aside, comprehensive planning exercises do not guarantee a satisfactory plan for environmental protection: success in the early stages of the process does not guarantee success later on. The production of land-use-related data is important, but it may not lead to agreement on the questions of value that arise when the time comes to interpret the data. Land-use decisions, in the last analysis, are political: political factors may produce a plan that some of the parties affected reject or may prevent any plan from taking shape. Alternatively, a plan may be created, then exceptions may be made in order to accommodate the needs of a major resource developer.

These possibilities explain why comprehensive land-use planning is increasingly coming into question in the North. Those groups—particularly

native people—who feel threatened and politically weak are increasing
interpreting land-use planning exercises as just another vehicle for th
implementation of southern-oriented programs or projects. They fear th
land-use planning will only be initiated in circumstances in which fund
mental policy decisions precede and constrain the planning process. Fo
example, the Mackenzie Delta Regional Plan anticipated that natural-ga
wells and a gas-gathering system would be constructed in the Delta, a
assumption that soured many native people on the exercise. The pla
resulting from such a study might well have the consequence of rationalizin
a policy that native people feel runs counter to their interest. For instance,
may merely recommend ways of mitigating the destructive consequences (
an undesirable development because it is not empowered to recommen
rejection. Indeed, the whole process might be undertaken to provide th
appearance of official concern in order to still the controversy surroundin
the announcement of a project. Many native people feel that participation i
this type of process is simply an exercise in co-opting that allows th
initiators of the process—or the more senior policy makers who have seen th
public-relations potential of a planning process to which their subordinate
are sincerely committed—to claim that the final plan meets native nee
because native people participated in its development. This possibility ha
led native people to question the legitimacy of comprehensive land-us
planning. Doubting its legitimacy and uncertain of the uses to which the
contribution may be put, native people may shun the planning process. T
the extent that they do, however, the expert knowledge they—in many case
alone—possess about renewable resources and their harvesting will not for
part of the information base on which the plan rests. The plan will therefor
be less sound and less credible to the native people, regardless of the
opinions about its legitimacy. Of course, a plan whose legitimacy an
credibility are suspect is unlikely to possess the authority to command respec
and voluntary compliance with the management regime it proposes.

The problem is a difficult one because it ultimately turns not on th
question of the viability of planning theory but on the question of powe
Planning is a tool: it has little power in and of itself; rather, it relies on th
power and authority of those who implement it and sanction its implementa
tion. So long as the motives of those who control planning in the North toda
are suspect by native people, planning itself will be suspect. For the nativ
people, although of course not necessarily for northerners or southerner
with interests in the North, the answer to the problem is to vest authority fo
land-use planning—and for the implementation and administration of th
plan—in the historic regulators of northern land use—the native people.

Native Claims as a Vehicle for Environmental Protection

Most of the northern native claims have argued that control over all of th
affected territory or at least over wildlife and the environment be vested in th

ative groups that are to be created as part of the claims settlements. They ave argued that such an approach would place land-use decision making in he hands of a single body, comprised of people who have traditionally cared or the land, or who—at the very least—could not produce a worse record han Ottawa has. In the native peoples' view, native customary law has roven itself to be the best available renewable-resource management nechanism; the failure of whites to acknowledge this fact is to the natives nore a consequence of ethnocentric science and a need to rationalize the orm of growth through technology than a reflection of the history of the North.

For reasons already discussed, it would be against Ottawa's interest to ccept such a line of argument. However, some modifications of it may be olitically more viable. For example, joint native–territorial government gencies might be created to negotiate plans to cover certain types of land use nd to manage wildlife resources, which, of course, migrate through what ill be both native and non-native lands. Out of this type of structure might volve a form of partial land-use planning in the North.

Conclusion

Comprehensive land-use planning, enforced through a regulatory structure, vould provide the surest approach to environmental protection. Such a egime should differ in a variety of ways from that currently in operation. First, it should recognize the rights of the native people, who are directly ffected by proposed developments in the North; ultimately, the attainment f this objective turns on the just settlement of the northern native claims.

Second, land-use decisions should be based on a set of fundamental rinciples established in advance of consideration of particular applications. The existence of such principles should reduce the tendency to *ad hoc* lecision making and to granting of approval in principle to projects, a ractice that creates such a presumption in favour of the project in question hat it may be very difficult politically for government to turn down the roject, even if it has failed to satisfy the conditions attached to the earlier artial approval.

Third, these principles should be informed by scientific information on he northern environment that has been produced by properly designed tudies, rather than the hasty and all-too-often project-related research that as tended to be the norm.[66] Also of great importance is the need to involve ative people more directly in the design of research. This involvement vould contribute to making research priorities more relevant to their needs. t would permit scientists to benefit from the intimate native knowledge of he North. It may also dispel the native people's suspicion that research indings might form part of the basis of southern society's assault on orthern native life, while at the same time it may sensitize scientists to the olitical context in which their studies proceed.

Fourth, the process should provide for an adequate process of publi
participation. Such a process would require the fullest possible disclosure t
the public of information concerning the project, public-informatio
programs in the communities most affected, funding for those wishing t
make presentations or to question those bringing forward developmer
applications, and enough notice to give them time to prepare properly. It i
fashionable in industry and some government circles to condemn publi
hearings. However, they have proven valuable in identifying seriou
deficiencies in projects that would have been much more expensive c
environmentally damaging had their problems not been brought to light i
the course of public hearings.[67]

Sixth, a single agency should be established to be responsible for judgin
northern megaproject proposals so that the confusion surrounding th
currently fragmented process can be significantly reduced.

Finally, the entire process needs to be enshrined in legislation so tha
fewer of the protections it offers rely on official discretion rather than on lega
guarantees.

Ultimately, however, the legislative framework involved is a les
important question than the degree to which governments are committed t
environmental protection. To date, Ottawa has not demonstrated grea
commitment to protecting the natural heritage of the North. It has no
allowed the Department of Fisheries and Oceans to become a major player i
the northern environmental-protection game; it has stinted on the funding c
environmental-protection programs[68] and biological research;[69] and it ha
failed to produce a coherent and unified regulatory process for considerin
proposed northern megaprojects. On several occasions, Ottawa has approve
projects, such as the routing of the Alaska Highway pipeline along th
Klondike Highway (a routing that was replaced by an all-Alaska Highwa
routing during negotiations with the United States) on the basis of virtuall
no environmental-assessment information.[70] This situation undoubtedl
reflects Ottawa's dual interest in both environmental protection and eco
nomic development in the North. However, so long as this ambivalenc
continues, land-use planning will continue to be poorly informed, reactive
and *ad hoc*: the result will generally favour the interests of resourc
megadevelopers. It is now fully recognized that northern megadevelopmen
is going to occur. The policy challenge of the 1980s will be to manage tha
development in the public interest. An acceleration of a comprehensiv
planning process or the creation of a plan of modest proportions would hel
put this management on a systematic, informed, and legitimate basis
However, before such a development will come about, Ottawa will have t
have a change of heart.

Notes

[1] Robert F. Keith and Janet B. Wright (eds.), *Northern Transitions*, 2 vols. (Ottawa: Canadian Arctic Resources Committee, 1978), Vol. II, p. 152.

[2] Thomas R. Berger, *The Report of the Mackenzie Valley Pipeline Inquiry*, 2 vols. (Ottawa: Supply and Services Canada, 1977), Vol. II, p. 8.

[3] This point is elaborated in Peter J. Usher, "Renewable Resource Development in Northern Canada," in Keith and Wright, *op. cit.*, p. 160.

[4] Berger, *op. cit.*, Vol. I, p. 100.

[5] *Ibid.*, p. 101.

[6] J.C. Stabler, "The Report of the Mackenzie Valley Pipeline Inquiry, Vol. I: A Socio-Economic Critique," in Keith and Wright, *op. cit.*, p. 190.

[7] In this regard, Stabler cites a survey done by Derek G. Smith in 1975 in which native students in Grades 7 through 12 in the Mackenzie Delta were asked to rank a variety of adult jobs in order of their attractiveness. Smith found that the students attached little value to "the seasonal, unskilled, rural and outdoors sorts of occupations with which Native people have so consistently been identified in the past." *Ibid.*, p. 195.

[8] An example of this analysis and the calculations of the value of the wildlife harvest in the western Arctic and Mackenzie Valley are presented in Berger, *op. cit.*, Vol. II, pp. 15-34.

[9] Peter J. Usher, "A Reply to J.C. Stabler," in Keith and Wright, *op. cit.*, p. 201.

[10] Peter J. Usher, "Renewable Resource Development in Northern Canada," in Keith and Wright, *op. cit.*, p. 171.

[11] *Ibid.*, p. 155.

[12] Peter A. Cumming and Neil H. Mickenberg (eds.), *Native Rights in Canada*, 2nd ed. (Toronto: Indian-Eskimo Association of Canada and General Publishing, 1972), Ch. 20, provides a useful introduction to the laws on native hunting rights.

[13] Forestry in the North is described in T. Fenge *et al.*, *Land Use Programs in Canada: Northwest Territories* (Ottawa: Supply and Services Canada, 1979), and D.K. Redpath, *Land Use Programs in Canada: Yukon Territory* (Ottawa: Supply and Services Canada, 1979), Ch. 7.

[14] Berger, *op. cit.*, Vol. II, pp. 35-43.

[15] *Ibid.*, p. 36.

[16] Inuit Development Corporation, *Intersettlement Trade: A Survey of the Prospects and a Development Plan* (Ottawa: Inuit Development Corporation, 1980).

[17] Berger, *op. cit.*, Vol. II, p. 39.

[18] *Ibid.*, p. 40.

[19] *Ibid.*, p. 43.

[20] *Ibid.*, p. 43.

[1] These are described in National Parks Branch, Parks Canada, "National Wilderness Parks North of 60°," in Keith and Wright, *op. cit.*, pp. 233-36.

[2] This proposed park is described in C. Hunt, R. Miller, and D. Tingley, *Wilderness Area*, Northern Yukon Series, Research Monograph 2 (Ottawa: Canadian Arctic Resources Committee, 1979).

[3] The policy issues involving this herd are described in Nancy Russell LeBlond, *Porcupine Caribou Herd* Northern Yukon Series, Research Monograph 3 (Ottawa: Canadian Arctic Resources Committee, 1979), and are summarized in *Northern Perspectives*, Vol. VII, no. 7.

[4] Richard D. Revel, "The International Biological Programme in the Subarctic and Arctic Regions of Canada," in Keith and Wright, *op. cit.*

[5] The difference between the two types of status is that hunting is completely forbidden in sanctuaries, but is permitted by subsistence hunters in preserves. T. Fenge, *op. cit.*, p. 203.

[6] Redpath, *op. cit.*, p. 185.

[7] Fenge, *op. cit.*, p. 208.

[28]This legislation is discussed in detail in both *Land Use in Canada*, volumes cited above, an with evaluative comments in A.R. Lucas, D. MacLeod, and R.S. Miller, "Regulation of Hig Arctic Development," in M.J. Dunbar (ed.), *Marine Transportation and High Arc Development: Policy Framework and Priorities* (Ottawa: Canadian Arctic Resources Cor mittee, 1979).

[29]SOR 77-210.

[30]Fenge, *op. cit.*, p. 53.

[31]Lucas, MacLeod, and Miller, *op. cit.*, p. 101.

[32]Redpath, *op. cit.*, pp. 202-05.

[33]*Ibid.*, p. 207.

[34]R.S.C. 1970, c. 2 (1st Supplement).

[35]R.S.C. 1970, c. 28 (1st Supplement).

[36]Dunbar, *op. cit.*, p. 131.

[37]W. MacLeod, *Water Management in the Canadian North* (Ottawa: Canadian Arc Resources Committee, 1977), p. 89.

[38]*Ibid.*, pp. 106-07.

[39]*Ibid.*, pp. 30, 88.

[40]R.S.C. 1970, c. F-14, amended by R.S.C. 1970 c. 17 (1st Supplement), R.S.C. 1970, c. 14 (2r Supplement), and S.C. 1976-77, c. 35.

[41]MacLeod, *op. cit.*, p. 86.

[42]SOR 79-82.

[43]A 1980 memorandum written by a DIAND official and reprinted in *Northern Perspectives*, Vo VIII, no. 6, p. 12, indicates that this continues to be a very real problem.

[44]A variety of examples could be cited, of which two are the protection of the environmen around placer-mining operations discussed above and the permitting of dredging McKinley Bay on the Tuktoyaktuk Peninsula in 1979. *Northern Perspectives*, Vol. VIII, no. 2

[45]The process is described in *A Guide to the Federal Environmental Assessment and Revie Process* (Ottawa: Federal Environmental Assessment and Review Office, 1977), and in D. Pau Emond, *Environmental Assessment Law in Canada* (Toronto: Emond-Montgomery, 1978 Ch. 5, and A.R. Lucas and E.B. Peterson, "Northern Land Use Law and Policy Developmen 1972-78 and the Future," in Keith and Wright, *op. cit.*, pp. 74-77.

[46]Quoted in Lucas and Peterson, *op. cit.*, p. 74.

[47]*A Guide to the Federal Environmental Assessment and Review Process*, p. 12.

[48]See Emond and Lucas and Peterson.

[49]Robert Page, "Environmental Concerns, Government Controls and Economic Develop ment," a paper presented to the Symposium of the Royal Society of Canada on "A Century c Canada's Arctic Islands 1880-1980" (Yellowknife, August 13, 1980), p. 17.

[50]Emond, *op. cit.*, pp. 220-21.

[51]*Ibid.*, p. 222.

[52]Environment Canada, *Final Report of the Federal Task Force on Environmental Impac Policy and Procedure* (Ottawa: 1972). Ironically, this document has never been released to th public. However, portions of it are on reserve at the Osgoode Hall Law Library of Yor University in Downsview, Ontario.

[53]Emond, *op. cit.*, pp. 231-32.

[54]Lucas, MacLeod, and Miller, *op. cit.*, p. 152.

[55]D.J. Gamble, "Destruction by Insignificant Increments," *Northern Perspectives*, Vol. VII, no. (1979).

[56]*News/North* (September 12, 1980), p. A15.

[57]This change was urged in the EARP Reports on Eastern Offshore Drilling—South Davis Strai (No. 6) and Lancaster Sound Drilling (No. 7).

[58]*Arctic Seas Bulletin*, Vol. 2, no. 11 (1980).

[59]*Northern Perspectives*, Vol. VII, no. 6 (1979), p. 2.

[1]John B. Robinson, "Policy, Pipelines and Public Participation: The National Energy Board's Northern Pipeline Hearings," in O.P. Dwivedi (ed.), *Resources and the Environment: Policy Perspectives for Canada* (Toronto: McClelland and Stewart, 1980), p. 193.

[1]John K. Naysmith, *Land Use and Public Policy in Northern Canada* (Ottawa: DIAND, 1975), p. 165.

[2]*Ibid.*, p. 166.

[3]*Ibid.*, pp. 125-26.

[4]William E. Rees, "Development and Planning North of 60°: Past and Future," in Keith and Wright, *op. cit.*, pp. 49-54.

[5]*Northern Perspectives*, Vol. VII, no. 6 (1979), p. 2.

[6]The problems of northern scientific research and the criteria for adequate programs of research are discussed in Lucas and Peterson, *op. cit.*, pp. 71-74, and in Science Council of Canada, *Northward Looking: A Strategy and a Science Policy for Northern Development* (Ottawa: Science Council of Canada Report No. 26, 1977).

[7]Robinson, *op. cit.*, 193.

[8]See for example, *Northern Perspectives*, Vol. VIII, no. 6 (1980), p. 12.

[9]Lucas and Peterson, *op. cit.*, pp. 72-73, describes the decline in recent years in basic ecological research in the North.

[10]It has been argued that when the Mackenzie Highway was being built during the first half of the 1970s, environmental assessment was taking place during the construction rather than before it. Dickinson, "Northern Resources: A Study of Constraints, Conflicts and Alternatives," in Peterson and Wright, *Northern Transitions: Northern Resource and Land Use Policy Study* (Ottawa: Canadian Arctic Resources Committee, 1978), p. 267.

6/Northern Politics in the 1980s

In the last ten years, northern Canada has experienced a dramatic politic[a]
evolution, compressing into a single decade developments that took muc[h]
longer to unfold in southern Canada. During the 1970s the North becam[e]
politicized: new groups formed, grew, defined their philosophies, and joine[d]
battle against long-established interests. The lines of conflict hardened as th[e]
various interests came to shun the middle ground in the pursuit of goals tha[t]
had either not been articulated in the political arena before or had alway[s]
held unquestioned sway. However, as the decade drew to a close, norther[n]
politics were maturing. On the one hand, native and environmental group[s]
were acknowledging the inevitability of non-renewable southern-oriente[d]
resource development and emphasizing the need to pace and manage tha[t]
development rather than block it. They and the territorial government[,]
while still not able to match resources with Ottawa and the oil industry, we[re]
developing both the practical experience in dealing with the feder[al]
government and developers and the technical resources to press credibly for [a]
fuller role in the making of decisions about the future of the North. On th[e]
other hand, Ottawa and the development industry were beginning t[o]
recognize the legitimacy of or at least the potential political clout behind th[e]
broader concerns being raised about northern development.

However, while the 1970s did close on a note of greater moderation tha[n]
existed in the middle of the decade, the actual progress primarily involve[d]
second-order issues. The basic conflicts of northern politics did not chang[e]
substantially over the decade and they are unlikely to fade in the futur[e.]
Indeed, during the energy-conscious 1980s they will intensify. Continue[d]
conflict can be predicted with confidence because it rests on such a durabl[e]
base—the ongoing colonial relationship between the North and the South i[n]
Canada. Ultimate constitutional power lies with the government of Canad[a,]
which has far too much at stake in the North to relax its hold on any of th[e]
powers that might affect its ability to realize its goals in the North. This i[s]
precisely the message of the Canada Oil and Gas Act; as Ottawa implement[s]
the National Energy Program it will use the full weight of its legislativ[e]
authority to pursue its fundamental interests in the North.

Of course, where fundamental interests are not at issue, Ottawa can b[e]
more flexible. This flexibility will permit the politics of the norther[n]

territories to evolve to some degree spontaneously in response to the evolution of their social structures and local needs. However, the limits of this evolution will be set by Ottawa. Moreover, the most powerful engines of change will be the megaprojects that the South will propose for the North. Some of these will never proceed beyond the proposal state. However, even as proposals, they will influence the agenda of northern politics by requiring the northern governments and interest groups to focus their resources on responding to them. If they are approved, even more resources will have to be diverted from alternative uses in order to maximize the northern benefits and mitigate the costs of the projects. Whatever their fate, it will be for the North to react and the South to determine. It will be in this context that Ottawa will respond to the demands of northern native people for settlements of their aboriginal claims and to the pursuit by the territorial governments of the devolution of authority to bring them closer to the status of provinces. Ottawa will respond with some sympathy to these claims, in that they promise to help realize certain subsidiary goals that Ottawa holds in the North. However, increasingly in the 1980s, the goal for Ottawa in these political tradeoffs will be unfettered control over non-renewable-resource development, particularly over energy megaprojects. In this sense, the basic question of northern politics is simply how closely Ottawa will feel it must rein in northern ambitions in order to ensure for itself the kind of control it needs.

The answer to this question lies in the evolution of bureaucratic politics and the definition of the national interest. The two northern policy themes of the 1970s were, first, responding to the challenge of rapid change and, second, the implementation of bias. The tremendous rate of change overloaded policy makers who faced a compounded challenge. They not only had to regulate developments, but also more fundamentally to create the basic policies to be applied in specific cases. Even more fundamentally, they had to sort out the institutional relationships within government by means of which these basic policies were to be fashioned. The inevitable result was that policy makers frequently were forced to produce *ad hoc* solutions based on inadequate information and consultation and generally to let policy evolve in interaction with actual cases while they themselves struggled to learn from the "on the job training" inherent in such a rapidly unfolding policy area. Not surprisingly, the policy makers faced with such a monumental task made mistakes, failed to act as responsively to northern interests as they might have, and to some extent deliberately excluded interest-group adversaries from full participation in the policy process simply for self-protection.

Some policy makers sincerely attempted to come to grips with the claims of northern natives, the growing independence of the territorial governments, and the challenges of decision making posed particularly by the northern-pipeline and offshore-drilling applications. However, others took the extremely fluid situation as an opportunity to push megadevelopment in the North to the hilt. For these policy makers, concerns about the adequacy of the policy process—its public information and participation component, its basis in scientific research, the unity and coherence of regulatory reviews— were at best subsidiary, or at worst obstructive, to the already predetermined commitment to proceed with northern energy development.

The shape of Ottawa's northern policies and policy processes will be determined by the respective contributions of these two groups of policy makers to the policy end product. Of course, any division of public servants and the arrays of interest groups into merely two categories is a gross simplification, but also necessary to outline the debate, albeit onesided, on Ottawa's northern policy. The point is that the first group of policy makers has tended to be more in touch with the local impacts—social, economic, and political—of northern megadevelopment than has the second group, and to attach a higher priority to these impacts than does the group committed to northern megadevelopment. The first group has at least been grappling seriously with the northern impacts of southern-initiated projects. It has been willing to consider seriously—if not necessarily to endorse—the claims made by northerners. It shows promise of learning from its mistakes. The second group has tended to pay less attention to northern claims and to view them as second-order matters—impacts to be mitigated and compensated for—rather than as determinants of the basic decisions about proposed projects. This mentality condemns this group to repeat past policy errors rather than to mellow with experience.

In the 1970s the northern-oriented sensibilities of the first group achieved some reflection in efforts to bolster scientific research in the North, strengthen the northern governments, fund native claims, and attach terms and conditions to the acceptance of northern projects. While such policy efforts will continue in the 1980s, they will be overshadowed in Ottawa by the ever-increasing political weight of the second type of sensibility—the view that aggressive northern energy development is unquestionably in the national interest, indeed so preeminent a concern as to invalidate any objection that might be raised to it. The champions of this perspective form a very impressive coalition. The Department of Finance has always occupied a starring role on the Ottawa stage. It can be counted on to stress the balance-of-payments and governmental-revenue benefits of northern energy develop-ment. Industry, Trade and Commerce will point to the industrial benefits of such developments and hear its position echoed by the Department of Regional Economic Expansion to the extent that the industrial spinoffs from northern energy development can be anticipated to benefit the less prosper-ous regions of Canada. External Affairs will approve the sovereignty-bolstering implications of northern energy projects—and who in Ottawa will not applaud a lessening of Canada's reliance on the recalcitrant energy-producing provinces? Finally, the bureaucratic heavyweight of the late 1970s, destined to be the administrative darling of the 1980s—the Department of

Energy, Mines and Resources—will actively promote the search for and development of northern energy in order to fill what will increasingly be seen as the major issue of the 1980s—the need to assure a satisfactory energy future for Canada.

In opposition to this coalition stand the Department of the Environment and parts of the Department of Indian Affairs and Northern Development. DOE has always had difficulty making itself heard in the melee in Ottawa and is unlikely to have much impact on the timing or shape of northern megadevelopment.[1] However, while DOE's next ten years are likely to suffer from the same limitations as its first decade, the major change of the 1980s is that DIAND's star will decline as much as EMR's will rise. Because of this, the fraction of DIAND's members who do display a northern sensibility will be in a much weaker position to apply it to the really crucial northern policy decisions in the 1980s.

To appreciate the causes of this evolution, it is necessary to understand the beleaguered position of DIAND today. In part, DIAND's weakness is a legacy of its history. During the 1970s, DIAND suffered from a variety of problems. It had the unenviable task of championing an unpopular group in Ottawa—native people. Because its client group was politically weak, DIAND was unable to benefit from the type of private support that, for example, the manufacturing interests of Canada give to the Department of Industry, Trade and Commerce. To the contrary, because of its earlier history of paternalism directed more at a social control than at development,[2] DIAND suffered from bitter and increasingly strong attacks from its client group. In significant instances, these attacks were aimed at policies that had been decided elsewhere in government, yet that DIAND had to implement. Thus, the opposition by native people to the whole unsympathetic thrust of federal-government policies focused on DIAND, despite the fact that it was only partly responsible for these policies.

Wherever the responsibility lay, the hostility of DIAND's client group and the obvious failure of its policies to improve the material condition of Canada's native people greatly undermined DIAND's credibility in Ottawa. In the North, DIAND appeared particularly incompetent because of the internal contradiction of its mission. In effect, it was supposed to embody both of the sensibilities sketched above. As a protector of the northern environment and northern society it was called on to judge rigorously and modify the very northern megaprojects it was also required to promote. The practical result was that DIAND had great difficulty in reconciling contradictory interests, particularly in the period when confrontation and extreme expressions of position dominated. Much energy was used up in conflicts within the department. Coherent and anticipatory policies and processes of decision making and regulation could not be created because the debates within the department could not be resolved, particularly because cabinet persistently avoided giving DIAND the clear policy direction it needed to deal on other than an *ad hoc* level with specific projects. These internal problems served to exaggerate the fecklessness the department appeared to have in dealings with a client group that was both hostile to and out of favour in Ottawa.

Entering the 1980s, DIAND must confront new challenges that promise to weaken it even further by reducing its Northern Affairs Programme to a vestige of its present status. In the 1970s, the Northern Affairs Programme was responsible for about a quarter of DIAND's budget, spending more than $330 million in 1979-80.[3] By the end of the 1980s, it may well only handle a few residual tasks required under miscellaneous pieces of legislation.

The most important cause of its likely demise is that Ottawa has come to view northern megadevelopment as too important to be entrusted to DIAND. This view may well have contributed significantly to the announcement that the Canada Oil and Gas Act will lead to the integration of the oil-and-gas-related activities of DIAND with the northern responsibilities of the Department of Energy, Mines and Resources.[4] While the resulting agency will be responsible to both ministers, the likelihood is that it will take the direction of the more powerful of the two, the Minister of Energy, Mines and Resources. At the very least, the change puts some distance between DIAND and the oil-and-gas-related functions formerly integral to it. Taken further, it may simply be a transitional stage leading to the incorporation of the new agency within EMR itself. If this does come to pass, it will simply provide an institutional reflection of EMR's evolving dominance over northern-development policy.

At the same time, the gains made by the two territorial governments during the 1970s put them into a better position than ever to press for further devolutions of power to bring their status increasingly in line with that of the provinces. It can confidently be predicted that they will not receive in the foreseeable future any degree of control over northern megadevelopment proposals or revenues that might in any way challenge Ottawa's interests in these areas. However, in the other senses in which they are still territories subject to DIAND's powers that the provinces wield independently for themselves, Ottawa is likely to concede devolution gradually. The Drury Report points to this evolution in the N.W.T. and has already been acted on: the financial relations between the territorial and federal governments have been brought more in line with those between Ottawa and the provinces.[5]

The net result of these changes will be to gut the once-substantial Northern Affairs section of DIAND. It can be expected that the Northern Affairs Programme will resist this evolution. Its members feel committed to the policies they have evolved, confident of their abilities to continue to manage these policies, and, in all likelihood, dubious of the capacity of those who will be taking over from them to guide the North in the right directions.

Their resistance will mean that, during the transition, the North will continue to suffer from a lack of coherent direction at a crucial time in its history. Just as it is experiencing changes that will be definitive in determining the outcome of native claims—and with them the viability of a lifestyle option for native people—the North will have to go it alone; the agency supposed to oversee these changes will itself be experiencing upheaval. The result will be to perpetuate the paradox of purposeful drift so striking in northern policy making in the 1970s.[6]

The drift reflects Ottawa's lack of will to put into place a policy process that will bring to bear the full range of concerns on northern-megaprojects decisions. For example, legislation has not been passed requiring comprehensive project assessments. The federal Environmental Assessment and Review Process operates at ministerial discretion only in an advisory capacity, and without the support of adequate legislative statements identifying environmental and social concerns in the North as questions of high priority. The National Energy Board enjoys a more authoritative position in examining proposed megaprojects, but its hearings focus only on selected aspects of projects. The division of regulatory responsibility between these two reviews and the roles played in the approval process by a range of additional government agencies contribute to the fragmentation of the decision-making process—thus contributing to delay, uncertainty, and a general loss of focus in government. By default in such a situation, northern-development interests seize and hold the initiative. Far from being compelled to accommodate themselves to Ottawa's definition of the national interest as clearly set out in legislation and coherently administered by a single regulatory agency, they define the issues.

The existing review process puts at a disadvantage those who wish to ensure the best possible response by developers to northern social and environmental needs. Inadequate funding for baseline research means scientific information that could help identify undesirable impacts of proposed projects and thus the need for modifications is often unavailable. Crucial information on projects may be inaccessible because legislation does not compel its disclosure. The cost of preparing presentations at regulatory hearings may be prohibitive or may force northern residents and others who might wish to question a development to present arguments that, for lack of funding, cannot possibly match the depth of those brought forward by project proponents.

These problems erode the rationality of the northern-megaproject regulatory process and promote drift in government policy by reducing the likelihood that the regulatory process will effectively scrutinize projects. A similar consequence has followed simply because federal agencies lack the personnel and funding to fully keep pace with the rapid evolution of project proposals. Both factors contribute to drift, but the drift is towards the dominant sentiment in Ottawa in favour of northern megaprojects. Having been bitten once by the experience of the Mackenzie Valley Pipeline Inquiry, Ottawa is shy about creating any institutional focus around which opposition to a megaproject can organize. Megaprojects are seriously scrutinized by

Ottawa, but in relation to an artificially narrow definition of the national interest applied in such a limited setting that effective participation is restricted primarily to those who share a pro-development bias.

This bias and the evolution of the intergovernmental relations that Ottawa is promoting will preoccupy northern politics in the 1980s. The unfolding of the decade will witness the territorial governments' increasingly assuming from DIAND the responsibility for their internal operations and for most of the kind of programs handled by the provinces in southern Canada. At the same time, southern-oriented megadevelopment will exert a constant pressure. The combined result of these two developments will be to intensify the northerners' stress from actual or anticipated development and to commit their governments even more resolutely to seeking a hand in turning megadevelopment to their own purposes. In general, they will press as hard as possible for a substantial role in judging proposals and attaching conditions to their approval. In other words, they will continue to press Ottawa to divest itself of precisely the residual power that Ottawa sees as most critical for the attaining of its northern goals. They will also try to wrest from Ottawa and from project proponents significant concessions on specific projects, such as were suggested in Chapter 4. Ottawa can be expected to resist concessions on specifics where they conflict with its interests and to refuse to share ultimate authority over the approval of megaprojects.

In the 1970s, conflicts over northern development pitted weak territorial governments against a powerful federal government and relatively weak but not insignificant elements of the federal establishment (most notably in DIAND and DOE) against a stronger coalition of federal agencies. Increasingly in the 1980s, the lines of battle will shift. DIAND will fade from the picture. Its northern role will become vestigial, leaving it to carry out in the North only its Canada-wide mandate to administer policy on status Indians and Inuit. This development will result in strengthened territorial governments and an increasingly ideologically homogeneous federal government struggling for control of northern development. With the lion's share of the political resources, Ottawa will not find it difficult to hold off the territorial assault. Rather, the consequence of this protracted struggle will be the continued colonial shape of the northern political agenda, with the attendant waste of energy.

The territorial governments will expend substantial effort in the intergovernmental struggle; they will therefore be less able to focus on the severe social problems facing their people. The territorial governments will be further distracted from their business by the need to respond to development proposals and to projects once they are approved. They may also find themselves distracted from the important business at hand by preferring to condemn the distant southern government or tilt with it rather than to confront the unpalatable task of dealing with social problems of northern origin or with northern solutions. All of these likely developments, which really only represent a further working through of an evolution already in progress, will manifest the ongoing political colonialism of the North.

However, the news is not all bad. In the 1980s, northerners will become more experienced in operating their maturing political institutions; hence, the administrative competence of their governments will grow. If an accommodation can be fashioned between the native and non-native segments of northern society—an accommodation that is taking shape in the Northwest Territories, although, regretably, not yet in the Yukon—the evolving political maturity of the North will produce policies to deal effectively with northern needs. However, more effective northern governments are only as helpful as those governments are powerful. To the extent that the basic directions of northern economics—hence, social change and politics—will be determined in the South, the politics of the North in the 1980s will continue to be marred by incoherence and dissonance.

To determine the plausibility of this scenario, one need only consult the National Energy Program. Whatever its other merits, the NEP demonstrates Ottawa's acute reliance on developing energy resources in the North. Feeling such desperation, Ottawa is hardly likely to throw away one of the few high cards it holds in the energy poker game. The victims of its determination, the northerners who will have to adjust to the consequences of the new northern-development thrust of the 1980s, will not even enjoy a seat at the table. Their historic allies in government, never strong at the best of times, can be counted on to hold losing hands.

The end result will be federal policies that leave the North where Ottawa has always left it—in the wilderness. While a choice of futures does arguably remain for the North at the start of the 1980s, the odds are that the die is cast. In Ottawa, the purposeful drift will accelerate. In the North, the costs of economic dependence will remain very much in evidence. The frustration of colonial politics, while diminished, will persist—an apparently permanent feature of the northern political landscape.

Notes

[1] The dimensions of DOE's recent budgetary difficulties are reported in Michael Whittington, "Department of Environment," in G. Bruce Doern (ed.), *Spending Tax Dollars: Federal Expenditures, 1981* (Ottawa: School of Public Administration, Carleton University, 1980).

[2] See for example, J.R. Ponting and R. Gibbins, *Out of Irrelevance* (Toronto: Butterworth, 1980), p. 100.

[3] DIAND, *Annual Report, 1979-80* (Ottawa: Supply and Services Canada, 1980), p. 40.

[4] *News/North* (March 13, 1981), p. 1.

[5] See Ch. 3.

[6] See for example, Couchiching Study Group, "Analysis," in E.B. Peterson and J.B. Wright (eds.), *Northern Transitions: Northern Resource and Land-Use Policy Study* (Ottawa: Canadian Arctic Resources Committee, 1978), and A.R. Lucas and E.B. Peterson, "Northern Land Use Law and Policy Development: 1972-78 and the Future," in R.F. Keith and J.B. Wright (eds.), *Northern Transitions: Second National Workshop on People, Resources and the Environment North of 60°* (Ottawa: Canadian Arctic Resources Committee, 1978).

Appendix
Methodological Approaches to Northern Politics

The North is experiencing change at a great and ever-accelerating rate. This means that many of the details presented in this or any other book on the North are bound to become dated. What will not become dated, however, are the three perspectives this appendix presents in simplified form. Political sociology, the colonial model, and policy analysis provide enduringly valuable tools for organizing the ever-changing details of northern politics. The first and the last are universal approaches to politics. The colonial situation of the North may change in matters of detail, but is not likely to dissipate in the foreseeable future. In other words, the three perspectives presented in this appendix provide lasting methodology for studying the northern issues this book has discussed.

The Political Sociology of the North

The Canadian North is both a society in its own right—actually several societies—and a colony. Its politics can only be understood if this duality is kept in mind. The North is not unique in form, for modern technology and economics have created a world where such a thing as a closed society no longer exists: a society's politics can no longer be explained satisfactorily solely in terms of events and forces within it. While politics in all societies owes something to the external relations of the society, few experience the degree of formal as well as practical dependence that characterizes the Canadian North. For this reason, political analysis in the North must always consider both the social structure of the North and the pattern of forces that impinge on it from outside.

Politics is an integral part of the life of all societies. While there are almost always specifically political structures distinct from other institutions in society, politics itself can more usefully be interpreted as an aspect of social structure. It can only be understood in the context of the society in which it evolves. In any society, politics is the set of relationships among the members of the society by means of which decisions binding on the members of the society are made and implemented. The decisions must be made because differences of opinion or interest need to be resolved if conflict is to be contained and society is to be able to function peacefully. The source of these differences is the diversity within each society—in other words, social structure. The task of political sociology is to describe this structure and to assess its implications for the politics of the society being studied.

To form a general impression of the politics of any society, it is necessary to proceed through several steps. The first is to identify all politically relevant groups in the society. This does not mean all groups in society, but only those groups whose members share some characteristic—occupation, location, race—that may lead them to make some demand on the political system. Second, the group's interests must be identified. It is possible to argue that groups have certain objective interests regardless of whether they recognize them. However, whether or not the observer agrees with the views of the groups' members, what counts are the interests that the group members believe they share and wish to promote in the political arena. For this reason, it is not sufficient merely to attempt to infer a group's interest from its objective characteristics. Rather, the empirical method of examining the statements and actions of the members and leadership of the group provides the best indicator of the group's interests as its members perceive them. The group's historical experiences and culture can explain how objective circumstances translate into felt needs and how these needs may come to be passionately sought. However, these factors are more effective in explaining than in defining the group's view of its political interest, which is best assessed using the straightforward empirical method.

The third task of the political sociologist in the Canadian North or elsewhere is to assess the political resources each group possesses. A political resource is any value on which a relationship of dependence can be based. If one individual needs something that another possesses, then that something is a political resource. If that something is of enough value to the first person, he may be compelled to obey the second person's directions in exchange for a share of the resource. Familiar political resources include money, votes, and the ability to use or not to use violent force. Equally, if not more important, in the North are two other resources. The first is information. If an individual, corporation, or government possesses certain information that is not available to other participants in northern politics, it is in a position to deny them the understanding to undermine the position of the holder of the information. In this sense, knowledge can be power. It can be a potent form of power, for its use is often not fully understood by the person or group over which it is wielded. Resistance in such a situation is difficult. For example, if an oil-exploration firm encounters in its drilling geological formations or underground pressures that pose environmental risks, then withholds this information from the government officials responsible for regulating the environmental safety of the operation, the officials cannot possibly properly carry out their job. Information can also both affect and reflect power relationships when the question arises about what information will be accepted as accurate and relevant and what will be considered spurious or, worse yet, "unscientific." This issue frequently surfaces at the hearings of regulatory boards when the proponents and opponents of a given project cal expert witnesses whose testimony is contradictory.[1] Information also be comes an issue when natives' knowledge of northern species, climate, or othe matters is rejected as not scientifically based.

A second political resource operates particularly prominently in th North: the "legal position." For example, while it is popular to discuss th ethical aspects of the northern native claims and to consider the implication of various possible forms of settlement on the future integration of norther society and politics, the claims rest on a legal foundation. The strength o that foundation will be the major determinant of the outcome of the claims Similarly, both territories' claims for greater self-government will be judged not by their people, but by Ottawa because Ottawa possesses the lega authority to decide. The adversaries in northern political issues usually prefe to avoid litigation, primarily because they are uncertain of the outcome However, this route remains open to them if they wish to pursue it and thei day-to-day relationships owe a great deal to the strength of their lega positions. Political resources are not very interesting in the abstract. The only become relevant when they are used to achieve power. For this reasor any political assessment should consider as an important trait of a politica group the intensity of commitment it brings to an issue. A group with fev resources but tremendous commitment can defeat a rival with much greate resources but little inclination to use them.

It should also be remembered that political resources only contribute t power in a comparative setting. It is never sufficient in describing the powe relationship between two individuals or groups to assess the resources and commitment of one of them. Power rests on the comparison between the resources of the two, keeping in mind, first, that the extent to which the resources are actually resources depends on a subjective factor, the depen dence of each actor on the resources and, second, that this dependence ma vary from time to time as may the individuals' stocks of political resources Thus, power is relative and variable, not absolute and fixed.

Influence is analytically distinct from power because it involves actin; out of deference to a person or interest rather than because of any compulsion Of course, the powerful tend to be influential because they are well endowec with the political resources such as credibility and privileged access t decision makers, which underlie influence relationships. However, the possibility of influence is politically important for the weak, because i represents a last hope that they may win the respect of the powerful and receive some consideration in the policy process. Influence is all the mor important because it is the cement of the alliances in much of politics. Thus to assess successfully the evolution of a political issue, the influence as well a the power of the individuals and groups involved should be studied.

A completely comprehensive study of a political issue should identify a the relevant social groups and their respective political resources. After this has been done, the fourth task of the political sociologist is to describe the total system that these groups constitute—that is, the relationships of power and interest among the various groups. To the extent that interests are shared or even complementary—different, but mutually supportive—alliances are possible and can greatly improve the prospects for individual groups by combining their political resources. For example, it was the combined weight of the native, environmental, and church social-action lobbies that delayed approval of the Canadian Arctic Gas pipeline proposal until Ottawa realized its weaknesses. No one of these groups could have accomplished this feat alone.

The description of the political alignments in a society forms the basis for the fifth step, describing and explaining the strategy and tactics. Each group's leadership will perform the kind of calculation that has been described, then decide what form of political action holds the greatest promise of success. In making these decisions, leaders will be influenced by factors such as their past experiences, cultural values which particularly suggest certain options and make others illegitimate, and expectations of how the other groups will act to promote their interests. Out of all of this will come a set of strategies and tactics that constitute the politics of the society. In many cases, the strategies and tactics will lead to relatively lasting ideas about politics and to the creation of durable political structures, such as parties and interest groups. They may also lead to some private groups' gaining credibility with government or some branch of it, so that government can no longer be said to be above the issue. For example, it has been argued that the government of Canada has been so eager to promote oil and gas development in the North that in the 1970s relationships developed between it and the oil and gas industry over this question which virtually excluded other interests.[2]

Political action and political structures are the visible elements of politics. However, they are only the tip of the iceberg. Because what lies beneath shapes what lies above, the sociological approach is invaluable when studying any political issue. First identify all the relevant groups. Second, identify their perceived interests and their commitment to them. Third, assess their political resources. Fourth, place them in the context of the other groups relevant to the issues and compare them in terms of interests and resources. Fifth, while also being sensitive to the ways the political process is evolving as new experiences are encountered, identify the regularities of culture and behaviour that channel politics in certain directions and give it its pattern and meaning. This analysis may appear dry and abstract, but when it is actually put into practice, it will make sense of the richness of detail of northern—or any other—politics and give meaning to what would otherwise appear to be a jumble of unconnected pieces of evidence.

The Colonial Reality of the North

The North can be studied as a society—actually a set of several societies—but it can only be understood as a colony. Basically, a society is colonial to the extent that major decisions affecting it are made outside it. Colonialism is weakness and dependence. As Chapter 3 details, the North is totally dependent constitutionally on Ottawa. It is also a colony as a matter of practical politics, in that the territories lack the political resources to sway Ottawa. They elect only three of 282 members of Parliament and have been represented in only one of the federal cabinets since 1945. The territorial governments lack the funds to engage in massive public relations in the South and lack the moral authority in lobbying Ottawa they would enjoy if northerners were united in strong support of them. In addition, they may find that they have to take a back seat to southern or foreign-based firms that are well positioned to lobby Ottawa on questions of northern development.

The territories have no legal ability to block Ottawa's cherished goal of attaining this development by means of large-scale projects. The economic stagnation of the North discourages them from attempting such a strategy in any case. The Yukon government is desperate for economic development and would scarcely threaten to obstruct it in order to pressure Ottawa. The government of the N.W.T. is concerned about the social impact of large-scale developments—particularly before the settlement of the native claims—and about obtaining a share of the revenues generated by resource developments. However, it recognizes the need to stimulate the territorial economy and would be reluctant to attempt to use a resource project as a hostage in bargaining with Ottawa, even if it could.

The final political resource the North possesses is the appeal to ethics. Precisely because the North is a colony of the South, all Canadians have an ethical responsibility for what is done in their name to Canadians over whom Ottawa wields absolute authority. For this reason, northerners may be able to gain a sympathetic response in segments of the southern population, but, as has been noted above, this approach only works if it does not run up against a policy or program to which Ottawa is firmly committed. As with the other political resources, moral claims give to the North the degree of power that usually characterizes colonies—very little.

As a consequence of its colonial legal and political situation, the political process of the North differs from that of Ottawa.[3] First, the political institutions in the North are imposed on it rather than indigenous to it. Not only have they not been created by northerners, but their operation does not reflect the traditional native political processes. The imposition of and weakness of governmental structures reduce their legitimacy for all northerners. Over and above this, their southern pattern of adversarial debate tends to confuse, insult, or at least discomfort native people who are accustomed to consensus politics and who in practical political terms are at a disadvantage in unfamiliar institutions. In this way, the structures of government are doubly illegitimate for northern natives, thereby adding to the division that sets apart the native and non-native populations of the North.

The second element of colonial politics is that it largely defines the agendas of northern government. The governments of the Yukon and the N.W.T. are modern governments that operate almost the whole range of programs that Canadians associate with provincial governments. However, much of the time and energy of politicians and the attention of the northern media are consumed in relating to the colonial status of the North. Undoubtedly, the issues that provide the focus of this book—native claims, political development, and economic policy—are integral parts of provincial politics. However, they form more of a preoccupation in the North and tend to be defined much more in colonial terms because Ottawa holds the bulk of the power to decide the outcome of issues. More importantly, initiatives in these areas tend to come from Ottawa rather than from the territorial governments. Ottawa's initiatives force the territorial governments to devote their limited human and other resources to reacting at the expense of initiating programs. This distorts the territorial governments' priorities and may delay the implementation of policies important to them.

The Office of the Secretary of State gave fledgling native groups the funds to get established and has supported their ongoing activities, and DIAND has funded these groups in preparing their claims. Without this funding, decided on outside the North, the political agenda of the North would undoubtedly be much different from what it is today. Finally, the agenda of the North is colonial, in that political discourse tends to revolve around the awareness of colonialism and to inject the colonial sensitivity into all issues. However, it is becoming increasingly difficult to claim that the North is different from southern Canada in this regard, given the prominence of federal-provincial tensions.

The economic colonialism of the North is as confining as the political. Basically, economic activity in the North depends heavily on the interests of the South. The small population, harsh climate, and vast size of the North mean that few economic activities of a substantial size can be created solely to serve northern needs. Economic growth occurs only when the South needs something the North possesses. Even then, the economics of projects may be such that they require the active support of government in terms of financial aid or the sympathy of regulatory agencies. Because Ottawa controls these forms of support, it effectively controls the megaproject side of northern development.

Even when large-scale economic development does occur in the North, it shows the colonial tendency of providing relatively little benefit to the colony. The usual "multiplier effect" of stimulating the local economy by purchasing goods and services in it is reduced by the tendency to supply megaprojects from the South. Similarly, the profits produced by these projects tend to move to the homes of the owners of the project, leaving relatively little surplus in the North for financing further economic growth. Finally, as explained in Chapter 1, the Northern economy tends to be colonial not merely because it consists of two sectors—the large-scale, capital-intensive resource sector and the small-scale, labour-intensive hunting, fishing, trapping sector—but also because of the relationship between them. Specifically, the former undermines the latter in a variety of ways causing social and economic dislocation and increasing native society's dependence on the first sector. To summarize, colonial economies are weak, dependent, and caught in processes likely to keep them that way. Thus, it is likely that the external economic relations of colonies will remain colonial long after the political vestiges of colonialism have ended. The economy of the Canadian North follows this model and any analysis of northern political economy should keep this point in mind.

Colonialism is more than just a political, economic, and social phenomenon because the objective realities have a subjective side: what might be termed a "colonial culture." The colonial political culture tends to emphasize opposition to the metropolis, yet focuses political activity on the metropolis because that is where power lies and because the colonial governmental institutions, being both weak and imposed by the metropolis, enjoy little popular credibility. The Canadian North is no exception. In addition, the depth of the gaps in its society and the profound differences and values in the assumptions and motives of its native and non-native groups have contributed to a high degree of political confusion and incoherence. All of these factors have limited the territorial governments' abilities to be responsive to the needs of their citizens and to improve their legitimacy on the basis of their proven responsiveness, although the government of the Northwest Territories now seems to be putting this vicious circle of colonial politics behind it.

Colonial culture usually involves self-perceptions of the colonials' lack of worth and efficacy. Styles, media, and ideas from the metropolis tend to be favoured. This pattern can in part be explained by the ability of metropolitan markets to support more sophisticated media production than can the small populations in the hinterland. However, an additional explanation is usually required to account for the intensity of the colonial craving for what is metropolitan. This explanation is a cultural one, simply that what is metropolitan is seen as good and what is colonial is, by definition, inferior. In a similar sense, the colonial culture may involve habits of dependence, of relying on the metropolis to achieve some desired change, rather than achieving it oneself. The sense of inefficacy that leads to passiveness has its roots in the economic and political facts of dependence, but after a period of time it can assume an independent status of its own and reinforce the initial dependence.

While this is a common colonial pattern, it does not seem particularly prominent in the North. Northerners are often frustrated in their dealings

ith the South, but they do not interpret their failures as implying some
nadequacy on their own part. Rather, they bring a determination and an
ndependence of mind to their relationship with Ottawa. The native people
ave always felt themselves separate from the mainstream of Canadian
ociety. However, they are now losing their colonial acceptance of their low
ocial and economic status as due to some personal failing on their part. They
re "decolonizing" their thinking. For their part, northern non-natives also
el distinct from other Canadians and attribute to their own lifestyles a
ariety of positive attributes they do not see in the South. In the elan of this
elf-definition, the northern culture is definitely not colonial.

With this exception, however, many aspects of the Canadian North
ome into sharper focus when viewed in terms of the colonial perspective.
he weakness of the colony and the undertone of conflict between the colony
nd the metropolis are defining traits of colonialism. In the North they are
ever far from the surface of politics.

he Policy Process

his Appendix has offered two tools—political sociology and the colonial
model—for describing and explaining northern politics. A third tool, policy
nalysis, is equally valuable because its subject matter, the making of
olitical decisions, is the subject of this book.

Policy analysis has spawned a large literature in both political science
nd management studies.[4] While it is not possible to replicate the detail and
ichness of that literature, the rest of this appendix will highlight some
nsights from policy analysis that are particularly helpful in interpreting
northern policy processes.

ome Distinctions

olicy can be defined as patterns of government action. This definition is a
road one, in that it acknowledges that governmental actions can be
onsidered policies even if they are not formally stated as such. The test is
vhether government acts. However, the breadth of the definition should not
e taken to suggest that all policies are equally significant. The student of
ublic policy should differentiate among policies:

. That are announced but not actually implemented through legislation or
   the drafting of the necessary regulations;
. That are expressed in regulations or legislation, but not fully implemented either by cabinet decision or by public-service unwillingness or
   inability to pursue the policy; and
. That are actually legislated and implemented fully.

These distinctions are important in determining what the government is
ctually doing with a political issue as contrasted with what it might wish the
ublic to assume it is doing.

A second important distinction is that between "policy output" and "policy outcome." Output is policy; it is what government does. Outcome is the consequence of policy rather than the policy itself. Frequently, the outcome of a policy diverges quite dramatically from what the policy maker had in mind. For this reason it is fallacious to assume that the outcome a policy actually produces was in fact the goal the creators of the policy were seeking. For example, the process of moving native people from their small and isolated camps in the North into towns has produced severe problems for native people. However, only the most cynical would suggest that the desperation, violence, and family breakdown that have been some of the consequences of this policy were actually what Ottawa had in mind when deciding to move native people into communities. Similarly, the Liberal government in 1974 could not possibly have willed the outcome of its creation of the Berger Inquiry. Output and outcome must always be distinguished when describing policy.

Policy as Process

Common sense suggests that a policy is something that is fixed and certain for a period of time. After a while it may change into something else that is also unchanging, but at any time it is static. Such a view suggests that policy is an event. In reality, policy can only be understood as a process.

The policy process can be viewed as a series of stages, so long as it is remembered that such a view is highly simplified. The process does not proceed neatly from the first stage to the next to the next. Rather, the issue may return to an early stage in the process for reformulation of the work done at that stage, or an issue may skip several stages in the process because of lack of time, hard data, or theoretical understanding of the problem or because it serves the interests of a powerful actor. Quite possibly, several stages will proceed at once. Still, for purposes of analysis the policy stages can be seen as

1. **Identification of the Issue.** There are many unfilled needs in society and many differences of perspective on particular questions. However, only a fraction of these needs and conflicts come to be seen by decision makers as having sufficient political relevance that they should be considered by government. Identifying such issues is the first stage of the policy process.
2. **Definition of the Issue.** A given social problem can be interpreted in a variety of ways. For example, is the essence of native claims the self-determination of peoples or the compensation of groups of individuals for agreeing to some kind of real-estate transaction? Similarly, are high rates of native infant mortality a medical problem or a social problem? The way the question is posed will influence its answer by precluding certain solutions that would be perfectly plausible if the issue were only defined differently.
3. **Identifying alternative solutions.**
4. **Specifying the costs and benefits of each of these solutions.**

5. **Choosing among the alternatives on the basis of a set of values.**
6. **Legislating.**
7. **Implementing.**
8. **Receiving and assessing information on the impact of the policy** to permit a redefinition of the problem and another passage through the policy process.

The crucial fact to keep in mind about this process is that it does not proceed as some abstract search for the truth. Rather, it is political at every stage. That is, the process is affected by the values of the people who shape it and the power and influence these people possess will determine their ability to shape the process. The blunt truth is that the ability to shape the process of policy making is the ability to shape policy. Thus, any actor who has the means to prevent issues from entering the policy process enjoys a privileged position: government will never make a decision that harms that individual's interest because government will never make a decision on that issue. For example, so long as Ottawa chose to leave the education of northern native children in the hands of the Christian missions, they were unrestricted in teaching the curriculum they preferred to teach. The other side of this coin is that those who cannot force an issue past the political gatekeepers find themselves in a weak position.

Power rules at the other stages of the process as well. The definition of an issue can easily benefit one actor at the cost of others and the selection of alternative solutions may only include those that benefit the powerful. For example, the Yukon territorial government has expressed a willingness to offer Yukon natives their choice of a variety of formats of minority participation in the government, a choice that hardly meets the wishes of the native people. The weighing of costs and benefits obviously will proceed in terms of the values of the powerful, not the weak.

The student of public policy should recognize several consequences of this interplay of power. The first is that there is no such thing as a "public interest" or a "national good" that exists in any objective sense. The public interest is simply the honorific title bestowed on the end product of the decision-making process. It is what those with power define it to be. Thus, a policy should not be explained in terms of how it relates to the observer's image of the national interest as if that was the only goal that guided the policy's creation. Policy must be explained in terms of the interplay of interests and values of the various actors involved in the decision-making process.

A second consequence of the process of policy making is that not all of the actors may be involved at all the stages of the process. This fact alone is useful in explaining policy outputs, in that decisions taken early in the process are likely to send the process in certain directions that cannot be altered by those who enter the process in its later stages. The advantages of privileged access to the decision-making process lead interest groups to engage heavily in what may be called positional politics—not so much seeking certain policies, but seeking to participate to the maximum in the making of policies while their rivals languish in the cold.

A third consequence of the nature of the policy process is that it leaves a great deal of room for irrationality, or at least non-rational results. Politics may dictate that crucial stages in the process be omitted and the benefits of their analysis lost. Different sets of actors may be involved in the various stages of the process. To the extent that their values and assumptions differ, the policy may take on a shape that would not represent the preferences of any of the groups and that might be internally contradictory. The length of time the process may take leaves open the possibility that the context in which the early decisions were made might change substantially by the time the decision is actually reached. This could result in a policy's being produced that is far from the best response to the changed situation. Finally, the information required to undertake a proper policy analysis may not be available or may be deliberately slanted or withheld by those who are in a position to engineer and to benefit from such a tactic. Thus, a major criticism of environmental-assessment procedures in the North is that they depend on environmental assessments by the very interests proposing developments. This situation invites abuses that can reduce the rationality of decision making.

A fourth consequence of the policy process follows from the burdens it places on decision makers. The process is extremely time consuming because it involves several stages, some of which may have to be repeated in protected rounds of reformulations, consultations, and renewed approvals of revised texts. In addition, most policies rest at least to some degree on theoretical or technological expertise. The politician—a generalist who lacks this base of special skills and must divide his attention among a large number of issues— finds himself or herself at a great disadvantage in attempting to control the policy process, particularly in the crucial intermediate stages when policy alternatives are being prepared for his or her consideration. The sheer impossibility of the politician's being everywhere at once confers by necessary default substantial power on public servants. The ultimate authority rests with the elected politician, but the pressures of the position result in a great deal of discretion flowing to officials. For this reason, bureaucratic biases and the often obscure workings of bureaucratic politics may be important factors in explaining particular policies. In other words, government is much more than politicians. Put another way, not all the politicians in government are elected.

To summarize, policies cannot simply be explained by deductions based on the contents of the policy itself. Thus, the decision to create the Arctic Waters Pollution Prevention Act or the Northern Pipeline Act involved more than simply safeguarding the northern ocean and expediting a pipeline. To be understood, they must be seen as the product of lengthy, complex processes in which the power and the interests of a variety of political actors lurched and heaved toward particular conclusions. It is in the interplay of power and interest and the particular shape of the process in which they interacted that the explanations of these policies lie.

Of course, in seeking these explanations, it is necessary to appreciate the context in which the policy process unfolds. Richard Simeon has usefully described this context in terms of environment, ideas, and institutions.[5] By environment is meant the objective factors in society that give rise to issues. For example, Canada's high level of energy consumption and the uncertainty surrounding future supplies of oil and gas have led Ottawa to look northward in the hope of improving Canada's energy situation through a program of northern hydrocarbon exploration and development. In a narrower sense, the policy under study may be linked in the minds of policy makers with another issue that causes them to produce a different solution to the first issue from what they otherwise would have. For example, it has been suggested that Ottawa would not have provided such generous tax incentives in support of oil and gas exploration in the North in the late 1970s were it not for the federal yearning for deposits to be found to improve Ottawa's bargaining power by reducing Canada's dependence on Alberta hydro-carbons. Thus, a northern policy decision may well have been grounded in federal-provincial considerations.

Simeon's reference to ideas emphasizes the importance of the subjective in politics. Some aspects of subjectivity are sufficiently patterned and constant that they can be termed cultural and may prove useful in explaining why certain proposals emerged from the policy process, while others received little consideration. Culture is not definitive, in that it does not itself determine the specifics of policy, but it does define the boundaries of political debate, influence the shape of political processes, and set general priorities. Other ideas that may not actually be elements of culture can also influence the policy process if they involve perceptions of specific issues and the alternatives that the issues present. What must always be remembered is that politics is a subjective process and accordingly can only be explained in terms of what the participants thought to be the case at the time they were taking part in the making of the decision. This fact makes it essential to ask what concerns the participants brought to an issue rather than to impose one's own interpretation of the issue and the context onto the process. It is also important to try to accept that political actors whose views differ from one's own views actually do hold those views. It is psychologically comforting to believe that someone with whom you disagree does not actually hold views contrary to yours, but rather is cynically feigning these beliefs for personal advantage. This presumption is usually incorrect and to apply it to policy analysis is to risk missing the point completely. Thus, environmentalists ought to accept that petroleum-corporation executives believe that they are working in the national interest. Similarly, Ottawa's politicians would do well to try to comprehend the depth to which the Dene truly believe that they constitute a nation. Perceptions that are realities to those involved in political processes should not be dismissed as unreal by observers simply because the observers do not hold these views. The views may or may not be accurate, but they govern the behaviour of the political actors and for this reason they form a necessary part of a successful explanation of the political process being studied. Empathy is essential to this policy analysis.

Finally, institutions are important because, like the policy process, their structure can assist certain interests and undermine others. Institutions, such as the territorial status of the North, distribute power differentially and the details of this distribution should always be considered by the student of public policy.

To summarize, policy analysis stresses (1) the evolutionary nature of policies, (2) the importance of positional politics, (3) the possibility of non rationality and accordingly the difficulty of simply inferring the causes of a policy from its terms, (4) explanation in terms of the interplay of power and interest, not the pursuit of some abstract public interest, and (5) the role of the context of the policy process, including the ideas the participants bring to the process, ideas that must be approached empathetically.

Notes

[1]Two such debates discussed in this book are the differences over the extent and health of the native economy of the North (Chapter 5) and the conflicting interpretations of the ability of pipeline proponents to control the problem of "frost heave" (Chapter 4).

[2]Edgar Dosman, *The National Interest* (Toronto: McClelland and Stewart, 1975).

[3]An interesting question, which is avoided here completely, is the extent to which various provinces manifest the politics of colonies.

[4]This literature is reviewed in Richard Simeon, "Studying Public Policy," *Canadian Journal of Political Science*, Vol. LX, no. 4 (December 1976).

[5]*Ibid.*, pp. 566-68, 570-75.

Selected Bibliography

Northern Canada has attracted the attention of a great many authors; their works are far too numerous to list here. In keeping with the principle governing the footnotes to this book, the following bibliography emphasizes works that are recent, reasonably accessible, and relevant to public-policy questions, and does not include fictional, biographical, or overly specialized items.

Periodicals and Annuals

News/North and *The Native Press*, both published in Yellowknife, and the *Whitehorse Star* and the *Yukon Indian News* are the best northern news sources; *News/North* provides the fullest coverage of a broad range of policy areas.

Northern Perspectives, published regularly by the Canadian Arctic Resources Committee, has established a reputation for expert, analytic, and fair commentary, which makes it obligatory reading for anyone interested in northern policy issues.

The *Musk-Ox*, published by the Institute for Northern Studies of the University of Saskatchewan, contains scientific, cultural, economic, and historical articles as well as a valuable news digest that often includes transcripts or excerpts of documents of particular interest to observers of northern public policy.

Northern Titles is an index of English-language periodicals, northern newspapers, native-published newspapers, and government documents relating to the North. It is prepared by the Boreal Institute for Northern Research of the University of Alberta and is available for online searching through QL Systems. This invaluable service is available through the libraries of the following institutions: Wilfrid Laurier University; McGill University; the University of Saskatchewan; the University of Calgary; the Calgary Public Library; the University of Western Ontario; the Faculty of Environmental Studies, York University; the University of Waterloo; and the Yukon Archives; as well as in the original at the Boreal Institute. The Boreal Institute Vertical Files on Northern Affairs, available on microfiche, comprise clippings from major southern Canadian newspapers on northern affairs, the northern parts of provinces, and Canada's native peoples.

The Canada Yearbook contains many statistics pertaining to the two northern territories.

The Canadian Annual Review contains separate essays describing developments in the two territories.

Government Documents

Canada, Department of Indian Affairs and Northern Development. *Annual Report*. Ottawa: published annually.

Canada, Department of Indian Affairs and Northern Development, Advisory Committee on Northern Development. *Annual Northern Expenditure Plan*. Ottawa: DIAND, published annually.

———. *Government Activities in the North*. Ottawa: DIAND, published annually.

Northwest Territories, Government. *Annual Report*.

Northwest Territories, Government, Bureau of Statistics, *Statistics Quarterly*. Yellowknife: published annually.

Northwest Territories, Legislative Assembly, *Hansard* [Entitled *Debates* prior to the fourth session of the Ninth Assembly, 1981].

Yukon, Government, *Annual Report*. Whitehorse: published annually.

Yukon, Government, Economic Research and Planning Unit, *Yukon Economic Review*. Whitehorse: published annually.

Yukon, Legislative Assembly, *Hansard*.

Monographs

The numbers following each entry indicate the chapter or chapters of this book to which the item cited is most relevant.

Beauchamp, Kenneth P. *Land Management in the Canadian North*. Ottawa: Canadian Arctic Resources Committee, 1976. (4, 5)

Berger, Thomas R. *Northern Frontier, Northern Homeland: Report of the Mackenzie Valley Pipeline Inquiry*. 2 vols. Ottawa: Supply and Services Canada, 1977. (1, 2, 4, 5)

Bregha, Francois. *Bob Blair's Pipeline*. Updated ed. Toronto: Lorimer, 1981. (4)

Brody, Hugh. *The People's Land*. Harmondsworth: Penguin, 1975. (1, 3)

Canada, Advisory Commission on the Development of Government in the Northwest Territories: A.W.R. Carrothers, Chairman. *Report to the Minister of Northern Affairs and National Resources*. Ottawa: 1966. (3)

Canada, Department of Energy, Mines and Resources. *The National Energy Program 1980*. Ottawa: 1980. (3, 4, 6)

Canada, Department of the Environment, Environmental Assessment Panel. *A Guide to the Federal Environmental Assessment and Review Process*. Ottawa: 1977. (5)

Canada, Department of the Environment, Lands Directorate. *Federal Lands: Their Use and Management.* Land Use in Canada Series, No. 11. Ottawa: 1978. (4, 5)

Canada, Department of Indian Affairs and Northern Development. *The James Bay and Northern Quebec Agreement.* Quebec City: DIAND and Government of Quebec, 1976. (2)

Canada, Science Council of Canada. *Northward Looking: A Strategy and Science Policy for Northern Development.* Report No. 26. Ottawa: 1977. (1, 5)

Canadian Arctic Resources Committee. Mackenzie Delta: *Priorities and Alternatives.* Ottawa: Canada Arctic Resources Committee, 1977. (4, 5)

Crowe, Keith J. *A History of the Original Peoples of Northern Canada.* Montreal: Arctic Institute of North America and McGill-Queen's University Press, 1974. (1, 2)

Cumming, Peter A., and Mickenberg, Neil H., eds. *Native Rights in Canada,* 2nd ed. Toronto: General Publishing, 1972. (2)

Dosman, E.J., ed. *The Arctic in Question.* Toronto: Oxford University Press, 1976. (1, 4)

——— . *The National Interest: The Politics of Northern Development, 1968-75.* Toronto: McClelland and Stewart, 1975. (4)

Drury, C.M. *Constitutional Development in the Northwest Territories: Report of the Special Representative.* Ottawa: Supply and Services Canada, 1980. (3)

Emond, D. Paul. *Environmental Assessment Law in Canada.* Toronto: Emond-Montgomery, 1978. (4, 5)

Fenge, T., et al. *Land Use Programs in Canada: Northwest Territories.* Ottawa: Supply and Services Canada, 1979. (4, 5)

Fumoleau, Rene. *As Long as This Land Shall Last.* Toronto: McClelland and Stewart, n.d. (1, 2)

Gibson, Robert. *The Strathcona Sound Mining Project.* Background Study No. 42. Ottawa: Science Council of Canada, 1978. (1, 4, 5)

Griffiths, Franklyn. *A Northern Foreign Policy.* Wellesley Paper 7/79. Toronto: Canadian Institute of International Affairs, 1979. (1)

Hamelin, Louis-Edmond. *Canadian Nordicity: It's Your North Too.* William Barr, trans. Montreal: Harvest House, 1978. (1, 2, 3)

Hunt, C.; Miller, R.; and Tingley, D. *Wilderness Area.* Ottawa: Canadian Arctic Resources Committee, 1979. (5)

Keith, R.F., et al. *Northern Development and Technology Assessment Systems.* Background Study No. 34. Ottawa: Science Council of Canada, 1976. (4, 6)

Keith, R.F., and Wright, J.B., eds. *Northern Transitions: Second National Workshop on People, Resources and the Environment North of 60°.* Vol. II of *Northern Transitions.* Ottawa: Canadian Arctic Resources Committee, 1978. (1, 2, 3, 4, 5)

LeBlond, N. Russell. *Porcupine Caribou Herd*. Ottawa: Canadian Arctic Resources Committee, 1979. (5)

Lysyk, K.; Bohmer, E.; and Phelps, W. *Report of the Alaska Highway Pipeline Inquiry*. Ottawa: Minister of Supply and Services Canada, 1977. (1, 2, 4, 5)

MacLeod, W. *The Dempster Highway*. Ottawa: Canadian Arctic Resources Committee, 1979. (1, 4, 5)

————. *Water Management in the Canadian North: The Administration of Inland Waters North of 60°*. Ottawa: Canadian Arctic Resources Committee, 1977. (5)

National Energy Board. *Reasons for Decision: Northern Pipelines*. 3 vols. Ottawa: Supply and Services Canada, 1977. (4)

Naysmith, John. *Land Use and Public Policy in Northern Canada*. Ottawa: Department of Indian Affairs and Northern Development, 1975. (5)

Nicholls, W.G. *Aishihik: The Politics of Hydro Planning in the Yukon*. Ottawa: Canadian Arctic Resources Committee, 1981. (4, 5)

Peterson, E.B., and Wright, J.B., eds. *Northern Transitions: Northern Resource and Land Use Policy Study*. Vol. I of *Northern Transitions*. Ottawa: Canadian Arctic Resources Committee, 1978. (1, 4, 5)

Pharand, Donat. *The Law of the Sea of the Arctic*. Ottawa: University of Ottawa Press, 1973. (1)

Pimlott, D.; Brown, D.; and Sam, K. *Oil Under the Ice*. Ottawa: Canadian Arctic Resources Committee, 1976. (4, 5)

Ponting, J. Rick, and Gibbins, Roger. *Out of Irrelevance: A Socio-Political Introduction to Indian Affairs in Canada*. Scarborough: Butterworth, 1980. (2, 5)

Rea, K.J. *The Political Economy of Northern Development*. Background Study No. 36. Ottawa: Science Council of Canada, 1976. (1, 4)

Redpath, D.K. *Land Use Programs in Canada: Yukon Territory*. Ottawa: Supply and Services Canada, 1979. (4, 5)

Theberge, John B.; Nelson, J. Gordon; and Fenge, Terry; eds. *Environmentally Significant Areas of the Yukon Territory*. Ottawa: Canadian Arctic Resources Committee, 1980. (5)

Watkins, Mel., ed. *Dene Nation: The Colony Within*. Toronto: University of Toronto Press, 1977. (1, 2, 5)

Williams, Peter. *Pipelines and Permafrost*. London: Longman, 1979. (1, 4)

Wright, J.B., ed. *Marine Transportation and High Arctic Development: Policy Framework and Priorities*. Ottawa: Canadian Arctic Resources Committee, 1979. (1, 4, 5)

Index

Note: The entries used in this index assume the adjective "northern." Thus, for example, "economics," "geography," "native claims" are intended to refer to "northern economics," "northern geography" and "northern native claims."